The Oxford Guide to Library Research

The Oxford Guide
to Library Research

Thomas Mann

New York   Oxford
Oxford University Press
1998

Oxford University Press

Oxford New York
Athens Auckland Bangkok Bogotá Bombay
Buenos Aires Calcutta Cape Town Dar es Salaam
Delhi Florence Hong Kong Istanbul Karachi
Kuala Lumpur Madras Madrid Melbourne
Mexico City Nairobi Paris Singapore
Taipei Tokyo Toronto Warsaw

and associated companies in
Berlin Ibadan

Published by Oxford University Press, Inc.
198 Madison Avenue, New York, New York 10016

Oxford is a registered trademark of Oxford University Press, Inc.

Library of Congress Cataloging-in-Publication Data
Mann, Thomas, 1948–
The Oxford guide to library research / by Thomas Mann.
p. cm.
Rev. and updated ed. of: A guide to library research methods.
1987
Includes bibliographical references and index.
ISBN 0-19-512312-3
ISBN 0-19-512313-1 (pbk.)
1. Library research—United States. I. Mann, Thomas, 1948–
Guide to library research methods. II. Title.
Z710.M23   1998
025.5'24—dc21   98-5888

1 3 5 7 9 8 6 4 2

Printed in the United States of America
on acid-free paper

For
Jack Nabholtz

Contents

complements library catalog: advantages and disadvantages—Scattering of subjects—Exploiting the library's internal structure—Continuing need for classified bookstacks in computer age—Ways to find the right classification areas—Browsing in other situations

Preface

Real libraries and virtual libraries are not the same; if you want to be a good researcher you have to be aware of the trade-offs. While the electronic virtual libraries overcome, in some respects, the *where* restrictions of libraries with walls, they do so only at the cost of imposing other significant restrictions of *what* and *who*—that is, either they limit what is available to begin with (offering copyright-free material); or, if they do mount copyrighted sources, and hope to protect them, they then impose major restrictions on who has access to them (those who can pay stiff fees at the point of use, or those who can pay subscription costs for passwords).

In the overall universe of information records there are three considerations that are inextricably tied together: (1) copyright protection; (2) free "fair use" use of the records by everyone; and (3) a localized *where* restriction. The first two cannot be combined without the presence of the third. It is precisely this third element that real libraries alone provide. The only way to overcome the inevitable *what* and *who* restrictions in cyberspace, to provide free access to a wide range of copyrighted works, is to limit their use to a particular place. (I will extend this discussion in Chapter 10.)

Printed books and journals, as physical objects in nonbroadcastable formats, have built-in *where* restrictions that enable them to be offered for free use within the walls of real libraries; indeed, even the more desirable parts of the Information Superhighway itself—its copyrighted databases—become *freely* available to users only when they are restricted by site licenses to the *where* localities of specific terminals within real-library walls. You cannot get "everything" freely online from your home or office, nor will you ever be able to. The information world simply does not work without major trade-offs of *where, what,* and *who* limitations.

Another significant difference between real and virtual libraries is the format of the material they present. Very few people can stand to read book-length narrative or expository texts—say, 150 pages or so—on screen display formats. Nor do they like the point-of-use expense of printing reams of individual sheets. (Even the cyberprophets who predict the end of real libraries are making their predictions, ironically, in printed and copyrighted books, which are freely available to everyone only in the real libraries they belittle.) Format is an important and real consideration because it is linked to a kind of hierarchy in the world of learning:

1. *Data* are the unorganized, unfiltered, and unevaluated raw materials of thought, comparable to sense experiences.
2. *Information* reflects an organization of data to the point that statements can be made about it, either true or false, and coherent or incoherent with other information. At this level, too, attitudes of approval or disapproval can appear, whether justified or not.
3. *Opinion* is a level of thinking with an added weight of confidence attached to a belief, prior to objective confirmation by other people. (The lack of confirmation may be due to a time delay, to inadequate communication, or to the opinion's simply being wrong in the first place.)
4. *Knowledge* reflects a still higher level of organization to the point that truth or falsity can be assured by tests of correspondence to, and coherence with, the world of experience and of other ideas; this level includes discernment of patterns within information and the making of generalizations that are accessible to, and acceptable by, other people.
5. *Understanding* is a higher level of thought in that it comprehends not just patterns and generalizations but the *causes* or *reasons* behind them. An understanding of physical causes gives one a measure of predictability, the hallmark of the sciences. The humanities, on the other hand, are grounded on the assumption of the nonillusory nature of free will and the reality of chosen goals as motivating factors; their hallmarks are philosophical justification of reasons, and explanatory integration of experience in narrative forms of

beginnings and middles leading to ends. (The social sciences mix both scientific and humanistic criteria of explanation.)

6. *Wisdom* is the highest level of all, in that it *evaluates the worth* of knowledge and understanding according to ultimate criteria of value in areas of truth, goodness, and beauty—within ultimate frameworks or philosophies of what counts as evidence, or what counts as an explanation, to begin with.

The important point is that, not to put too fine a point on it, the higher levels of this progression cannot be attained by people with brief attention spans. The conveyance and reception of the highest levels of thought—insofar as such levels are transmissible at all—require the absorption of written texts in narrative or expository forms that are of a considerable length. And while both screens and books can *contain* texts of any length, it is becoming more apparent that the book format is much more successful at *conveying* the higher levels of thought—which is not the same thing as merely recording them. The difference is somewhat like having water in liquid or frozen formats; the identity of chemical composition still does not make chewing ice satisfying to thirsty people. Why this is so, I will leave to psychologists; I have simply noticed, repeatedly, that the large majority of people who advocate the replacement of real libraries by virtual ones have themselves seldom read any book-length narratives or expositions in the format they would so cavalierly impose on everyone else. I can only conclude, at least provisionally, that there is a bias in the screen display formats toward the visual, the audio, the colorful, the animated, the instantaneous connection, the quickly updated, and the short text—which most readily convey the levels of data, information, opinion, and (to some extent) knowledge. The higher levels of thinking, however—which are not ultimately separable from lengthy verbal narratives and expositions—are still conveyed, and absorbed, more readily through the different medium of book formats.

A concern for the maintenance of real libraries that provide *free* access to *books* is thus not in the least "sentimental"; rather, it is reflective of a justifiable and very serious care that our culture not lose its higher levels of thought. Simply having book-length texts available electronically—and limiting the set to copyright-free works at that—by no means assures that they will actually be read in online formats.

This book maps out nine major roads, and some important side paths, to lead you efficiently into the realm of humanity's accumulated thought records, with, frankly, a concentration on what you can find in real research libraries. (The real entirely include the virtual, in that libraries can make the same Internet connections you make from home; but the virtual do not entirely include the resources of real libraries because of the *what* and *who* restrictions of copyright and because of the important format differences.) With reference to the above hierarchy of intellectual levels, I hope this book will get you to the level of understanding, not just of the trade-offs between real and virtual libraries, but also of the equally important trade-offs among several distinct methods of searching them.

Most guides to research are organized either by subject ("These are the resources for education, these for history, these for nursing," and so on) or by type of literature (dictionaries, handbooks, directories, databases, etc.). This one is different. Although it makes some use of both these traditional schemes, this *Guide* is primarily structured around nine different *methods* of subject searching:

- Controlled vocabulary searching
- Browsing and scanning subject-classified bookstacks
- Keyword searching
- Citation searching
- Related-record searching
- Searching through published bibliographies
- Boolean combination searching (with some other computer manipulations)
- Using the subject expertise of people sources
- Type of literature searching

Each of these methods is potentially applicable in *any* subject area; each has both strengths and weaknesses, advantages and disadvantages; and each is capable of turning up information that cannot be reached by the other eight.

I have found through experience that this overall scheme simply works better than the traditional alternatives. (Indeed, it encompasses them.) My own background includes work as an academic researcher at the doctoral level, a private investigator, a graduate student in library science, a free-lance researcher, a reference librarian at two universities, and a general reference librarian for fifteen years at the largest library in the world. A second forming element derives from my having observed tens of thousands of other researchers over two decades. What the aggregate of all this has suggested to me is that most people unconsciously work within a framework of very limited assumptions about the extent of information that is easily and freely available to them; and, further, most have only very hazy notions of anything beyond general computer searches.

It strikes me, too, that previous writers on this "research" subject who are not librarians have overlooked some fundamentally important steps and distinctions in telling their audiences how to proceed; and many have even perpetuated harmful notions. On the other hand, some librarians who have written on the subject have not placed the weight and emphasis on certain matters that scholars and other investigators require; indeed, library guides frequently offer little more than lists of individual printed and electronic sources with no overall perspective on methods or techniques of *using* them. And the recent spate of "cyber" guides to research tend to dumb down the whole process by suggesting, or even stating, that "everything" is available on the Information Superhighway—thereby confining researchers' views, right from the start, to only one galaxy of sources within an information universe that is truly much larger. Moreover, very few writers of any sort give concrete examples of what to do—or of what *not* to do, which may be the more instructive.

Much of what I've discovered over the past twenty-some years I have had to learn "the hard way," and I especially hope to save the reader from some of the more egregious mistakes and omissions I've been guilty of myself at one time or another. Unlike many people whom I've had occasion to help, I have had the fortunate (although painful) experience of having had such mistakes systematically brought to my attention by the several shifting professional perspectives I've had on the same types of problems. What this has done for me, I think, is to make certain patterns in research behavior more evident, specifically:

- Patterns in the types of questions that people ask, and in how they ask them

- Patterns in the usually unconscious assumptions they hold about what can be done
- Patterns in the bad advice they are sometimes given by teachers, employers, and colleagues
- Patterns in the mistakes and omissions that reduce the efficiency of their research

Viewed collectively, these patterns tend to suggest the areas in which most people need the most help; and it is on this group of concerns that I wish to concentrate. I hope especially to give readers a sense of the principles and rules involved that are applicable in any situation, not just an annotated list of particular subject sources. I also hope that, through the examples I've come across in my own research projects and in helping others (from which I've sometimes created composite examples for this book), this guide will give readers a sense of the trade-offs that are always involved in choosing one research option rather than another. I especially hope to provide a perspective of how the different trade-offs balance and compensate for each other's weaknesses in the total information system.

This book could not have been written without the help and expertise of many people. I especially want to thank D. W. Schneider and Fred Peterson, without whom an earlier version, under the title *A Guide to Library Research Methods* (Oxford, 1987), would never have left the ground; and Francis Miksa, who provided a solid grounding in the principles of library science when I was in graduate school. A number of colleagues have provided useful advice, information, or criticisms of the manuscript. I wish to thank Adele Chwalek, Lucinda Conger, Sally Fleming, Nanette Gibbs, Gary Jensen, Carolyn Lee, Maria Laqueur, Rodney Phillips, Roberta Scull, Paul Wasserman, and Steve Zink for the help with sections of the first book, some of which have survived a thorough rewriting for the second. Eugene Garfield and Edward D. Leonardo from the Institute for Scientific Information, and Charles Chadwyck-Healey and his staff in Alexandria, Virginia, were most helpful in providing information about their databases. I am grateful once again to the H. W. Wilson Company to quote extensively from some of their promotional literature. Marilyn Halpern at the Educational Testing Service was most helpful in responding to my inquiries, as was Chris Barstad of Information Handling Services and Jim Hornstra of NewsBank.

The list of people from whom I have learned much at the Library of Congress would include whole sections of the Library's staff directory. For help in preparing the first book I am especially indebted to Sam Andrusko, Carol Armbruster, Pat Bernard, George Caldwell, Agnes Ferruso, Judy Furash, Ann Gardner, Anne Marie Gwynn, Annette Hale, Victoria Hill, Richard Howard, Anna Keller, Brent Kendrick, Sandy Lawson, Sarah Pritchard, Judith Reid, Bill Reitwiesner, Dave Smith, and Virginia Wood. John Feulner, a master of the process, was especially helpful in suggesting ways of using people sources. This new book has again drawn on the advice, suggestions, and help of many of the same LC staff, especially Judith Reid for her list of genealogical Web sites; and also several others, among them Beverly Brannan, Connie Carter, Mary Jane Cavallo, Chi Wang, Jennifer Cutting, Art Emerson, Kathryn Engstrom, Jan Herd, Mindy Hetrick, Grant Harris, Judy Krone, Jim McGovern, Chris Murphy, Cathy O'Connor, Peggy Pearlstein, Lynn Pedigo, James Scala, Dick Sharp, Joan Sullivan, Allen Thrasher, and Carole Zimmermann. I've also learned much from many of the Library's regular readers who have provided what, to a reference librarian, is an invaluable contribution: feedback on what actually works and what doesn't, in real research situations. Among these are Ellon Carpenter, Melissa Conway, Phoebe Fleurat, Abby Gilbert, George Gingras, Carrie Johnson, Ken Kitchell, Edward Luft, Fred Maxwell, Irvin Matus, Josephine Pacheco, Muriel Parry, Ruth Price, Betty Rowe, Al Schoen, Claire Sherman, Jon Simon, Julia Thompson, and Jan Wepsiec. I must also reluctantly acknowledge a debt to various administrators at the Library's upper levels who have been responsible for lowering the quality of its cataloging and classification so much since the early 1990s, and who have restricted both the hours and levels of access to its onsite collections; without their influence I would never have gained so much experience in trying to explain the fundamental needs of researchers in very simple language and with concrete examples. (Perhaps this book will find an outside audience more willing to heed the message on the need for quality and consistency in categorization and labeling, and on the importance of real libraries.) A special thanks to Colleen Hoppins for her unfailing encouragement and inspiration. The editors and staff of Oxford

University Press, especially Elda Rotor, have done a wonderful job in shepherding the manuscript through production; I am grateful to all of them, and to Rick Balkin, agent extraordinaire, who has done his usual fine job of making the whole process run smoothly.

While this book assembles the insights of many people, I must emphasize that its shortcomings are attributable only to myself. The opinions, value judgments, and criticisms expressed within it are also my own; they should not be taken to represent the official views or policy of any organization with which I am or have been affiliated.

Washington, D.C.   T. M.
June 1997

The Oxford Guide to Library Research

1

Initial Overviews: Encyclopedias

The best way to start many inquiries is to see if someone has already written an overview that outlines the most important facts on the subject and provides a concise list of recommended readings. This is precisely what a good encyclopedia article does. Unlike most Web sites, encyclopedia articles have usually gone through a process of editorial review by reputable publishers whose continuance in the marketplace depends on their reputation for accuracy; in addition, the selection of encyclopedias by libraries is in itself another hurdle of review. One of the main problems with the Internet, that it often gives researchers so many hits that they can't find good overviews within the welter, is thus often solved quickly and easily by encyclopedias.

Unfortunately, the *misuse* of encyclopedias tends unnecessarily to limit their effectiveness both for the student writing a term paper and for the business executive, professional, or independent learner the individual will become after leaving the classroom. This misuse comes in two forms: (1) in expecting an encyclopedia to be the beginning *and end* of a complex inquiry, and (2) in expecting the general encyclopedias that everybody knows about to provide a level of detail found only in the specialized encyclopedias that very few people know about. When students get inadequate results from general sets (or their computer versions), they frequently tend to change their overall assumptions regarding the future use of all encyclopedias.

The first important point, then, is that encyclopedias should be regarded as good starting points for nonspecialists who need a basic overview of a subject or a background perspective on it—but they should not be seen as compendiums of "all knowledge" that will make further specialized research unnecessary. Nor should one expect currency from such sources—it is the newspaper, the journal article, or the Web site and not the encyclopedia that one should turn to for current events (a distinction that seems to be lost on many encyclopedia salesmen). Part of the problem people have with encyclopedias is that schools (and even universities) tend to leave students with only hazy notions of what *other* sources lead quickly to the more specialized or current information, and so researchers often don't perceive what should be starting points within a clear context of what lies beyond. (This book will provide that context.)

The second point to be emphasized is that a deeper level of the specialized information is indeed available in encyclopedias if one knows enough to look beyond the familiar *Britannica, Americana, World Book,* or *Collier's.* There are thousands of specialized sets, or sometimes one-volume works, covering particular fields of knowledge—"specialized" in the sense of concentrating on certain subject areas, not in the sense of being written in the jargon of specialists. The whole purpose of any encyclopedia is to provide an orientation to someone who is not already conversant with the subject being discussed. A real expert will usually not need an introductory overview within his or her own field but may require one for other areas.

Sometimes, however, experts will indeed require a large overview of recent or technical developments within their own fields; but the sources providing these perspectives are not introductory and they are written in a way that assumes the reader already knows the basics. For this kind of overview the researcher will turn to review articles, not encyclopedias. The business executive, professional, or independent learner who has left academia will get the most mileage out of encyclopedias by using the specialized sets in conjunction with, or as background for, these review articles (see Chapter 8).

But even researchers still in school will usually get farther into a subject and find more information by using specialized rather than general encyclopedias. People seeking introductory articles in the sciences, for example, will often be better served by the *McGraw-Hill Encyclopedia of Science and Technology* (20 vols.; McGraw-Hill, revised irregularly), which is the standard set in its field, rather than the *Britannica, Ameri-*

cana, Collier's, or *World Book.* Similarly, those in the social sciences will frequently be better off turning to the authoritative *Encyclopedia of the Social Sciences* (15 vols.; Macmillan, 1930–35) and its successor and supplement, the *International Encyclopedia of the Social Sciences* (19 vols.; McGraw-Hill, 1959–91). Students in the arts, too, should consult the specialized works in these areas, among them the excellent *Encyclopedia of World Art* (15 vols.; McGraw-Hill, 1959–68), the *Dictionary of Art* (34 vols.; Grove's Dictionaries, 1996), and the *New Grove Dictionary of Music and Musicians* (20 vols.; Macmillan, 1980). (Don't be misled by the term "dictionary"—in library and publishing terminology it refers simply to the alphabetical arrangement of articles without regard to their length, so it is often synonymous with "encyclopedia.")

Note also a particularly important point: While many general encyclopedias are now starting to appear in online or CD-ROM versions, the "bells and whistles" of the electronic formats—such things as moving images and sound bites of speeches or music—should not distract you from the fact that their content remains at a relatively general level. Much deeper levels of subject content can be found in the specialized encyclopedias; and most of these appear, and remain, in print format only, to be consulted in real rather than virtual libraries.

Among the thousands of relatively little-known specialized encyclopedias, the above titles are especially good; other works that are considered standard in their fields include the following:

Dictionary of American History (8 vols.; Scribner's, 1976; 2-vol. supplement, 1996)

Dictionary of American Biography (20 vols.; reprint, 11 vols. and supplements; Scribner's, 1927–)

Dictionary of National Biography (22 vols. and supplements; Oxford University Press, 1917–)

Dictionary of Scientific Biography (16 vols.; Scribner's, 1970–80)

Dictionary of the History of Ideas (5 vols.; Scribner's, 1973–74)

Dictionary of the Middle Ages (13 vols.; Scribner's, 1983–89)

Encyclopedia of Religion (16 vols.; Macmillan, 1987)

Encyclopedia of Philosophy (8 vols.; Macmillan, 1967; reprinted in 4 vols., 1972; 1-vol. supplement, 1996)

Routledge Encyclopedia of Philosophy (10 vols.; 1998)

New Catholic Encyclopedia (18 vols.; McGraw-Hill, 1967–89)

Interpreter's Dictionary of the Bible (4 vols.; Abingdon, 1962; 1 supplementary volume, 1976)

New Palgrave Dictionary of Economics (4 vols.; Macmillan, 1988)

Encyclopedia of Education (10 vols.; Macmillan, 1971)

International Encyclopedia of Education (10 vols.; Pergamon, 1985)

International Encyclopedia of Higher Education (10 vols.; Jossey-Bass, 1977)

International Encyclopedia of Psychiatry, Psychology, Psychoanalysis & Neurology (12 vols.; Van Nostrand Reinhold, 1977)

Funk & Wagnalls Standard Dictionary of Folklore, Mythology, and Legend (2d ed.; Funk & Wagnalls, 1972)

Encyclopedic Dictionary of Mathematics (2 vols.; MIT Press, 1977)

Grzimek's Animal Life Encyclopedia (13 vols.; Van Nostrand Reinhold, 1972–75)

Grzimek's Encyclopedia of Mammals (2d ed., 5 vols.; McGraw-Hill, 1990)

Although the above are certainly important, they by no means exhaust the field. Some other representative titles that may suggest the range of available works include:

Anchor Bible Dictionary (6 vols.)

The Australian Encyclopedia (6 vols.)

Biographical Dictionary of American Labor

Biographical Dictionary of American Mayors, 1820–1980

Biographical Dictionary of the American Left

Companion Encyclopedia of the History and Philosophy of the Mathematical Sciences (2 vols.)

Dictionary of Afro-American Slavery

Dictionary of American Communal and Utopian History

Dictionary of Concepts in Literary Criticism and Theory

Dictionary of Literary Biography (160+ vols., ongoing)

Dictionary of Mexican American History

Dictionary of Mexican Literature

Dictionary of Named Effects and Laws in Chemistry, Physics, and Mathematics

Dictionary of the Literature of the Iberian Peninsula

Encyclopaedia Judaica (16 vols.)

Encyclopaedia of Food Science, Food Technology, and Nutrition (8 vols.)

Encyclopaedia of Islam, New Edition (in progress)

Encyclopaedia of Religion and Ethics (13 vols.)

Encyclopaedic Dictionary of Physics (9 vols. and supplements)

Encyclopedia of Accounting Systems (3 vols.)

Encyclopedia of African-American Civil Rights

Encyclopedia of African-American Culture and History (5 vols.)

Encyclopedia of American Economic History (3 vols.)

Encyclopedia of American Foreign Policy (3 vols.)

Encyclopedia of American Political History (3 vols.)

Encyclopedia of American Religions

Encyclopedia of American Social History (3 vols.)

Encyclopedia of American Spy Films

Encyclopedia of Anthropology

Encyclopedia of Architecture: Design, Engineering & Construction (5 vols.)

Encyclopedia of Asian History (4 vols.)

Encyclopedia of Banking and Finance

Encyclopedia of Bioethics (5 vols.)

Encyclopedia of Continental Women Writers (2 vols.)

Encyclopedia of Crafts (3 vols.)

Encyclopedia of Crime and Justice (4 vols.)

Encyclopedia of Cultural Anthropology (4 vols.)

Encyclopedia of Democracy (4 vols.)

Encyclopedia of Earth Sciences (a series of 1-volume encyclopedias covering Oceanography, Atmospheric Science and Astrogeology, Geochemistry and Environmental Sciences, Geomorphology, World Regional Geology, etc.)

Encyclopedia of Educational Research (4 vols.)

Encyclopedia of Electronics

Encyclopedia of Engineering Materials and Processes

Encyclopedia of Fluid Mechanics (6 vols.)
Encyclopedia of Higher Education (4 vols.)
Encyclopedia of Historic Places (2 vols.)
Encyclopedia of Human Behavior (2 vols.)
Encyclopedia of Human Biology (8 vols.)
Encyclopedia of Jazz in the Seventies (a companion volume to *Encyclopedia of Jazz in the Sixties*)
Encyclopedia of Language and Linguistics (10 vols.)
Encyclopedia of Library and Information Science (58+ vols., ongoing)
Encyclopedia of Library History
Encyclopedia of Management
Encyclopedia of Microscopy
Encyclopedia of Military History from 3,500 B.C. to the Present
Encyclopedia of Modern Architecture
Encyclopedia of Mystery and Detection
Encyclopedia of Neuroscience (2 vols.)
Encyclopedia of Physical Science and Technology (2d ed., 18 vols.)
Encyclopedia of Prehistoric Life
Encyclopedia of Psychology (4 vols.)
Encyclopedia of Recorded Sound in the United States
Encyclopedia of Sociology (4 vols.)
Encyclopedia of Southern Culture
Encyclopedia of the South
Encyclopedia of Special Education (3 vols.)
Encyclopedia of Spectroscopy
Encyclopedia of Strange and Unexplained Physical Phenomena
Encyclopedia of the American Constitution (4 vols. and 1 supplement)
Encyclopedia of the Holocaust (4 vols.)
Encyclopedia of the United Nations and International Agreements
Encyclopedia of Themes and Subjects in Painting
Encyclopedia of Urban Planning
Encyclopedia of World Cultures (10 vols.)
Facts On File Dictionary of Chemistry
Facts On File Dictionary of Classical, Biblical, and Literary Allusions
Facts On File Dictionary of Mathematics
Facts On File Dictionary of Military Science

Facts On File Dictionary of Numerical Allusions
The Great Soviet Encyclopedia (32 vols.)
Grzimek's Encyclopedia of Evolution
Guide to American Law: Everyman's Legal Encyclopedia (12 vols.)
Historical Dictionary of Reconstruction
Historical Dictionary of the New Deal
International Encyclopedia of Communications (4 vols.)
International Encyclopedia of Education (2d ed., 12 vols.)
International Encyclopedia of Higher Education (10 vols.)
International Encyclopedia of Statistics (2 vols.)
International Military and Defense Encyclopedia (6 vols.)
Kodansha Encyclopedia of Japan (9 vols.)
McGraw-Hill Encyclopedia of Energy
Macmillan Encyclopedia of Architects (4 vols.)
Macmillan Illustrated Animal Encyclopedia
A Milton Encyclopedia (9 vols.)
The Modern Encyclopedia of Russian and Soviet History (58 vols.)
Mrs. Byrne's Dictionary of Unusual, Obscure, and Preposterous Words
    (new and expanded edition)[1]
New Grove Dictionary of American Music (4 vols.)
New Grove Dictionary of Musical Instruments (3 vols.)
New Grove Dictionary of Opera (4 vols.)
Oxford Companion to Philosophy
Sexuality and the Law: An Encyclopedia of Major Legal Cases
Standard Encyclopedia of Southern Africa (12 vols.)
Van Nostrand's Scientific Encyclopedia
World Encyclopedia of Peace (4 vols.)
World Encyclopedia of Political Systems and Parties (2 vols.)
World Press Encyclopedia
Worldmark Encyclopedia of the Nations (5 vols.)
Worldmark Encyclopedia of the States

Some of the subjects suggested here are covered by other specialized works, too; and then there are encyclopedias for many other subjects as well.

There are several ways to determine whether a special encyclopedia covers your area of interest. Note, however, that a particularly important factor in the search process is that you *begin by assuming that such a source exists, even when you don't know if it does.* Reference librarians will tell you that proceeding on such an assumption always makes the discovery more likely, as it provides a stronger motive to venture into uncharted waters.

A particularly good shortcut is to use an amazing reference book titled *First Stop: The Master Index to Subject Encyclopedias* (Oryx Press, 1989). This is a cumulative keyword index to the titles of articles in 430 specialized encyclopedias (and some other reference sources, such as the Cambridge history series). The articles indexed here must be at least 250 words in length and must also include a bibliography for further research. *First Stop* tells you immediately which encyclopedias cover your topic—and there may be several.

Not all specialized encyclopedias are covered in *First Stop,* however, so you need to know about a few other sources as well:

Guide to Reference Books (American Library Association; supplemented and revised irregularly). The current edition of this venerable source is usually referred to as "Balay," after Robert Balay, its editor. It is a comprehensive list of reference sources in all subject areas, categorized by types of literature—including dictionaries and encyclopedias. If you want to know if a specialized encyclopedia exists, look for the listings of this type of literature within any subject category you're curious about.

Dictionary of Dictionaries and Eminent Encyclopedias, by Thomas Kabdebo (2nd ed.; Bowker-Saur, 1997). This is a critical guide to more than 6,000 dictionaries and encyclopedias; works discussed can be monolingual, bilingual, or multilingual as long as English is one element. It will often tell you the *best* such source in an area, and compare it to other sources. It has a very good index.

Kister's Best Encyclopedias: A Comparative Guide to General and Specialized Encyclopedias, by Kenneth Kister (2d ed.; Oryx, 1994). This provides detailed descriptions and comparisons of more than 160 general and 400 specialized English-language encyclopedias, including electronic versions; a few foreign-language sources are also briefly covered.

ARBA Guide to Subject Encyclopedias and Dictionaries, edited by Susan C. Awe (2d ed.; Libraries Unlimited, 1997). This provides annotated descriptions of 1,061 sources.

Encyclopedias, Atlases & Dictionaries, edited by Marion Sader and Amy Lewis (R. R. Bowker, 1995). This is a comparative and evaluative guide to 185 English-language sources in print and electronic formats.

Dictionaries, Encyclopedias, and Other Word-Related Books, by Annie M. Brewer (2 vols., 4th ed.; Gale Research, 1988). This is a listing of about 30,000 works arranged in the order of Library of Congress Classification numbers, with an index of subjects and titles. Entries reproduce nonevaluative library catalog records.

Catalog of Dictionaries, Word Books, and Philological Texts, 1440–1900, compiled by David E. Vancil (Greenwood Press, 1993). A good source for historical research, this is an inventory of the Cordell Collection of Dictionaries at Indiana State University; it is the world's largest, with more than 5,100 pre-1901 imprints plus several thousand more for the twentieth century. Indexes are by date, by language, and by subject. Entries are not annotated.

Anglo-American General Encyclopedias: A Historical Bibliography: 1703–1967, by S. Padraig [James Patrick] Walsh (New York: R. R. Bowker, 1968). Another good source for a historical overview; its 419 entries are extensively annotated. Indexes are by Editors and Publishers/Distributors; there is also a chronological listing of titles.

Note that none of these sources is computerized; all of this information is available only through paper format materials. Note, too, that a problem common to all of the above finding guides is that, once published, they become dated. On the other hand, it is also important to realize that becoming dated does not necessarily mean becoming *out*dated, especially since encyclopedias aim to summarize knowledge that is regarded as "established" to begin with.

If you wish to check continually updated finding guides, however, to determine if new encyclopedias have appeared, there are two in particular to consult. The first is the annual *American Reference Books Annual*, or *ARBA* (Libraries Unlimited, 1970–), which lists, with evaluative annotations, most of the English-language reference sources published within the past year (accessible by a subject index). The second is your library's computer or card catalog, which is another continually updated source. Specialized encyclopedias—both new and old—usually will be listed under one of these forms of heading:

[Subject heading]—Dictionaries
[Subject heading]—Encyclopedias
[Subject heading]—[Geographical subdivision]—Dictionaries
[Subject heading]—[Geographical subdivision]—Encyclopedias

The important thing to watch for here is that either of the subdivisions ("—Dictionaries" or "—Encyclopedias") may turn up a good source. (The several ways to find the right subject heading in the first place—the crucial first element in the string—will be discussed in the next chapter.)

The utility of specialized encyclopedias is often discovered by students writing short papers.

- A student looking for a good article on the history of bookbinding found that the *Britannica* and *Americana* articles were too short; but when a librarian referred him to the *Encyclopedia of World Art,* which he had never heard of, he found a more detailed discussion that amply suited his needs.
- A researcher seeking orientation on the subject "U.S. isolationism between the world wars" found less than a column of material in *Britannica;* about two pages' worth, scattered among four articles, in *Americana*; about a column's worth, over three articles, in *Collier's;* and about the same, over four articles, in *World Book.* In the *Encyclopedia of American Foreign Policy,* however, she found a ten-page article on the whole history and philosophy of "Isolationism," about four pages of which were devoted to the interwar period. In addition, the extensive bibliography at the end of the article was much more specifically on target than those in the other encyclopedias.
- A student of theology was interested in finding discussions of twentieth-century scholars on the concept of "the Church as sacrament." Her main problem was that she could not find a subject heading that matched this topic in either the library catalog or the journal indexes. In turning to the *New Catholic Encyclopedia*, however—which has a vocabulary more tailored to Church-related subjects—she found an article "Sacrament of the Church," and it had a good-sized bibliography appended.

- A researcher looking for information on the phrase *Senatus Populusque Romanus* could find nothing in the various general encyclopedias; but a quick look in *First Stop* directed him to the *Cambridge Ancient History* set, where he found what he needed.
- A bibliographer looking for information on the concept *ut pictora poesis* also found nothing in the general sets but located an eleven-page article in *The Dictionary of the History of Ideas* (5 vols.) by consulting *First Stop.*

In emphasizing specialized encyclopedias, I do not mean to suggest that the general sets are unimportant. Indeed, there are a few specialized features within the general sets that are particularly useful. The *Encyclopedia Americana,* for example (unlike other encyclopedias), sometimes prints the full texts of historic documents in addition to providing information about them. When you look up "Declaration of the Rights of Man and the Citizen" or "*Mayflower* Compact," or "Washington's Farewell Address," for instance, you get not just a summary but actual texts. *Americana* also offers articles on each individual century (e.g., on the Fifth Century or the Nineteenth Century) that are sometimes useful, and also articles on each book of the Bible, as well as many brief articles on individual works of art, literature, and music (The *Winged Victory* statue, the novel *Middlemarch,* the ballet *The Firebird*, etc.).

The *Britannica* set covers philosophy particularly well, including a book-length article "Philosophies of the Branches of Knowledge," which no other encyclopedia offers. The annual *Britannica Book of the Year* supplement is very good in its presentation of statistical data on political, social, demographic, and economic conditions in the countries of the world; and it provides them in two sections, the first by country and the second by subject, so that comparisons can be readily made among the countries. The *Macropaedia* (long article) section of the *Britannica* also does something the other sets don't—it clusters what would otherwise be many alphabetically separated small articles within larger theme articles, often book length. Thus "Musical Instruments" gathers in one place articles on percussion, stringed, keyboard, wind, and electronic instruments; and the article "Transportation" includes sections on history, motor vehicles, railroads, aircraft, ships, freight pipelines, urban mass transportation, traffic control and safety, and so on. The *Micropaedia* (short length) section articles often serve as overviews of the longer treatments in the *Macropaedia* section. The set's one-volume *Propaedia* is a fascinating classification of all of the articles in the *Britannica* in a logical order, showing relationships and linkages not apparent from the alphabetical sequence of the articles themselves.

Collier's is particularly good for articles that give practical "how-to" tips on dealing with problems of childhood and child development, on buying insurance, or interior design or sewing techniques. Its index is also excellent.

The *World Book* is exceptionally good in providing quick, "look it up"-type information—on flags, state flowers, first aid, gardening instructions, symptoms of illnesses, metric conversion tables, football rules, summaries of Shakespeare's plays, and so on.

General foreign-language encyclopedias are also often particularly good in turning up biographical information on obscure figures who played roles in the history of various countries. Their illustrations are also sometimes more useful than those in the English-language sets. These sources, however, are overlooked much too often.

There are also many encyclopedias that focus specifically on *biographical* information. For an overview of your options in this area, see the Appendix of this book.

When you need an article on a particular subject (a substantive but less than book-length source), five possibilities should occur to you:

1. An encyclopedia article (generally written as an overview for non-specialists)
2. A journal/periodical or newspaper article
3. A "state of the art" review article (generally written as a summary for specialists)
4. An essay in an anthology
5. A Web site on the topic

Each of these latter four forms is accessible through sources that will be discussed later. For an encyclopedia article, however, you should start by assuming there is a *specialized* encyclopedia covering your area of interest and then look for it.

Note

1. The editor's introduction to this remarkable work, by Mrs. Byrne's ex-husband, is, by itself, famous among bibliophiles: "Working alone and without government support (or even comprehension) she managed to assemble the six thousand weirdest words in the English language. Nobody asked her to do it because nobody thought such a thing was possible. In fact, I asked her *not* to do it."

2

Subject Headings and the Library Catalog

A card or computer catalog lists a library's book holdings; and although it also list the titles of the various journals in the collections, it does not record the individual articles that appear within them. (For those you will need separate journal indexes, databases, and CD-ROMs, discussed in Chapters 4 through 9). Each entry in the catalog will provide you with a call number enabling you to locate the desired volume on the shelves.

As a rule, every book held by the library will appear in several places within the filing sequence (either in card format or in a computer browse display). Each of these appearances will present an essentially identical description of the book; the only difference (in a card catalog) will be the top line, which determines where the card will be filed: One record of the book will be under the name of the author; one will be filed under the title of the work; and one or more will appear under subject category terms assigned to correspond to the contents of the book. In a computer catalog there will be variant brief displays on the browse screens (author, title, and subject heading lines) that lead you to the full entry that describes the book; but that basic entry, once found, will always be the same no matter which path leads you to it.

Some libraries with card catalogs are in "dictionary" format, which means they have author, title, and subject cards all interfiled in a single sequence, A through Z. Other libraries have "divided" catalogs, in which author and title cards are interfiled in one alphabet while subject cards appear in a separate file. Computer catalogs, especially those with "menu" rather than "command" softwares, may show similar file segrations of author, title, and subject sections.

Filing Conventions

Most searches for a particular author's books are relatively straightforward—you just look under the person's last name. There are several potential problems, however. If the surname begins with *Mc,* as in *McDonald,* a card catalog will usually file such entries as though they were spelled *Mac.* Also, in 1981 a major change in cataloging rules was adopted by most libraries, and it frequently causes confusion. Under the old rules an author's works would be listed only under the author's real name even though his or her books may have a pseudonym on their title page; thus, for example, works by Mark Twain would appear in the catalog under "Clemens, Samuel Langhorne" and not under "Twain." Under the new rules, however, books may be cataloged under whatever name appears on the title page. In some libraries you may save to search in one place for books cataloged prior to 1981 and in another for those that came after; it is a very expensive operation to go back and recatalog thousands of old entries under new rules, and so many libraries haven't done it. If there is more than one file, however, they should be linked by cross-references. So: *Follow cross-references.* In my own experience I have to confess that for years, before I became a librarian, I largely ignored them myself; but now having had so many experiences of finding *exactly* what I wanted by pursuing them—instead of finding just "something" relevant while ignoring the cross-references—I cannot emphasize this too strongly.

Searches for a particular title, too, are usually straightforward—you look under the first word of the title, disregarding the initial articles *A, An, The,* and their foreign-language equivalents. Thus Hemingway's *A Farewell to Arms* would be found in the *F* section of the file. It is a very common mistake among students to include initial articles when looking for titles in computer catalog "browse" displays (such as the RLIN BIB file; cf. Chapter 11); the result is that works actually in the collection are missed because they don't show up when the articles are typed in.

One noteworthy exception in title searching concerns the designations of some journals. Under the old rule, if the name of the sponsoring organization appears within the title of the journal, then the work would be filed under that name and not under the first word of the title. Thus, for example, the *Journal of the American Medical Association* would (under the old rule) appear as *American Medical Association. Journal*—that is, it would *not* appear under "Journal" as the first filing word.

A similar situation obtains for titles beginning with terms such as *Annals of, Bulletin of, Proceedings of, Transactions of,* etc., followed by the name of an organization. Note an important distinction, however: A title of the form *Journal of Psychiatry* would indeed appear under "Journal"; but a form such as *Journal of the Psychiatric Society* would appear under "*Psychiatric Society. Journal.*" The appearance of the name of an *organization* within the title determined the difference under the old rule.

Under the new rule, a journal may be cataloged under whatever form appears on the title page. A good rule of thumb is simply to check the alternate possibility if your first try doesn't work.

It is a very common mistake for researchers to overlook a library's holdings—specifically, its pre-1981 holdings—of such titles because they look under *Journal, Annals, Bulletin, Proceedings*, etc., rather than under the name of the organization.

Filing Sequence

Another of the most serious and persistent problems researchers have with card catalogs is that of misinterpreting the filing sequence, because it is customarily word-by-word rather than letter-by-letter filing, as many people expect. (This point applies only to card, rather than computer, catalogs.) The difference may be illustrated as follows:

Letter-by-letter filing (*not* used)

Nazareth
N.E.H.
Newark

New England
New Jersey
Newman, John Henry, Cardinal, 1801–1890
NEWMAN, JOHN HENRY, CARDINAL, 1801–1890
News
New York
N.Y.P.D.

Word-by-word filing (is used)

N.E.H.
N.Y.P.D.
Nazareth
New England
New Jersey
New York
Newark
Newman, John Henry, Cardinal, 1801–1890
NEWMAN, JOHN HENRY, CARDINAL, 1801–1890
News

The basic principle in word-by-word filing is that when you have multiword headings or names, you first group together all that have the same first word (and subarrange all of them according to the second word, then third, etc.) before moving on to any headings or names with a different first word.

Note that in this illustration the name "Newman, John Henry" in capital and lower-case letters is distinct from the name typed all in capitals. The first is an author heading (representing a work by Newman); the second is a subject heading (representing a work about Newman). Subject headings in card catalogs are always indicated by either of two signals: (1) the top line of the catalog card being typed in CAPITAL LETTERS; or (2) the top line being typed conventionally, but printed *in red ink*. These distinctions are important because they signal a crucial difference between *subject* and *title* entries, which will be discussed below.

Note also that initialisms (such as N.E.H. or N.Y.P.D.) are filed as though each letter were a separate word. They will therefore appear at the very beginning of their letter section in the catalog, ahead of the full words. (There are some exceptions; for example, I've seen UNESCO filed both at the beginning of the *U* drawers and in the middle, as though it were a word.) If there is any confusion, it's best simply to check both possible places. The important point is to know that there are indeed two places to look; ignorance of this regularly causes readers to assume that a library does not own acronym titles when they really are available. Many catalog users, for example, fail to find the journal title *PMLA* because it appears at the very beginning of the *P* filing sequence, ahead of words like *Pacific* and *Palestine*, rather than between *Plastic* and *Poetry*.

There may be still other disruptions of a normal alphabetical sequence within card catalogs, for the sake of creating logical groupings; for example, in some libraries all names of individuals (persons) file before all geographic names (places), which file before titles and subjects (things). Thus the personal name "Stone, William" would precede the place name "Stone, Ga.," which would precede the subject heading "STONE—BIBLI-OGRAPHY." If you get confused about anything, remember that it is the job of the reference librarians to help you.

Computer catalogs usually follow letter-by-letter conventions. And with them you won't have to worry about finding an entry word in relation to other entries; the machine will find it directly, wherever it is filed (assuming you type the entry correctly to begin with—some softwares are sensitive to spacing and punctuation).

Subject Headings

Aside from erroneously assuming that filing is letter-by-letter, the other most frequent problem people have in looking for books in the catalog is finding the right subject heading for their topic. For example, if a reader wants a book on morality, should she look under "Morality" or under "Ethics"? Or must she try both? The difference is considerable, since the two are nowhere near each other in the filing sequence. Similarly, if another reader wants information on sentencing criminals to death, should he look under "Death penalty" or under "Capital punishment"? And how does he know that he's thought up all of the right terms? Perhaps he should look under "Execution" or some other synonyms as well. Note that all three terms fall into quite different sections of the alphabet.

Reference librarians frequently run into people having problems in this regard—for example, one student became frustrated in looking for material on "Moonshining" because it is not under that heading. In a standard library catalog, works on this subject are filed under "Distilling, illicit." Another researcher wanted books on "Corporate philanthropy"; before asking for help she hadn't found anything because she was looking under "Philanthropy" rather than under the proper heading "Corporations—Charitable contributions." Similarly, researchers who want "Multinational corporations" often make the mistake of searching under that term when the proper heading is actually "International business enterprises"; and those looking for "Test tube babies" usually fail to search under the proper heading, "Fertilization in vitro, Human."

Not only the choice of words but also their order may be confusing—for example, should you look under "Surgical diagnosis" or "Diagnosis, surgical"? Under "Heavy minerals" or "Minerals, heavy"? Under "Fraudulent advertising" or "Advertising, fraudulent"? Inverted forms are not used consistently, so there is much room for error.

There are, however, systematic ways in which you can solve most of these problems. Specifically, there are four ways to find the right subject headings for your topic; two of them through using an annually revised, multivolume list of terms called *Library of Congress Subject Headings* (*LCSH*), and two through using the library's catalog itself. Before looking at the four ways, however, it is important to consider the principles governing the compilation and use of the *LCSH* list; they are uniform heading, scope-match specificity, and specific entry.

Uniform Heading.   Uniform heading is the principle that addresses the problem of synonyms, variant phrases, and different-language terms being used to express the same concept (e.g., "Death penalty," "Capital punishment," "*Todesstrafe*") and whose filing is scattered throughout the alphabet. Librarians who create systematic catalogs choose *one* of the many possible terms, in such cases, and file all relevant records under that single category term rather than repeat the same list of works under each of several terms scattered throughout the alphabet. Since the full list of relevant books appears under only one of the terms, the catalogers will insert *cross-references* at several of these other possible places in the alphabet to steer readers to the one main grouping.

Uniform heading also serves to round up the different *aspects* of a subject through the use of subdivisions of the single chosen term (e.g., "—Bibliography," "—History," "—Law and legislation," "—Study and teaching"). These various aspects may correspond to entirely different call number areas that are scattered throughout the classification scheme. For example, works under the *LCSH* term "Small business" usually get classed in HD (Economics) or KF (U.S. Law) areas; but if the books being cataloged are assigned the "—Accounting" subdivision, they switch to HF (Commerce) classes instead. If they receive the "—Finance" subdivision they are usually classed in HG (Finance); and if they are on the bibliographical aspect of the topic ("Small business—Bibliography") they are classed in Z7164.C81 (Business bibliography). All of these different class designations, while scattered in the bookstacks, nevertheless appear together in the catalog under the one heading "Small business."

Uniform headings thus round up, in one place, both *variant titles* for the same subject that are scattered throughout the catalog, and *variant class numbers* for the same subject that are scattered throughout the bookstacks. (Scattering of subject aspects in the classification scheme will be discussed further in Chapter 3.)

The advantage of uniform heading is that of the collocation function—you will not have to look in several different places for your subject. This subject grouping is brought about by the work that catalogers do in first creating and then adding to each bibliographic record an artificial point of commonality (the *LCSH* subject heading) that enables them to be retrieved together—a point of commonality that would not be retrievable or, indeed, that would not exist in the first place if catalogers merely recorded or transcribed data from the title pages of the books. Returning to "Capital punishment" as an example, note the wide variety of keywords that appear in only a brief sampling of titles that have been written on this topic:

The Ultimate Coercive Sanction
To Kill and Be Killed

A Life for a Life
Executing the Mentally Ill
Hanging Not Punishment Enough for Murtherers
Habeas Corpus Issues
In Spite of Innocence
The Unforgiven: Utah's Executed Men
Until You Are Dead
Fatal Error
Philosophy of Punishment

Hundreds of other keyword-variant titles could be listed—and in many different languages as well. Without the creation and assignment of the artificial point of commonality (the *LCSH* term "Capital punishment") to each record, a researcher looking for what the library had to offer on this topic would miss most of these works. Their natural language terms are simply too diverse to be rounded up systematically, or even guessed at with any efficiency.

Finding a whole group of relevant works categorized under a single term, however, enables you then to *recognize* within the one set a whole host of relevant titles whose variant phrasings—such as those above— you could never have specified in advance. This crucial element of serendipity or recognition on the retrieval end of library searches is a direct function of keyword-transcendent *categorizations* having been created by librarians at the input (cataloging) end of the operation. Cataloging is thus not at all the same as merely transcribing existing data from title pages or tables of contents. It is a process of *adding standardized terms* "on top of," or in addition to, the words provided by the book, rather than merely recording what is already there. Its major contribution lies in providing category terms that transcend the various expressions many different authors have used in talking about the same subject. And these category terms, unlike title keywords, can themselves be found through predictable and systematic means. The *LCSH* list is the record of what these uniform headings are.

Scope-Match Specificity.   Prior to the advent of computer catalogs, books, as a general rule, were seldom assigned more than two or three subject headings. This limitation was an important consideration in the creation of card catalogs, because filing individual cards for each book under a half dozen or more terms at different places in the alphabet would result in a catalog that was physically very bulky. The fewer category groups that were created, in other words, the more manageable was the size of the overall physical file.

Another important consideration—still relevant even in the age of computer catalogs—is the volume of work that catalogers have to do. Almost all libraries are chronically underfunded, and so catalogers who have to create records for dozens of books each day don't have the time to figure out ten or twelve headings for each one. (Again, cataloging is not simply a matter of transcribing words from tables of contents—or of simply adding existing headings from the *LCSH* list to records. It is also a matter of extending the list, creating new headings, and—the difficult part—integrating all of the new terms into a web of cross-referenced relationships to the existing headings.)

This is where scope-match specificity comes in. It means that catalogers will usually assign the minimum number of headings that indicate the subject content of a given book *as a whole*—that is, the catalogers will not assign a heading for each individual chapter or section of the book. Thus a book about "Orange" and "Grapefruit" will be entered under each of these two terms, because in combination they cover the whole scope of the work. If another book deals with these two topics plus "Tangerine," a third subject heading may be used. However, if a book deals with "Orange," "Grapefruit," "Tangerine," and "Lemon," it will not be cataloged under four different headings. When a work treats of four or more related topics, then a *single generic heading* representing all the topics comprehensively will be assigned—in this case, "Citrus fruits." While this is indeed a generic term, it is nevertheless the most specific term that covers the book *as a whole*. Catalogers traditionally aimed for this level of coverage. If there is no single term that expresses the subject of the book as a whole, they will try to sum up the book in as few headings as possible—usually about three.

The advent of computer catalogs has eliminated the need in some libraries to worry about bulky catalogs, so computerized catalog records often receive more than three subject headings. (A new rule of thumb for catalogers in the online environment is to assign a heading for any topic that takes up at least 20 percent of the book in hand.) Nevertheless, not all libraries have online catalogs; and even those that do have them still have to catalog too many books with too few catalogers, and it still takes less time to integrate three headings into a web of cross-references than ten or twelve—so the principle of scope-match specificity has not been rendered obsolete even in an age of computerization.

The most important implication of this principle for researchers is that it means you usually will not have ten or twelve chances to find the right heading for your topic in the catalog. Rather, you will usually have only about three to five chances. So it is particularly important to know how to find the *right* terms in a systematic manner.

Specific Entry.   This is by far the most important principle that researchers need to be aware of. It means that, given a choice between using specific or general headings for a book, catalogers will *predictably* choose *the most specific possible headings* for the book as a whole, *rather than the general headings* available in the *LCSH* list.

For example, if you are looking for material on nightmares, you should not look first under "Dreams" or "Sleep" but under "Nightmares" specifically. Similarly, if you want books on Siamese cats you should look under the specific heading "Siamese cat" and *not* under the general heading "Cats." One reseacher looking for material on Jewish children mistakenly assumed the proper heading would be "Jews." It isn't. It's "Jewish children," which was in a different drawer. Works under this specific heading are *not also* listed under the generic heading "Jews."

Another reader looking for books on management by objectives wasted a lot of time looking at records under the "Management" heading; he should have looked first specifically for "Management by objectives," which appears considerably farther back in the word-by-word filing. Again, such material will *not* be filed under *both* headings—you have to find the *most specific one* appropriate to the subject. Still another reader interested in the effects of divorce on children made the usual mistake of looking under the general heading "Divorce" rather than under the specific heading "Children of divorced parents." (There is also an even narrower term, "Adult children of divorced parents.") And—again!—

materials listed under narrower terms do not also appear under the broader term or terms because of the principle of uniform heading (that is, *one* term will be chosen from the range of possible headings). This is not to say that the more general headings may not also be useful, for they may; but *you should not start with a general heading if you really have a specific topic in mind.*

Note that this advice runs directly against the grain of what students are usually told ("Start with a broad idea and then try to narrow it down as you go"). While this may be good advice in other situations, *when you are using a library catalog it is better to do the exact opposite.* Start at the most specific level you can, and only *then* broaden out if adequately specific terms aren't available.

The problem with researchers starting with general terms is that they usually find a few sources that appear to be in the ballpark—but they simultaneously miss most of the best material without knowing it, and *they usually stop with their initial pool of general sources.* The researcher who looks under "Divorce," for instance, may indeed find a few books that have sections discussing the effects of divorce on children—but if he stops there (and most people do stop at the first level that seems at all relevant), he will miss all of the works under "Children of divorced parents," which are whole books (rather than just chapters or sections) on that topic.

The *LCSH* list of category terms contains both general and specific headings, of course. And the general terms are indeed used for books if they are written at the broad level. Thus some books are about dreams in general and will be given the broad heading, "Dreams" because that term is the "tightest fit" for those books. But other books, on children's dreams in particular, will be given only the narrower term "Children's Dreams" because it is the tightest fit for these books.

Another example: If you want information on the theory of the divine right of kings, do *not* look under "Kings" or "Monarchy" because the works recorded under the proper, specific heading "Divine right of kings" are *not duplicated* under the more general headings. They are *only* under the most specific heading. That's why an understanding of specific entry is so crucial.

When there are several possible levels of relevant headings available in *LCSH,* the virtue of specific entry lies in making the choice of which level to use *predictable*. Thus works on blue crabs *could* conceivably be cataloged under "Crabs," "Crustacea," or "Chesapeake Bay," or even under "Ecology," "Estuaries," "Invertebrates," "Marine biology," "Marine invertebrates," "Coastal fauna," "Oceanography," "Arthropoda," or any of two dozen other terms—all of which appear as valid headings in the red books (the *LCSH* list). The problem is that when you look in the direction of generality there is no logical or predictable stopping point; the solution is that when you search in the direction of specificity, there is. The right term to stop at in the *LCSH* list, here, is "Callinectes" (there is a direct cross-reference to this from "Blue crabs"). In all cases, as a rule, you should look in the direction of specific headings and stop only at the level of terminology that provides the tightest fit for your topic, rather than at the general levels above it. Look for general levels only *after* you've *first* tried to be as specific as possible, rather than vice versa.

So, then: How, exactly, do you find the right headings for your topic? There are two intertwined problems here: How do you get from the words you may think of ("Multinational corporations") to the often different terms used in the cataloging system ("International business enterprises"); and how do you find the most specific heading ("Children of divorced parents") when only the phrasing for the general subject ("Divorce") occurs to you? There are four ways to solve these problems.

1.   Follow cross-references in the *Library of Congress Subject Headings* list, especially the NT (Narrower Term) references.   As noted above, the *LCSH* list is an annual, multivolume set of terms that have been approved for use as subject category terms in library catalogs; it is often referred to as "the red books" because of the binding of the volumes composing it. The list also includes words and phrases that are not used, with cross-references to the proper terms. Thus if you look up "Morality" you will find a note, "*use* Ethics." Similarly, "Surgical diagnosis," which is not used, will tell you to *use* the acceptable form "Diagnosis, surgical."

Once you find the proper term, the *LCSH* books will also give you a list of other subject headings that are related to it so that you can systematically search either slightly different topics or different levels of generality. Thus "Death penalty," which is not used, refers you to "Capital punish-

Capital punishment *(May Subd Geog)*
  ₁HV8694-HV8699₁
  UF Abolition of capital punishment
      Death penalty
  BT Criminal law
      Punishment
  RT Executions and executioners
  NT Crucifixion
      Death row
      Discrimination in capital punishment
      Electrocution
      Garrote
      Hanging
      Last meal before execution
      Stoning
— **Religious aspects**
— — **Baptists, ₁Catholic Church, etc.₁**
— — **Buddhism, ₁Christianity, etc.₁**

Fig. 1

ment"; and under this term you will find a list of other headings that are preceded by different code designations. These codes are very important. They are UF, BT, RT, and NT. (See Figure 1.)

UF means "Used for"; thus, in Figure 1, "Capital punishment" in boldface type is *used for* "Death penalty." In other words, if terms are preceded by UF, do not use them. They are not acceptable forms; instead, use the boldface heading above them.

BT means Broader Term or Terms; these *are* valid headings that you can search under ("Criminal law," "Punishment").

RT means Related Term or Terms. RT references also refer to valid headings.

NT means Narrower Term or Terms; these, too, are acceptable search terms ("Crucifixion," "Death row," "Garrote," "Last meal before execution," etc.).

There are two crucial points here. The first is that the BTs, RTs, and NTs are *not subsets or subdivisions* of the boldface term above. They are *not included* in the coverage of the boldface term; if you want any of these subjects, *you must look for them directly*. Thus "Death row" and "Hanging" and "Punishment" are not included in the coverage of "Capital punishment"; if you want these topics you must search for them individually in the "D," "H," and "P" sections of the alphabet.

The second point is that the NT cross-references are by far the most important ones to follow up. They are usually the specific entry terms that you need to start with. And they may lead to other, even more specific terms. Thus, within the *LCSH* list, "Divorce" does not provide a direct NT reference to "Children of divorced parents," but it does start a series that leads to it. Specifically, "Divorce" provides an NT reference to "Divorced people"; this heading, in turn, provides an NT reference to "Divorced parents"; and this heading, finally, provides an NT reference to "Children of divorced parents"—which then provides still another NT reference to "Adult children of divorced parents" if you wish to pursue the subject to that still narrower level.

Knowledge of the narrower/broader nature of the cross-reference structure can help you to refine or expand your search, sometimes through an extended scale of headings, such as the following:

Descending order
Chordata
    NT Vertebrates
Vertebrates
    NT Mammals
Mammals
    NT Primates
Primates
    NT Monkeys
Monkeys
    NT Baboons
Baboons
    NT Hamadryas baboon

Ascending order
Hamadryas baboon
    BT Baboons
Baboons
    BT Monkeys
Monkeys
    BT Primates

Primates
    BT Mammals
Mammals
    BT Vertebrates
Vertebrates
    BT Chordata

Note that broader and narrower labels are always relative to other terms. For example, while "Dreams," on the face of it, is a rather general term (certainly in relation to "Children's dreams"), it is nevertheless a narrower term itself in relation to "Subconsciousness" or "Visions." "BT" and "NT" designations are thus not absolute labels. A heading that is "BT" or broader in relation to narrower terms below it will simultaneously be an "NT" or narrower heading in relation to broader headings above it. No matter where you enter the sequence, however, just remember to move in the direction of the tightest-fit headings for whatever level you ultimately have in mind.

    This, then, is the first way to find the right subject headings: Use the cross-references within the *LCSH* list and pay particular attention to the NT (narrower term) cross-references.

2. Look for narrower terms that are alphabetically adjacent to broader terms in the *LCSH* list. Not all narrower terms in the red books receive explicit NT cross-references pointing to them. In Figure 2, for example, note that the NT references under the general term "Afro-Americans" do not include any other headings that start with the element "Afro-"; and yet there are scores of such narrower headings that are alphabetically adjacent, in the list, to the general term. Thus, preceding "Afro-Americans" are dozens of more specific categories (and cross-references) such as "Afro-American aesthetics," "Afro-American wit and humor," and "Afro-American young men." And following it (not shown in Figure 2) are scores of other narrower terms such as "Afro-Americans and mass media," "Afro-Americans in business," and "Afro-Americans in veterinary medicine." The full roster of these terms starting with "Afro-" actually takes up eight full pages within *Library of Congress Subject Headings*.

    These narrower terms do not receive explicit NT cross-reference designations because they are already alphabetically adjacent to the broader

Afro-American women social reformers
>   *(May Subd Geog)*
>> UF Women social reformers, Afro-
>>   American
>> BT Women social reformers—United
>>   States

Afro-American wood-carving
>   *(May Subd Geog)*
>> UF Wood-carving, Afro-American
>> BT Wood-carving—United States

Afro-American young men *(May Subd Geog)*
>> UF Young men, Afro-American
>> BT Young men—United States

Afro-American youth *(May Subd Geog)*
>> UF Afro-Americans—Youth
>>   Negro youth *[Former heading]*
>>   Youth, Afro-American
>> BT Youth—United States
>> NT Church work with Afro-American
>>   youth

Afro-Americana
> USE Afro-Americans—Collectibles

Afro-Americans *(May Subd Geog)*
>   *[E185]*

Here are entered works on citizens of the United
States of black African descent. Works on blacks who
temporarily reside in the United States, such as aliens,
students from abroad, etc., are entered under Blacks—
United States. Works on blacks outside the United
States are entered under Blacks—[place].

>> UF African Americans
>>   Afro-Americans—United States
>>   Black Americans
>>   Colored people (United States)
>>   Negroes *[Former heading]*
>> BT Africans—United States
>>   Blacks—United States
>>   Ethnology—United States
>> SA *subdivision* Afro-Americans *under*
>>   *names of wars, e.g.* World War,
>>   1939-1945—Afro-Americans; *and*
>>   *headings beginning with* Afro-
>>   American
>> NT Associations, institutions, etc.—
>>   Membership, Afro-American
>>   Church work with Afro-Americans
>>   Mulattoes

Fig. 2

term; their omission as NTs enables the Library of Congress to save some printing costs—money can be saved by not repeating as NT terms those categories that can already be seen in the immediate neighborhood of a broader term. Nevertheless, because of the crucial principle of specific entry, these terms are every bit as important as the ones that do receive explicit NT listings.

You have to look in *two* places within the red books for the narrower terms, in other words: the NTs *and* the areas that are alphabetically adjacent to the general terms. It isn't difficult to do this; and yet it is a very common mistake for readers not to pay attention here, because the importance of finding the narrower (rather than the broader) headings is often not obvious.

Note, further, that the alphabetical contiguity of these narrower terms to their related broader heading is something that is almost entirely lost in computer browse screen displays. There, the interposition of scores of titles falling between the subject headings effectively scatters the narrower headings out of eye range; indeed, sometimes subject headings that are right next to each other in the red books may be scores of screens away from each other in the online displays of computer catalogs. (This is particularly the case with subject headings starting with the words "Business," "Television," and "Women." All of these broad headings have dozens of alphabetically adjacent narrower terms in the *LCSH* list, which simply cannot be seen next to each other when they are separated onscreen by hundreds of intervening *title* lines.) The point needs a certain emphasis these days because some libraries are trying to save money by saying that they no longer need to have expensive printed copies of the red books placed next to their computer terminals, asserting that "the same information is online anyway." This is nonsense. Access to information is not determined simply by its *existence*; its *format* of presentation is every bit as important. And the printed *LCSH* has a decided advantage in displaying those crucial alphabetically adjacent narrower terms that cannot be noticed onscreen, because the print format enables one's eyes to roam horizontally and diagonally, not just vertically.

3. Within the library catalog itself, look for subject tracings on relevant records that are retrieved by other means.   Sometimes a good

```
FILE:  LOCI:   You Browsed:  COCKNEY DIALECT
B01  Cockman.   F. G. (Frederick George)//(AUTH=5)
B02  Cockman.   Peter//(AUTH=1)
B03  Cockney//(TITL=1)
B04  Cockney boy in Essex//(TITL=1)
B05  Cockney camera//(TITL=1)
B06+ Cockney dialect & slang//(TITL=1)
B07  Cockney dialect and slang//(TITL=1)
B08  Cockney in Arcadia//(TITL=1)
B09  Cockney past and present//(TITL=1)
B10  Cockney, past and present//(TITL=1)
B11  cockney's farming experiences//(TITL=1)
B12  Cockpit//(TITL=3)
```

```
81-165873                          ITEM 1 OF 1 IN SET 1        (LCCC)

Wright, Peter, 1923-
    Cockney dialect and slang / Peter Wright. London : Batsford, 1981. 184 p.:
ill. ; 23 cm.

LC CALL NUMBER: PE1961 .W7

SUBJECTS:
    English language--Dialects--England--London.
    English language--Slang.
    London (England)--Social life and customs.

ADDED ENTRIES:
    Cockney dialect & slang.

DEWEY DEC:   427/.1 dc19

NOTES:
    Spine title:  Cockney dialect & slang.
    Includes index
```

```
FILE:  LOCI:   You Browsed:  ENGLISH LANGUAGE--DIALECTS--ENGLAND--LONDON--
B01  English language--Dialects--England--Lancashire//(SUBJ=6)
B02  English language--Dialects--England--Lancashire--G//(SUBJ=1)
B03  English language--Dialects--England--Lancashire--T//(SUBJ=2)
B04  English language--Dialects--England--Lincolnshire//(SUBJ=2)
B05  English language--Dialects--England--Lindsey//(SUBJ=1)
B06+ English language--Dialects--England--London//(SUBJ=20)
B07  English language--Dialects--England--London--Texts//(SUBJ=1)
B08  English language--Dialects--England--Maps//(SUBJ=6)
B09  English language--Dialects--England--Midlands//(SUBJ=1)
B10  English language--Dialects--England--Newcastle upc//(SUBJ=1)
B11  English language--Dialects--England--North Yorkshi//(SUBJ=1)
B12  English language--Dialects--England--Northamptonsh//(SUBJ=1)
```

Fig. 3

starting point can be secured in a catalog (either computer or card) by finding a good title rather than a category term from the red books. For example, a researcher looking for information on the Cockney dialect started his search by typing in the word "Cockney"; this led to a browse display that included the title *Cockney Dialect & Slang* and a few other works also starting with the same title word (see Figure 3). A glance at the bottom of the first title catalog record, here, shows that the proper *subject heading* is "English language—Dialects—England—London." The latter term groups together all of the works on this subject.

As Figure 3 indicates, searching "Cockney" turns up fewer than a half dozen titles that start with this word; but searching the proper *LCSH* category term turns up a score of relevant works—most of which do not even use the keyword "Cockney" at all in their title (*Ideolects in Dickens, The Early London Dialect, The Muvver Tongue, Bernard Shaw's Phonetics*, and so on). Most of what the library owns, in other words, would be entirely overlooked if the researcher simply confused a title display with a subject heading display. Such a researcher would find "something"—and probably stop searching at that point—while inadvertently missing most of what the library has to offer.

This is the crucial point to remember: In the catalog, *finding a title entry is not at all the same as finding a subject heading.* A title represents only one work; a subject heading, on the other hand, is a *category term* that groups together many individual titles that may refer to the same subject using a wide variety of unpredictable keywords, synonyms, or variant phrasings—and in foreign languages as well as English.

Tracings on relevant records can be searched in both computer and card catalogs. In the latter, simply look at the bottom of the card record for any relevant author or title entry to find the subject headings assigned to that book.

An example of using tracings in a card catalog is provided by the reader who was interested in the student riots in France in the late 1960s; he was having trouble finding a good subject heading to search under. He was already aware, however, of one book on the subject that he knew to be relevant: Patrick Seale's *Red Flag/Black Flag: The French Revolution, 1968.* The catalog card for this book is reproduced in Figure 4. Note that the tracings indicated that this work has been assigned two subject headings: "Paris—Riot, 1968" and "College students—France—Political activity." When the reference librarian showed him these tracings, he then found that other, similar works could be found under these category designations, and the works listed included, but were not limited to, English-language titles.

While searches for titles or relevant authors usually offer the best ways to start the process of finding subject tracings, *any* kind of search that turns up a single relevant starting point can do the trick. If the software of the computer catalog allows it, you can search first by keyword (appearing anywhere, not necessarily as the first word of a title), by author, or even by classification number to start the process. Indeed, the keyword search feature offered by many databases is often most useful not as the best way to

DC412
.S4   Seale, Patrick.
1968   Red flag/black flag; French revolution, 1968, by Patrick
        Seale and Maureen McConville. [1st American ed.] New
        York, Putnam [1968]

          252 p. illus., ports. 22 cm. $6.95

          1. Paris—Riot, 1968. 2. College students—France—Political ac-
tivity.   i. McConville, Maureen, joint author. ii. Title.

    DC412.S4   1968   944.3'6'083   68–57448

    Library of Congress   [5]

Fig. 4

find relevant records themselves, but rather as *the first step toward finding proper subject tracings* that lead to whole *groups* of records, the individual members of which may have entirely different keywords in their titles.

4. Within the library catalog, browse through all of the subdivisions of any relevant subject heading you find.   The fourth way to find the best subject heading for your topic is to look at the array of *subdivisions* of headings that show up in the catalog. There are three important points here:

1. A subdivision added to a heading (as in "Business intelligence— Case studies") makes an otherwise general heading more specific.
2. A subdivision added to a heading enables you to recognize a Boolean combination of elements that you would not have thought to combine yourself (see below).
3. Although some of these subdivisions are listed under their respective headings within the *LCSH* list itself, most of them are not. You have to look in the catalog itself rather than just in the red books set to see the full range of subdivisions that appear under any given heading.

There is a reason for the omission of most subdivisions in the subject headings list: Most of them are "free floating," which means they can be attached, with certain restrictions, to a variety of headings without the attachment being explicitly recorded in the *LCSH* list. This keeps the cost of the *LCSH* set manageable—if every possible heading-subdivision combination were actually recorded, the annual set would be so huge that many smaller libraries could no longer afford it.

For example, in the heading "Television—United States—History," neither of the elements "—United States" or "—History" is explicitly listed in the red books as being a search option under "Television." Nevertheless, they do appear as options that are displayed within the catalog itself. Note that subdivisions such as these, when appended to a general heading, thereby create a narrower and more specific category—and, again, library catalogers always seek to enter a book under the most specific heading appropriate to it. This is the only way to make predictable the choice of which level of generality to search under.

An additional benefit of subdivision is that it greatly increases discovery by serendipity; that is, it enables users to recognize relevant search options that they could never specify in advance. For example, I was once asked to help a reader who wanted information on Thomas Jefferson's views on religious liberty. Scanning through the array of subdivisions that are appended to Jefferson's name (as a subject) in the catalog produced an unanticipated variety of search options for answering this question:

Jefferson, Thomas, 1743–1826—Bibliography
                          * * *
                       —Quotations
                          * * *
                       —Views on freedom of religion

None of these subheadings appears under Jefferson's name in the *LCSH* list, but all of them nevertheless appear in the catalog itself.

- The third subdivision, "—Views on freedom of religion," is obviously directly relevant; it leads to Merrill D. Peterson's *Thomas Jefferson, Religious Liberty and the American Tradition* (Jefferson Institute, 1987), which is an entire book on the subject.

- The second subdivision, "—Quotations," leads to works such as *The Real Thomas Jefferson* (National Center for Constitutional Studies, 1983) and *Seeking the Moral Wisdom of the Founder of American Government* (L. Faucett, [1975?]), both of which are compilations of Jefferson's own words, *categorized by subject* (including the subject of religious liberty).

- The first subdivision, "—Bibliography," leads to both Frank Shuffelton's *Thomas Jefferson: A Comprehensive, Annotated Bibliography of Writings About Him (1826–1980)* (Garland, 1983) and Eugene L. Huddleston's *Thomas Jefferson: A Reference Guide* (G. K. Hall, 1982). Together, these two annotated bibliographies list *dozens* of sources on Jefferson and religious liberty.

When I first brought up the browse display of headings on the computer screen, I was consciously looking for the "—Views on" subdivision, but I was not specifically looking for either of the other two. Nevertheless, because I know enough always to scan through the full array, I could *recognize* the worth of the other subheadings even though it had not occurred to me to *specify them in advance*. And these additional search options, once noticed, led to dozens of additional and highly relevant sources.

Naive students of library science will sometimes say, "Libraries could save a lot of money if we simplify cataloging by eliminating multielement strings and simply record each element separately, because the computer software can combine the separate elements into the same results." While it is true that the computer could indeed combine "Jefferson" and "Quotations" as separate terms, or "Jefferson" and "Bibliography," the real problem is with the researchers—the human beings who use the computers. *They* cannot combine the two elements when they are separate (rather than linked in a string of terms) unless it occurs to them in advance that "Quotations" and "Bibliography" are indeed viable options. When catalogers have taken the trouble to create linked strings it is known as "precoordination" of terms; when the terms appear only as separate elements on the record, and have to be combined afterward by computer manipulations, it is known as "postcoordination." The important point is that precoordinated strings of subdivisions under a heading offer a major advantage to

searchers that cannot be matched by a postcoordinate system: A precoordinate system enables you to *recognize* many important search options that
simply would not occur to you to *specify in advance.*

That's why it is so important to look systematically at any and all subdivisions that appear under the headings you find in the library catalog—
they are likely to show you many relevant search options for your topic
that you didn't realize you had. And don't stop your search with only the
first relevant subdivision you find; make sure to look through *all* of them.
(This is another point that took years to "crystallize" for me. It is not
immediately obvious that you should look through *all* subdivisions of a
topic, and so most researchers just don't do it. But I've found through
experience that it works so well, and in such surprising ways, and in so
many instances, that it should be done consciously and deliberately.)

Some of the subdivisions that are possible—and that, as a reference
librarian, I have found most useful to look out for—are these:

[LC Subject Heading]—Bibliography
                —Bio-bibliography
                —Biography
                —Case studies
                —Civilization
                —Commerce
                —Costume
                —Criticism and interpretation
                —Description and travel
                —Diaries
                —Dictionaries
                —Directories
                —Economic conditions
                —Encyclopedias
                —Foreign economic relations
                —Foreign relations
                —Former Soviet Republics
                —Great Britain
                —Guidebooks

—Handbooks, manuals, etc.
—History
—History—Bibliography
—History—Sources
—Illustrations
—Japan
—Law and legislation
—Management
—Maps
—Personal narratives
—Pictorial works
—Rating of
—Relations
—Social life and customs
—Sources
—Statistics
—Study and teaching
—United States
—United States—Bibliography
—United States—History
—Views on [. . .]

Obviously not all of these subdivisions will appear under any one heading; but these are among the more important ones you should be on the lookout for. Recognizing options is fine; consciously looking for them is even more effective. Success in using subdivisions depends on your "getting the feel" of which ones you can expect to find. They are frequently overlooked in the catalog simply because readers aren't taught their importance and because there are so many of them. For example, in the card catalog of one library I worked in, the heading "Greece—History" is separated from the unqualified term "Greece" by the interposition of fifteen other subdivisions, such as "Greece—Description and travel" and "Greece—Foreign relations," plus a variety of titles starting with the name of the country. And, because of the principles of uniform heading and specific entry, most of the history books are entered under the subdivided form and *not* under

"Greece" by itself. So a researcher could easily miss them unless she suspects beforehand that a form such as "Greece—History" should exist farther back in the filing sequence.

The Library of Congress publishes a booklet called *Free-Floating Subdivisions: An Alphabetical Index* (revised irregularly). Researchers who wish to get a broad overview of what their options are in this area are well advised to study it. It is often used in library schools as a training tool for reference librarians. Copies may be ordered from the Library at 800-255-3666 (U.S. only) or 202-707-6100.

Many subjects can be subdivided geographically as well as topically; thus, for example, you would have an advantage if you suspected in advance that "Mass media—United States" may be a better heading than "Mass media" alone. At another university library where I worked, the two are separated by more than three dozen other subheadings; at the Library of Congress, in the old card catalog, they are in completely separate drawers. The point is that the most relevant works on a topic may very well have a "—United States" subdivision; but you may easily miss the form unless you are deliberately looking for it. The *LCSH* list provides a major clue in that it provides a parenthetical note "(May subd. geog.)" after all headings capable of being geographically subdivided; but the best way to avoid the difficulty is always to browse quickly through *all* subdivisions of a topic within the catalog, even if it involves skimming quickly through many computer screens or through a whole drawerful (or more) of cards. Many people don't want to take the time to do this; but doing it anyway is a hallmark that really distinguishes the technique of the efficient researcher from that of the novice.

A problem that students often have at the beginning of their projects is that of narrowing down their topic to manageable size. It should now be apparent that the subject cataloging system gives you several easy ways to do just this. (These aren't the *only* ways, of course; but they are indeed easy.) They are precisely the same four ways that lead you to the proper specific (rather than general) subject headings for your topic: Within the *LCSH* list, look especially for "NT" cross-references and alphabetically adjacent narrower terms; and within the catalog itself, look for subject tracings on relevant records turned up through title (or author, keyword, or class number) searches, and look for subdivisions of any relevant headings you come across. *Each of these procedures will enable you to recognize narrower and more manageable research topics—sometimes scores or hundreds of them—that you probably could not have specified in advance.* The process of following out any or all of these procedures is such that you will see, in a systematic manner, more clear and distinct options for researching various aspects of a broad subject than you would have thought possible.

A kind of "fifth way" to find the right headings for your topic is through computer combinations of two or more subject elements—that is, sometimes there isn't a single term that expresses the subject you want, but you can still hit the nail on the head, at a specific level, by combining separate headings (e.g., "Mexican Americans" and "Education, bilingual"). Such "Boolean combinations" will be discussed in Chapter 12.

It should be apparent at this point that there is much more system to the use of library catalogs than most people are aware of. There's nothing particularly difficult about the system; once it's explained, in fact, people catch on to it very quickly. The problem is that there's nothing particularly obvious about it, either, and it does have to be explained.

A further point: The *LCSH* list usually does not list *proper names* that can be used as subject headings. But they can still appear as valid headings within the catalog itself. Don't limit your formulation of questions to *only* the *LCSH* list, in other words—remember, again, that the catalog itself will provide you with search options that are not always explicitly recorded in the red books.

Another point to remember is that if you are specifically looking for foreign-language books on a subject, you still have to use the English-language subject headings to find them. For example, I once helped a reader who wanted only Italian books on the city of Venice. He was making the mistake of searching under "Venezia." Repeating that search today (in the Library of Congress's post-1968 database) leads to seven browse screens of individual titles that happen to start with that word. The proper *LCSH* form, however, is "Venice (Italy)"; searching under this heading leads to a set of more than 930 books, in all languages; this large set can then be limited to only those in Italian, which produces a result of more than 420 books. A large number of these Italian works on the subject do not themselves have the word "Venezia" in their titles; for example:

Il campiello sommerso
Veneto: itinerari ebraici
La chiesa del Tintoretto
Le sculture esterne di San Marco
Santi e contadini: lunario della tradizione orale veneta

All such Italian-language books on the subject "Venice (Italy)" are rounded up by the *English-language* category term.

Unfortunately, researchers need to be aware that a major problem in the *LCSH* system has been developing since about 1993. At that point, the Library of Congress (LC) began to accept "copy cataloging" from other libraries, in an effort to save money. This means that LC nowadays often accepts the subject headings created by other libraries for new books, if the other libraries have cataloged a book first. The problem is that many of the other 25,000 libraries from which LC draws these copied records are not nearly as careful as LC itself is in assigning headings at the proper level of specificity.[1] Headings created by others in the OCLC system (see Chapter 11) are very often—mistakenly—general rather than specific. (This may be due to the widespread practice, in many libraries, of relying on technicians rather than professional librarians to do much of their cataloging.) Such headings are not findable in a predictable manner, in other words. Researchers simply have to guess which level is being used, because the rule of thumb of specific entry, which makes the choice of levels predictable, has been largely abandoned in LC's uncritical acceptance and endorsement of these copied headings. One hopes that a blunder of this magnitude will ultimately be corrected in the future, as it adversely affects—indeed, directly undercuts—the *system* of retrieval in *all* research libraries throughout the English-speaking world. Until that correction is made, however, researchers need to be aware that "a hole in the bibliographic ozone layer" opened for the first time in the early 1990s and has been growing larger since then.

There are both advantages and disadvantages to pursuing information through the library catalog. The primary advantage—and it is an important one—is that anything you find in it is likely to be immediately available to you on the shelves; you needn't go to another library for the material or use the time-consuming interlibrary loan system. (If a book is not on the shelf where it should be, you should look for a daily computer-updated printout at either the reference or the circulation desks. Most libraries will have one; it will list all books checked out to individuals or placed on reserve. Some libraries now record this circulation information right in their online catalogs.)

One of the disadvantages, of course, is that the catalog will usually list only your own library's collections, which may not contain the best or the most recent books on your particular subject. Further, retrieval is complicated by the standard practice among catalogers of assigning as few subject headings as possible to a work—that is, only as many as summarize its contents as a whole. (This is the difference between subject cataloging and indexing.) With one notable exception, the best way to find out what's in the individual chapters is to browse through the contents of the books themselves, which you can locate in the stacks through their call numbers (see Chapter 3).

The exception involves collections of different essays by one or more authors. For most such works, the individual essays in the volume are each indexed separately in an ongoing publication called *Essay and General Literature Index* (H. W. Wilson, 1900–), which provides access by author or subject. And the subject terms it assigns tend to be the same *Library of Congress Subject Headings* used by the library catalog. This *Index* is very similar to a journal index; the only difference is that the articles it covers are in book anthologies rather than in periodicals. Each issue (semiannual with bound annual and five-year cumulations) contains a list of the anthologies it indexes; there is also a separate cumulative volume of *Works Indexed, 1900–1969*. The *Essay and General Literature Index* is a good supplement to the library catalog, for it provides deeper subject access into many books than the catalog does. And libraries frequently use its lists of works indexed as buying guides for developing their collections.

The *Index* is especially valuable to professors and graduate students because it supplies good access to scholarly *Festschriften*. It is noteworthy for undergraduates, too, because for every ten people who know of the existence of the specialized journal indexes and databases, only one will know of the *E&GLI*. Anyone who uses it is likely to be the only one in the class to have discovered the material it leads to. And, as a wise debater once said, "An expert is someone who can cite a source that nobody else knows about."

The *E&GLI* is not the only index that picks up essays from anthologies (*Religion Two, Historical Abstracts, MLA International Bibliography,* and *Anthropological Literature* are examples of others in specialized fields), but it is the best overall and multidisciplinary source of its type, and its coverage extends much farther back (to 1900) than the others.

The sources I am emphasizing in this book are those that allow access by subject; but there are other indexes analogous to the *E&GLI* that list and index individual items other than essays within anthologies—for example, poems, plays, and short stories. These can be identified through the reference sources discussed in Chapter 16.

The overall points to remember about subject headings are:

- You must find the subject term that is acceptable to the retrieval system, which will very often not be the term you think of by yourself.
- To find the right term or terms you need to consult the *Library of Congress Subject Headings* list, which is the standard roster of category terms used by libraries throughout the English-speaking world.
- Within the *LCSH* list you must follow the cross-references, paying particular attention to the NT (narrower term) references, which lead you to the *most specific* headings. Books are cataloged, as a rule, *only* under the most specific headings applicable to them and *not also* under broader or more general headings.
- Within the *LCSH* list there is a second way to find, systematically, the most specific appropriate headings: Look in the areas alphabetically adjacent to the general headings.
- Within the library catalog itself, you can find additional *LCSH* terms by "snagging" relevant records by other means (through author, title, keyword, or call number searches) and then looking at the *subject tracings* that appear at the bottom of those catalog records. These are the category terms you should look under to find other, similar books.
- Within the catalog itself, look for *subdivisions* of any relevant heading you come across. These subdivisions are frequently not listed in the red books *LCSH* set, but they will enable you to recognize many search options for your topic that you could never specify in advance.

- You should realize that many other catalogs, indexes, bibliographies, and databases tend to use the same *LCSH* list of subject terms. (These will be discussed in Chapter 4.)

Subject heading searches—or "controlled vocabulary" searches—however, are only one of several methods of gaining access to information. For the sake of providing a large overview, let me anticipate a few points to be discussed in subsequent chapters, and mention here that eight alternative methods of searching can be used when no subject heading exists or when you wish to turn up sources in addition to those turned up under subject headings:

- Systematic browsing or scanning (see Chapter 3)
- Keyword searches in both printed indexes and computer databases (see Chapters 5 and 12)
- Citation searches in printed indexes and computers (see Chapter 6)
- Related-record searches (see Chapter 7)
- Searches through published subject bibliographies (see Chapter 9)
- Computer searches (especially those involving a *combination* of terms or search elements; see Chapters 11 and 12); these can be done with subject headings, keywords, authors' names, or a variety of other elements
- Using people sources (see Chapter 14)
- Type of literature searches (see Chapter 16)

Each of these approaches—like searching with subject headings—has its own advantages and disadvantages; and, collectively viewed, each has a strength that compensates for a weakness in the others. An awareness of the basic structure of relationships among only these few distinct methods of searching can have a very large effect in increasing the efficiency of your research.

Note

1. Thomas Mann, "'Cataloging Must Change!' and Indexer Consistency Studies: Misreading the Evidence at Our Peril," *Cataloging & Classification Quarterly* 23, no. 3/4 (1997): 3–45.

3

Systematic Browsing, Scanning, and Use of Classified Bookstacks

Librarians sometimes meet with resistance when they suggest that if readers want certain information they should browse or scan the library's bookshelves in a particular area. Evidently some people assume—if it occurs to them at all—that browsing is at best a haphazard and inefficient way to do research. Others who cannot envision any resources beyond those that appear on computer screens also tend to disregard the importance of direct searches of the texts of printed books arranged in subject groups.

Such researchers are needlessly cutting themselves off from a primary avenue of access to recorded knowledge. Even in an age of computers, the systematic browsing or scanning of classified book collections is a very useful method of subject retrieval, and in some cases it is the most efficient method of all. Historically, the practice of shelving books in a classified arrangement (so that books on the same subject are placed next to each other in convenient groups) antedates the invention of the card catalog. Indeed, for many decades subject access to research collections was available *only* through the groupings of similar books together on the shelves. The great age for the development of classification schemes was at about the turn of the twentieth century, when the Library of Congress Classification (LCC) and Dewey Decimal Classification (DDC) systems were devised; few libraries had card catalogs then, so much effort was expended in creating precise categories and subcategories to reveal subtle relationships among subjects.

To understand the immense and continuing value of classified book arrangements—even in an age of computerization—it is worthwhile to consider the possible alternative methods of shelving books. A library could simply shelve them in the order of their acquisition—catalogers would then have only to assign sequential whole numbers to the books (1, 2, 3, . . .). Such a system would be capable of storing an infinite number of volumes; and, as long as the number that appears on the catalog record corresponds to the number on the book, readers who first find the catalog record would then be able to locate the corresponding volume on the shelves. The library would save thousands of dollars every year if this scheme were used, since it would require professional catalogers only for describing the books and devising subject headings for the catalog, and not for also creating systematic call numbers with intricate relationships to each other. It would save money, too, in preventing the need for redistribution of books caused by unanticipated bulges of growth in particular subject classes; in a whole number or "dummy number" system, the only area that needs room for growth is the very end of the sequence.

Another possibility is that the library could shelve books strictly according to their height—all six-inch-tall books together, all eleven-inch-tall books together, and so on. If this were done, then the vertical distance between bookshelves could be adjusted precisely so that there would be no wasted space above volumes caused by height differentials. Given that there are miles of shelving in any large library, this would enable storage to be much more space efficient, which would save a lot of money and allow room for larger collections. Just such a system, in fact, is used by the Center for Research Libraries in Chicago, which stores hundreds of thousands of little-used volumes that are available to other libraries through interlibrary loan. The New York Public Library also uses a system of shelving by height for a portion of its collections. Conventional subject groupings do not exist in such an arrangement.

Both these methods would be much less expensive to hard-pressed library budgets than the usual practice of maintaining a subject-class arrangement. So why is the latter still used when cheaper alternatives are available?

There are two major problems with the cheap alternatives: They preclude discovery of relevant books by simple recognition (as opposed to prior specification); and they rule out the possibility of in-depth subject scanning.

The first disadvantage, in other words, is that if someone wants a book on any subject, he or she *must know in advance specifically which book* is wanted in order to retrieve it from the storage system. There is no possibility of efficiently or systematically browsing the actual books when their subjects are irrelevant to their shelf arrangement. In a height system, if one volume on anthropology is six inches tall and another is ten inches tall, they may be shelved on entirely different floors; or, in a sequential system, if one book came into the system a year after the other, they may be separated by two hundred feet of cookbooks, car repair manuals, and Gothic novels.

One of the major advantages of a classified arrangement of materials, in contrast, is that it enables you to simply *recognize* relevant works that you could not specify in advance. It allows for—indeed, positively encourages—*discovery by serendipity*. The value of such discovery may be incalculable for any given search. One historian of prison labor, for example, found through stacks browsing the only known image of prisoners on a treadmill in the United States. "Neither the book title, nor the call number, nor the author led me to this report," he commented. "Only a hands-on shelf check did it."[1]

The second major problem with the nonclassified shelf arrangements is that all subject access to them is only at a relatively superficial level, via catalog surrogates within the library's catalog. You can't get down to the page and paragraph level within the books themselves in subject categories, in other words; you can search only catalog records in subject groups. And the *content* of the catalog records is necessarily much more superficial than that of the actual books they point to.

For example, I once had to answer a letter from a historian seeking information on traveling libraries that circulated among lighthouse keepers at the turn of the twentieth century; these were wooden bookcases, each with a different selection of books, that were rotated among the tenders in order to relieve the boredom and monotany of their isolated lives. I first tried searching the computer catalog of the books at the Library of Congress—with no luck. Even after searching other databases on the mainframe system, several CD-ROMs, and the largest commercial dial-up index to American history journals, I still found nothing—only, occasionally, the right words ([Lighthous? or Light(w)hous?] and [Book? or Librar?]) in the wrong contexts.

So I decided to scan the books on lighthouses in the library's bookstacks. The major grouping for this topic is at VK1000-1025 ("Lighthouse service"); this area had, by a quick count, 438 volumes on 12 shelves. I rapidly scanned all of this material.

I found 15 books that had directly relevant sections—a paragraph here, a half page there, a column elsewhere—containing descriptions of the book collections, reminiscences about them, official reports, anecdotes, and so on. I also found 7 sources of tangential interest—on reading or studying done in lighthouses, but without mentioning the traveling libraries—and photocopied these, too, for the letter writer. The primary 15 contained a total of about 2,100 words on the traveling libraries, including a partial list of titles.

Particularly noteworthy is the fact that, of the 15 prime sources, not one mentioned the libraries in its table of contents; and nine of them (60%) did not mention the libraries in their index, either—or did not even have an index to begin with. In other words, this information could not have been found *even if the books' tables of contents and indexes had been scanned into a database*. This level of research depth can be achieved *only* by inspecting the actual full texts in a systematic fashion—not by looking at *any* surrogate catalog records, no matter how detailed.

With the classification scheme's arrangement of books, however, the needed information could indeed be found both systematically and easily. Retrieving, via call slips, 438 books scattered by random accession numbers would be so time consuming and difficult as to be effectively not possible in the real world that actual researchers must work in. And determining in advance which 15 had the right information from the catalog would also be impossible—the surrogate catalog records just do not contain that *depth* of information. And so a reader who had to *guess* in advance which 15 of the 438 volumes had the right information would necessarily miss most of what the library actually had to offer—information that is readily available as long as we remember that *there are other ways to do full-text searches besides using computers, and that some of these ways simply cannot be fitted into computers.* The use of subject-classified arrangements of full texts—printed *books* arranged in subject groupings on bookshelves in libraries with walls—thus provides a *depth* of subject access that *cannot be matched by any computer searches of mere catalog surrogates.*

Thus, subject-classified books arrangements enable researchers to do both *browsing* (recognizing relevant sources that could not be specified in advance through use of the catalog or other sources such as bibliographies) and *scanning* (in-depth searching for specific information that is too particular to be recorded on catalog surrogates). Browsing is done when the searcher does not have a particular goal or question in mind—that is, when he or she simply wants to see "what's available." Scanning, in contrast, is done when the researcher does have a very particular question in mind—but one that cannot be answered by specifying in advance particular sources to answer it. In these cases, all that can be determined in advance is a *range of likely sources*—which must then be examined systematically at the level of full-text depth. The major advantages of the classified shelf scheme are thus two: (1) it enables and encourages discovery by *recognition* and *serendipity*, and (2) it allows a much greater *depth* of subject access to monographs than the catalog does.

The advantages and disadvantages of the library catalog and the book arrangement scheme are rather neatly complementary. One disadvantage of an online or card catalog is that it will tell you only the subject of a book as a whole, not the contents of individual sections, paragraphs, or sentences. This problem is corrected by the classified bookstacks—any book you find on the shelves will immediately present its full contents for your inspection. You will not have just two or three short subject headings to look at, but the table of contents, index, preface, introduction, full text, bibliography, and illustrations—and all of this information will be perceptible *in relation to* other full-text information on the same subject, immediately adjacent on the shelves.

One disadvantage of the shelf scheme is that any book within it can be shelved at only one call number, even though it may cover many subjects. A book such as *Women, Philosophy, and Sport: A Collection of Critical Essays* (Scarecrow Press, 1983), for example, could conceivably be assigned by a cataloger to either women's studies (HQ), philosophy (B), or sports (GV) classification areas—which are nowhere near each other on the shelves. In any such case, the cataloger simply must make a choice—which means that the book will be classed in only one of the three possible areas. And this means, in turn, that browsers or scanners who are looking for a book on this subject in the other two classes will not see it. This problem (that a book can be assigned to *only one* class area on the shelves) is remedied by the catalog, which provides multiple points of access for each record (i.e., author, title, class number, and usually at least two or three subject headings filed *at various places* in the catalog). The trade-off here is between the depth of access to a particular work and the number of points of access to it.

Conversely, a single subject may have many different aspects (philosophical, ethical, religious, biographical, historical, social, sociological, economic, political, legal, educational, musical, artistic, dramatic, fictional, medical, scientific, statistical, technical, military, bibliographical, etc.), and so the in-depth access you need may be impeded by the many relevant books being scattered throughout the classification scheme. For example, in the Library of Congress system the range of class numbers E51–99 contains a wealth of material on the history and culture of "Indians of North America." However, books on Indian languages are in PM101–7356; collections of fictional writings by Indian authors are in PS505 and PS5891; the history of Colonel William Crawford's Indian campaign is in E238; amateur Indian plays are in PN6120.16; Indian laws are in KF8201-8228; works on hospitals for Indians are in RA981.A35; and bibliographies on Indians are in Z1209.[2]

Similarly, while materials under the heading "Drinking and traffic accidents" have a home base at HE5620.D7, such materials also appear in nine different K and KF legal classes; in seven different RC medical classes; in seven different HV social pathology classes; and in several other areas, including AS36, J905.L3, QC100, TL152.3, and Z7164.T81—for a total of *thirty-two different browsing sections*. Anyone who simply looks at the HE5620.D7 area may miss at least as much important information as he or she finds. The situation with "Drug abuse" is similar: Even if one found the bulk of material contained in several different classes within the HV5800s, one would still be likely to overlook dozens of other areas, including AS36 (societies), BV4470 (pastoral theology), several H classes (social sciences) other than HV, several KF classes (U.S. law), LB1044 (teaching), a number of P (fiction) and R (medical) areas, QP37 (human physiology), TX943 (food service), and two different Z classes (bibliographies).

Since at least some such scattering is likely to be found with any subject, how do you identify all of the different classes into which the topic can fall? Here again the complementary nature of the library catalog comes to the rescue. Works that are scattered among many different classes in the bookstacks are grouped together under one subject heading within the catalog, enabling you to find which classes you should browse. (In the above examples the grouping function is achieved by the three subject headings that appear in quotation marks.) The trade-off here is between the depth of subject access to particular aspects of a broad subject and the range or extent of access to all of them.

A related problem is that the bookstacks provide no cross-references to other areas of the stacks that may contain related books. Works on the subject "Children's dreams," for example, tend to be classed in BF1099 (Dreams), whereas works on the related subject "Children—Sleep" tend to be classed in RJ (Pediatrics). Neither area of the bookshelves will alert you to the existence of the other. The subject heading system in the catalog, however, does provide the necessary cross-reference linkage between the two subject headings, under which you will *then* find the different call numbers recorded.

Thus, while the library catalog corrects the weaknesses of the classified stacks (by providing multiple points of access to works that can have only one position in the classes, by grouping together under one subject heading records that are scattered among many classes, and by providing cross-references to other topics in different classes), the shelf-browsing/scanning system in turn corrects the defects of the catalog (by providing in-depth access to full texts, free of the constraints and filters of an artificial vocabulary of subject headings arranged alphabetically rather than logically).

This complementary relationship is underscored by the policy of the Library of Congress in assigning subject headings to topical or documentary films. Since it is virtually impossible to browse a film collection for subject content (i.e., you cannot just pick up a film and flip through it), and since users must therefore rely almost entirely on catalog records for retrieval, LC provides such materials with extra subject headings.[3] Note the underlying assumption held by the librarians that this exception points out: In normal circumstances readers will *not* rely entirely on the catalog for subject access but will supplement its approach with shelf browsing or scanning.

If you don't use both approaches, in other words, you are not using the library as it is designed to be used—and you are probably missing half of what the library's monographs have to offer on your topic. The most efficient way to do library research is to match your retrieval technique to the library's storage technique, for in this way you will be exploiting the *internal structure* of the system. This structure *assumes* that you are aware of the complementary advantages and limitations of the catalog and book classification systems. You must be cognizant of the trade-offs involved, because the two do not duplicate each other, and if you use only one part and not the other, you are neglecting half of the basic retrieval system.

I emphasize the point for two reasons. First, there seems to be a kind of "theshhold of awareness" that many readers have to cross regarding the value of browsing in the bookstacks. While most researchers have had, at one time or another, experiences of serendipitous discovery in a library, many of them regard such experiences as more due to luck than to system. But it actually *is* the system that is working in such cases—and if you are aware of this, you can exploit that system *consciously* and *deliberately* rather than haphazardly. You can make your "luck" improve in a *systematic* way.

Second—and this is a relatively new concern—many librarians themselves are now moving away from the belief that there is a continuing need to arrange printed books in subject groups. The library profession as a whole has become so infatuated with visions of the "electronic library of the future" that many of its members now consider any records that cannot fit into computer workstations to be not worth bothering about. The problem is that while it is now technically possible to digitize entire book collections, it remains impossible to actually do so because of insurmountable legal (copyright), preservation, and cost problems. While grandiose visions of "virtual libraries" are being spun out by library theorists (whose muse for change seems largely unfettered by any personal experience in actually using real libraries), in the meantime attention is no longer being paid to the requirements of making nondigitized, printed-paper resources available in a systematic manner. Since the arrangement of printed books on actual shelves is not something that can "fit" into a computer workstation, it is being denigrated by information science professionals as a practice not worth continuing. Bookstacks are viewed as recalcitrant relics that are necessarily confined within physical walls—they simply do not fit into the worldview of those who see their goal as the creation of "libraries without walls."

Readers of this book who care about the future arrangement of academic libraries in particular need to monitor closely what their librarians are actually planning to do regarding the future maintenance (or abandonment) of classified bookstacks. I hate to point it out, but many librarians are themselves becoming the biggest threat to continued systematic access to printed books. The mere access to subject-classified *catalog surrogates* that they offer in exchange is simply not comparable—it does not and cannot provide systematic *full-text depth* of search capability. And most printed (and copyright-protected) books will *never* be digitized for full-text computer searching, no matter how often the contrary view is naïvely asserted. It is perhaps necessary to keep some hard data in mind on this: The Library of Congress alone has roughly 20 million volumes on more than 532 miles of bookshelves, and continues to receive more than 1,000 new printed volumes every working day. How much of *this* material will actually be fully digitized in the future "library without walls"? The answer is that virtually none of it will be converted—and yet full-text access is still needed for all of it.

A means of directly searching printed books—rather than catalog surrogates for them—continues to be essential for answering some types of questions. In working on a variety of research projects I have frequently found that scanning the subject groupings of books in the stacks is the *only* way to find the desired information. I once had to find information on the Civil War ironclad *Barataria*. "Barataria" is not a subject heading in the catalog; the best I found was "United States—History—Civil War, 1861–1865—Naval operations." The cards in the catalog under this heading led me to the E591–600 stack area; and in browsing through the hundreds of books there, paying special attention to tables of contents, chapter headings, and indexes, I found a great deal of specifically relevant material. Similarly, it was systematic scanning in the stacks that turned up information on Abraham Lincoln's pocket knives, an anecdote about James Thurber's mother, the date of construction of a monument to Christianity in Novgorod, and biographical information on a family of acrobats mentioned only in passing in the diary of Whistler's mother. The information on traveling lighthouse libraries, mentioned above, is another example. Although all of this information lay waiting within the library's books; *none* of it was specifically identifiable through use of the library's computer catalog, whether searched by class numbers, subject headings, or keywords.

The importance of scanning and browsing makes it essential that books actually be on the shelves where they should be so people can discover them. In this light, it is very detrimental to researchers that some college professors check out large numbers of books and keep them for whole semesters, or even years, in their offices. Subject access to these volumes is significantly diminished, for the material in them cannot all be identified through the library's catalog. It is all the more serious a problem because the books removed in this way are often the very best works on their subjects. Professors should remember to return *all* books they are not currently using, for simply to say "I'll return it if someone asks for it" is to display a fundamental disregard for the way researchers have to work.

There are two ways to find which classification number areas to scan for information on a topic. The first is to use the library catalog, looking under relevant subject headings and noting the call number ranges on the various records. The second way is to use the *Library of Congress Subject Headings* list directly. When you look up a heading you will frequently find that it tells you which ranges of class numbers correspond to that subject (see Figure 5). The *LCSH* list does not provide numbers for all subjects, however, nor does it give numbers for all aspects of a subject. That's why it's much better to use the catalog itself.

Using classified arrangements to enable yourself to recognize sources you could not specify in advance has applications beyond the use of the bookstacks. Even if the material being arranged in classified order is merely a set of cataloging records for books rather than the works themselves, the classified or logical groupings will still enable you to notice citations you might not perceive through an alphabetical sequence of subject headings. Some bibliographies are therefore arranged in this manner; one, the annually cumulated *American Book Publishing Record* (Bowker), is particularly noteworthy. It lists the year's production of American books in subject groupings that shade into each other; it is therefore a useful alternative to *Subject Guide to Books in Print,* which is arranged alphabetically by LC subject headings. Another good source is a microfiche set, the *Library of Congress Shelflist* (University Microfilms International),

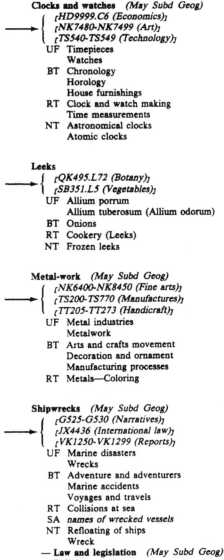

Clocks and watches   *(May Subd Geog)*
⟨HD9999.C6 *(Economics)*⟩
⟨NK7480-NK7499 *(Art)*⟩
⟨TS540-TS549 *(Technology)*⟩
　UF　Timepieces
　　　Watches
　BT　Chronology
　　　Horology
　　　House furnishings
　RT　Clock and watch making
　　　Time measurements
　NT　Astronomical clocks
　　　Atomic clocks

Leeks
⟨QK495.L72 *(Botany)*⟩
⟨SB351.L5 *(Vegetables)*⟩
　UF　Allium porrum
　　　Allium tuberosum (Allium odorum)
　BT　Onions
　RT　Cookery (Leeks)
　NT　Frozen leeks

Metal-work   *(May Subd Geog)*
⟨NK6400-NK8450 *(Fine arts)*⟩
⟨TS200-TS770 *(Manufactures)*⟩
⟨TT205-TT273 *(Handicraft)*⟩
　UF　Metal industries
　　　Metalwork
　BT　Arts and crafts movement
　　　Decoration and ornament
　　　Manufacturing processes
　RT　Metals—Coloring

Shipwrecks   *(May Subd Geog)*
⟨G525-G530 *(Narratives)*⟩
⟨JX4436 *(International law)*⟩
⟨VK1250-VK1299 *(Reports)*⟩
　UF　Marine disasters
　　　Wrecks
　BT　Adventure and adventurers
　　　Marine accidents
　　　Voyages and travels
　RT　Collisions at sea
　SA　*names of wrecked vessels*
　NT　Refloating of ships
　　　Wreck
　— **Law and legislation**   *(May Subd Geog)*
　— **Religious aspects**

Fig. 5

which lists all of the books in the Library of Congress (as of late 1978) in call number sequence. These sources can alert you to books, both current and retrospective, that don't happen to be held by your own library.

Systematic browsing is especially useful when dealing with primary records. Primary records are those generated by a particular event, by those who participated in the event, or by those who directly witnessed it; and they are often unpublished. Thus, for example, a researcher interested in World War II propaganda would be interested in such primary sources as copies of leaflets dropped from airplanes, typescript accounts of the flights written by those who planned or flew them, and firsthand accounts of civilians on the ground who found such leaflets. Secondary sources are the later analyses and reports written by nonparticipants, usually in published literature—although a published source can itself be primary if it is written by a participant or a witness or if it directly quotes one. Many collections of primary manuscripts or "raw materials" exist on an incredible array of subjects and can be identified through sources identified in the Appendix to this book. However, such collections are more often than not poorly indexed, or not indexed at all, so researchers usually must simply browse through them. The principle is the same, though: *First put yourself in a situation where the information you want is likely to exist, and then look around so you can recognize valuable things when you see them.*

One of the major themes of the present book is that a variety of techniques can be used to find information, that each of them has both advantages and disadvantages, and that no one of them can be counted on to do the entire job of in-depth research. What is required is usually a mixture of approaches so that the various trade-offs can balance each other. My observation, however, is that in this age of proliferating computer databases, the research technique of systematic browsing or scanning of printed books tends to be overlooked by researchers who are infatuated with the flashier electronic approaches. The fact remains, however, that the vast bulk of humanity's memory contained in books does not exist in digitized form, and never will; and researchers who neglect systematic browsing and scanning of the texts of books arranged in subject groupings are missing a vast store of material that cannot be efficiently retrieved in any other way.

Notes

1. David H. Shayt, quoted in the *Washington Post*, July 5, 1992, p. C8. A copy of the illustration Shayt found appears with his remarks.

2. This example is taken from a useful booklet titled *The Library of Congress Shelflist*, ed. Linda K. Hamilton (Ann Arbor, Mich.: University Microfilms International, 1979).

3. See Lois Mai Chan, *Library of Congress Subject Headings: Principles and Applications*, 3d ed. (Littleton, Colo.: Libraries Unlimited, 1995), p. 230.

4

Subject Headings and Indexes to Journal Articles

We have seen that a library's catalog usually does not provide in-depth subject access to monographs (i.e., at the chapter level or below) because it was designed not to duplicate a means of entry already provided by the shelf-scanning/classification scheme. Similarly, it does not provide access to individual articles within magazines or journals because a suitable alternative avenue exists: special journal indexes, in both printed and computerized formats. It is not cost-effective for a general library's catalog to duplicate a means of access that is already available elsewhere. Moreover, if we confine ourselves for a moment to speak of card catalogs, if such a file did provide author, title, and subject access to each article in every journal in the library, then it would be so bulky that it would take up an entire floor of the building and would be so much more difficult to use that access to monographs would be correspondingly diminished.

The problem of physical bulk does not arise, of course, with computer catalogs, which makes the prospect of combining databases (for book records and journal citations together) attractive. A different problem arises here, however: copyright restrictions. Computerized catalogs for books, created by libraries, usually aren't copyrighted; but the databases for journal citations are. Combining the two into a single file would thus create legal problems, especially if the catalog is made widely accessible through multiple terminals outside the library itself, or via the Internet. And so proprietary databases providing subject access to journal articles still tend to remain separate from those providing access to books. "One-stop shopping" in a single database covering "everything" is not a reality and never will be—unless, of course, you radically diminish your understanding of what constitutes "everything" to begin with.

Indexes to journals exist in all subject areas. As with encyclopedias, however, most people are aware of only a few general sets or databases (e.g., *Readers' Guide to Periodical Literature, InfoTrac*), but would be better served if they used the more specialized ones. The whole point is that the more you are conscious of the range and depth of resources available, beyond the superficial general sources, the more substantive and probing will be the questions you allow yourself to ask. Most people give up in their research way too soon because they are not aware of the best sources for their subject.

The most important journal indexes you need be aware of for basic library research are known collectively as the Wilson indexes, as they are published by the H. W. Wilson Company of New York, which also publishes *Essay and General Literature Index*. Each has a similar format, and in their print versions most provide author and subject (but not title) access to individual journal articles. CD-ROM and online versions exist for most of the sets, and these do allow title keywords to be searched; but there is a trade-off in that the computer versions usually cover only from the early or mid-1980s forward, whereas the print versions may extend back to the 1920s, or even to the turn of the twentieth century. (Another particularly important set of indexes is that produced by the Institute for Scientific Information in Philadelphia; these will be discussed in the next chapter.)

The Wilson indexes follow the general filing conventions of card catalogs (e.g., word-by-word rather than letter-by-letter alphabetization; the prefix *Mc* filed as though it were spelled *Mac* in the print versions; all author and subject entries interfiled in one alphabet). Each entry in the indexes provides the title of the article (although the entry itself is not *filed* under the title); the author's name; the title of the periodical and its date, volume, and page numbers; and very useful notes about the presence of illustrations, diagrams, or a bibliography may also be present. Each index has a separate "Book Review" section, too.[1] With the exception of *Art Index,* each of the Wilson indexes covers only English-language periodicals. The following are the ones you want to be aware of:

Readers' Guide to Periodical Literature (print, 1900– ; CD-ROM or online, 1/83– ; CD-ROM/online with abstracts, 9/84–).   This is the basic "umbrella" index covering all subject fields. *Readers' Guide* indexes 240 periodicals, many of which are of the popular "newsstand" type (i.e., the articles don't usually have footnotes), among them *Time, Newsweek, Better Homes and Gardens, Fortune, Good Housekeeping, Popular Photography*, etc. It comes out twice a month, generally, with quarterly and annual cumulations. There is also a separate two-volume *Nineteenth Century Readers' Guide to Periodical Literature*, which covers 51 periodicals published in the 1890s, with extra coverage of 14 of those titles back to 1850.

Social Sciences Index (print, 1974– ; CD-ROM or online, 2/83– ; *Wilson Social Sciences Abstracts* CD-ROM/online, 1/94–).   Like *Humanities Index* (below), it is a successor to *International Index* (1907–65) and *Social Sciences and Humanities Index* (1965–75). It provides access to 342 scholarly periodicals in the fields of anthropology, area studies, community health and medical care, consumer affairs, economics, environmental studies, ethnic studies, geography, gerontology, human ecology, international relations, law and criminology, minority studies, nursing, pharmacology, political science, psychiatry, psychology, public administration, public health, social work, sociology, and urban studies. One particularly noteworthy subject heading is "Tests and scales," which will lead you to information on psychological and other tests. The print version comes out quarterly, with annual cumulations; the disc version is updated monthly.

Humanities Index (print 1974– ; CD-ROM/online 2/84– ; *Wilson Humanities Abstracts* CD-ROM/online, 3/94–).   Successor to two other indexes going back to 1907, this sources covers 345 scholarly journals in the fields of archaeology, area studies, art, classical studies, dance, drama, film, folklore, history, journalism and communications, language and literature, literary and political criticism, music, performing arts, philosophy, religion, and theology. (Note especially that history is covered more in this index than in the *Social Sciences Index*.) It is published quarterly, with annual cumulations. The CD version is updated quarterly.

Business Periodicals Index (print, 1958– ; CD-ROM/online 7/82– ; *Wilson Business Abstracts* CD-ROM/online, 6/90–).   This currently covers

345 magazines and journals in the fields of accounting, acquisitions and mergers, advertising and marketing, automation, banking, building and construction, communications, computers, economics, electronics, engineering, finance and investment, government regulations, industrial relations, insurance, international business, labor, management, occupational health and safety, oil and gas, personnel, public relations, publishing, real estate, small business, and taxation. It is especially valuable for picking up articles on individual companies and biographical articles about business leaders. The print version comes out quarterly with annual cumulations; the CD is updated monthly. The version available through the OCLC First-Search service has changed its title to *Wilson Business Abstracts*. Coverage prior to 1958 is provided by the *Industrial Arts Index* (1913–57).

General Science Index (print, 1978– ; CD-ROM/online, 5/84– ; *Wilson General Science Abstracts* CD-ROM/online, 3/93–).   A relatively new source, *GSI* covers 139 periodicals in the areas of astronomy, atmospheric sciences, biological sciences, botany, chemistry, earth sciences, environment and conservation, food and nutrition, genetics, mathematics, medicine and health, microbiology, oceanography, physics, physiology, psychology, and zoology. It appears monthly, with quarterly and annual cumulations; the computer version is updated monthly.

Applied Science and Technology Index (print, 1958– ; CD-ROM/online, 10/83– ; *Wilson Applied Science & Technology Abstracts* CD-ROM/online, 3/93–).   Another successor to *Industrial Arts Index* (1913–57), this venerable source covers 391 periodicals in the fields of aeronautics and space science, artificial intelligence and machine learning, chemistry, computer technology and applications, construction industry, electricity, energy resources and research, engineering (civil, electrical, mechanical), engineering materials, environmental sciences and waste management, fire and fire prevention, food and food industry, geology, industrial and mechanical arts, machinery, marine technology and oceanography, mathematics, metallurgy, meteorology, petroleum and gas, physics, plastics, robotics, telecommunications, textile industry and fabrics, and transportation. Like *General Science Index* it provides only subject (not author) access. In addition to a separate index of book reviews (a usual feature in the Wilson indexes), this index also has a separate index of product reviews. It is a monthly publication, with quarterly and annual cumulations; in CD form it is updated monthly.

Biological and Agricultural Index (print, 1964– ; CD-ROM/online, 7/83–). A successor to *Agricultural Index* (1916–63), this source indexes 225 periodicals in the areas of agricultural chemicals, agricultural economics, agricultural engineering, agronomy, animal husbandry, bacteriology, biochemistry, biology, biotechnology, botany, conservation, cytology, dairying, ecology, entomology, environmental sciences, fishery sciences, food sciences, forestry, genetics, horticulture, limnology, livestock, marine biology, microbiology, mycology, nutrition, pesticides, physiology, plant pathology, poultry, soil science, veterinary medicine, virology, wildlife, and zoology. It appears quarterly, with annual cumulations; the CD is updated monthly.

Index to Legal Periodicals (print, 1908– ; CD-ROM/online, 8/81–). This set covers 620 legal periodicals, including law reviews, bar association journals, yearbooks, and government publications originating in the United States, Puerto Rico, Canada, Great Britain, Ireland, Australia, and New Zealand. Topics covered include banking, constitutional law, criminal law, environmental protection, labor law, landlord/tenant decisions, malpractice suits, multinational corporations, public law and politics, securities and antitrust legislation, and tax law and estate planning. The useful subheading "Cases" appears under specific subject headings, and there is also a separate "Table of Cases" arranged by names of plaintiffs and defendants, and a "Table of Jurisdictions." It is published quarterly, with annual cumulations; the CD version is updated monthly.

Education Index (print, 1929– ; CD-ROM/online, 6/83– ; *Wilson Education Abstracts* CD-ROM/online, 8/94–). This indexes 400 English-language periodicals, yearbooks, and monographic series from around the world. It covers administration and supervision, adult education, the arts, audiovisual education, classroom computers, comparative and international education, competency-based education, counseling, personnel service, educational technology, English-language arts, government funding, health and physical education, higher education, language and linguistics, library and information science, literacy standards, multicultural/ethnic education, preschool and elementary education, psychology and mental health, religious education, science and mathematics, secondary education, social sciences, special education, teacher education, teacher/parent relations, teaching methods and curriculum, and vocational education. Like *Social Sciences Index,* it has a very useful subject heading "Tests and scales." It is published monthly, with quarterly and annual cumulations; the CD version is updated monthly.

Biography Index (print, 1946– ; CD-ROM/online, 7/84–).   This is more than just an index to journal literature. In addition to picking out biographical articles that are covered in more than 1,000 periodicals of every kind, it also covers English-language *books* of individual and collective biography (more than 1,800 annually), plus *New York Times* obituaries. It is one of the best sources providing overall access to all types of biographical materials, including autobiographies, bibliographies, critical studies, diaries, drama, fiction (biographical novels), interviews, journals, juvenile literature, letters, memoirs, pictorial works, and poetry. Its entries are by names of the biographees, including birth and death dates, nationality, profession, and full bibliographic citation. There is also a separate index by names of occupations and subject categories (e.g., "Architects," "Economists," "Handicapped," "Murder victims"). It comes out quarterly, with annual and two-year cumulations; the CD is updated quarterly.

Art Index (print, 1929– ; CD-ROM/online, 9/84– ; *Wilson Art Abstracts* CD-ROM/online, 1/94–).   This covers 213 domestic and foreign art-related journals and museum bulletins, including those in foreign languages, with coverage of advertising art, antiques, archaeology, architecture and architectural history, art history, arts and crafts, city planning, computers in art and architecture, fine arts, folk art, glassware, graphic arts, industrial design, interior design, jewelry, landscape design, motion pictures, museology, painting, photography, pottery, sculpture, television, textiles, video, and woodwork. It appears quarterly, with annual cumulations, and the CD version is updated quarterly.

The Wilson Company publishes a variety of other indexes, too (e.g., *Bibliographic Index, Book Review Digest, Library Literature, Play Index, Short Story Index, Children's Catalog, Fiction Catalog*, etc.), so this list is not complete. If you wish to find out if there is an index in some subject not covered above, see Chapter 16.

The vocabulary control of the subject headings used in the Wilson indexes is worth noting. They have their own system of headings and cross-references within each index, so it is especially important always to look for and follow "see" references to other subject headings. Beyond this, however, the indexes consult the *Library of Congress Subject Headings* list for much of their terminology. They are not limited to this list (hence the importance of following the cross-references to variant terms); but they use it often enough that you should exploit the relationship. My own experience is that frequently an *LCSH* heading that works in the book catalog *also* works in the Wilson indexes—and vice versa. Four examples:

- A reader was interested in the matter of parents legally abdicating responsibility for rearing their children but was having trouble finding a relevant subject heading. In looking through the *Index to Legal Periodicals*, however, she found several relevant titles of articles under the heading "Parent and child (Law)." She then tried this same heading in the library catalog and found pertinent books.
- A drama student interested in the avant-garde "Living Theatre" group of the 1960s found that the right subject heading to use in the *Humanities Index* is "Experimental theatre." She then used the same heading in both the card catalog and *Bibliographic Index* (a subject index to published bibliographies) and found additional useful sources, among them Margaret Croyden's *Lunatics, Lovers, and Poets: The Contemporary Experimental Theatre* (McGraw-Hill, 1974). This volume has a 45-page chapter on the Living Theatre and an extensive bibliography.
- The woman who wanted material on the effects of divorce on children found that the right subject heading to use in the catalog is "Children of divorced parents" (not "Divorce"). She then found that

the same heading is used in the *Social Sciences Index* and in *Readers' Guide*.

- An example of the difference between *LCSH* and Wilson terminology is provided by the student who wanted material on job interviews. He found that the relevant *LCSH* term is "Employment interviewing," and this worked well in the catalog. However, when he looked up the same term in *Business Periodicals Index* he found a note, "*see* Recruiting of employees—Interviewing"; and when he tried it in *Social Sciences Index* another note told him, "*see* Interviews and interviewing." Thus the Wilson indexes, here, did not use the *LCSH* term—however, the important point is that they still listed it and provided a cross-reference from it to their own terms. Starting with the *LCSH* list can still provide you with a hook into the vocabulary of the journal indexes. Again, this technique does not *always* work—but it works often enough that you should consciously use it.

A company that is in competition with Wilson is Information Access Company (IAC). It, too, publishes basic indexes, although not in as many separate fields as Wilson; and it also tends to use *Library of Congress Subject Headings*. All of the Information Access products are CD-ROMs; in general, each covers at least the current year of periodicals, and libraries have the option to add an additional four-year backfile. In other words, figure that these indexes cover at most the current five years of their subjects. Collectively they are known as *InfoTrac*; but any given library that offers InfoTrac may not offer all of its component databases.[2] Some of the more popular IAC CD-ROMs are:

- *The Magazine Index.* This database covers 400 periodicals, including all of those in *Readers' Guide*, plus coverage of the current two months of the *New York Times* and the *Wall Street Journal*. Most citations contain abstracts. A corresponding *Magazine Collection* microfilm set of the actual articles is also available. Some libraries may also offer *Magazine Index Plus*, which provides ASCII digital versions of the full texts of about 100 of the periodicals covered in the *Index,* for a rolling period of the most recent two years.

- *Business Index.* This CD covers 850 business periodicals cover-to-cover, including the *Wall Street Journal*, the financial section of the *New York Times*, the *Asian Wall Street Journal*, and the *Financial Times of Canada*. Most references contain abstracts. It is linked to a *Business Collection* microfilm set of the actual articles; there is also a *Business ASAP* CD-ROM available that provides computerized full texts of articles from more than 350 of the journals covered by the *Index*, for two full years plus the current year. (See also the "Business" section in the Appendix of this book for descriptions of other IAC databases.)
- *General Periodicals Index.* This is kind of a hybrid of the *Magazine* and *Business* indexes, covering more than 1,100 titles. It is also linked to the *Magazine Collection* and *Business Collection* microfilm sets that provide the full texts of articles.
- *Academic Index.* This CD covers more scholarly journals than *Magazine Index* does; it indexes 550 academic publications from all disciplines in humanities, social sciences, and sciences, as well as general interest magazines and "news magazines." A larger version called *Expanded Academic Index,* covers approximately 1,500 journals.
- *National Newspaper Index.* This database covers the current year, and three retrospective years, of the *New York Times*, the *Washington Post,* the *Wall Street Journal,* the *Christian Science Monitor,* and the *Los Angeles Times*.
- *LegalTrac.* This covers all articles in more than 800 legal periodicals from 1980 forward.

Although these three provide broader coverage than their Wilson counterparts, fewer libraries will own them, whereas almost all will have the Wilsons.

A particularly good British source with subject headings of its own devising is the *British Humanities Index* (Bowker/Saur, quarterly with annual cumulations, 1962–). This is an author and subject index to journals and newspapers published in Great Britain; it is the successor to the old *Subject Index to Periodicals* (1915–61, with a gap from 1923 to 1925). The *Canadian Index* (Toronto: Micromedia Limited, 1993–), monthly with semiannual cumulations, covers 550 journals and newspapers. It is also available online and in CD-ROM as the *Canadian Business & Current Affairs (CBCA)* database.

An alternative avenue of access to the Wilson indexes (or, rather, to online versions that have the same time-period limitations as the CD-ROM versions) is the OCLC FirstSearch service, which enables local libraries to tap into scores of databases mounted on the OCLC company's computers in Ohio. Although, of course, each library must pay a subscriber's fee for the access, there are no direct charges passed on to individual users. Searching in FirstSearch is much like using CD-ROM databases, except that the files are mounted elsewhere rather than in the building where you're doing the search; and the OCLC software and command structure will be different from the commands you would use on the CD-ROMs. FirstSearch currently offers most of the Wilson indexes—if your library chooses to subscribe to them. Scores of databases are actually available through the service, but your own library may, for budgetary reasons, offer only a limited selection.

A service in competition with OCLC FirstSearch is the RLG, or Research Libraries Group, Eureka set of databases (see Chapter 11); like FirstSearch, the RLG system enables libraries to subscribe to scores of databases that provide access to citations of journal articles—again, with the usual qualification that only recent years are covered in the computer versions. (Both OCLC FirstSearch and RLG Eureka also offer document delivery features, enabling you to order actual copies of most of the articles you identify. Since the charge is usually about $10 per article, however, you will probably prefer free access to your library's copies. Make sure, though, that your library isn't canceling subscriptions because "the same" journals they used to subscribe to are now "accessible" via high-priced document delivery services. The cost of such services is usually more than enough to discourage most nonbusiness and nonlegal use of them.)

No matter which online (or CD-ROM) services are or are not available to you, it is still useful to think of the Wilson indexes and databases as the "basic" sources for library research in journals and periodicals. The important point is that you know in advance that many specialized indexes exist beyond *Readers' Guide to Periodical Literature*. If you remember *at least* the range of Wilson sources, you'll be in pretty good shape; beyond them, there are so many hundreds of other options that no one can remember all of them.

•   •   •

The fact that so many of these basic indexes to journals tend—more or less—to use *Library of Congress Subject Headings* for their vocabulary control is important in cross-disciplinary inquiries. If you find a valid LC term, you can sometimes use it in a surprising range of sources. The reason for this is that each index covers not merely the subject indicated in its title but, in addition, *other subjects from the perspective of that discipline.*[3] Unfortunately, very few researchers ever exploit this fact. To choose only one example, a researcher looking under "Indians of North America" would find much material in the book catalog and in *Social Sciences Index* and *Humanities Index*. But he would also find an amazing amount of coverage—under the same heading—in *Applied Science & Technology Index, Art Index, Biological and Agricultural Index, Business Periodicals Index, Education Index, Essay and General Literature Index, General Science Index, Index to Legal Periodicals, Readers' Guide, Magazine Index, Business Index,* and the *LegalTrac* file. (And, to press the inquiry on to other sources not discussed in detail so far, he could also use the same term in *Bibliographic Index, Cumulative Book Index, Fiction Catalog, Monthly Catalog of U.S. Government Publications, National Newspaper Index, Public Affairs Information Service, Short Story Index,* and *Subject Collections* [a guide to libraries with special strengths in various subject areas].)

You could similarly use almost the full range of sources on many other subjects (e.g., Aged, Art, Blacks, Communications, Computers, Developing countries, Management, Religion, Shipwrecks, Tea, Women, et al.). The point is that virtually no subject is limited to a single index; rather, all the indexes may cover any subject, but from differing perspectives. And the relatively frequent use of *LCSH* terminology greatly facilitates parallel searches in different disciplines. My experience as a reference librarian is that the question "Which indexes use LC terms?" is often more important than "Which index covers *X* subject?"—for *dozens* of indexes may cover a particular topic, and if a researcher uses only one or two, then he may well miss more than he finds.

Sometimes the cross-disciplinary potential of the various indexes is surprising, as shown in the following examples.

- *Business Periodicals Index* picks up an article titled "Case Study of a Decision Analysis: Hamlet's Soliloquy" from the journal *Interface*.

- *Index to Legal Periodicals* cites a law review article "Hamlet and the Law of Homicide," plus others, such as "Shakespeare in the Law," "Shakespeare's *Henry the Fifth* and the Law of War," "'Let's Kill All the Lawyers': What Did Shakespeare Mean?" and "William Shakespeare and the Jurisprudence of Comedy."
- *General Science Index* locates an article "Was Shakespeare a Playwright?" from *Science Digest*.
- *Art Index* picks up such things as an article in an architectural journal on the reconstruction of the Globe Theatre in London, and an *Art News* report on the discovery of a long-lost portrait of the Bard.
- *Biological and Agricultural Index*, too, occasionally indexes an article on the Shakespeare Garden in Central Park in New York; in 1987 it also picked up an essay on the use of a medicinal term in one of the Shakespeare plays.
- An issue of *Applied Science & Technology Index* has cross-references under "Art" to "Architecture," "Ceramic art," and "Photography and sculpture"; under "Art and science" there is an article titled "Robots Take the Lead in Ballet." Similarly, a volume of *General Science Index* has references under "Art" to the following:

    Animals in art
    Biological illustrations
    Birds in art
    Computers—Art uses
    Fish in art
    Paintings
    Plants in art
There are also articles or references under:
    Art, Prehistoric
    Art and mathematics
    Art and mental illness
    Art and science

Of course, in most cases a researcher will not need to use the full range of perspectives available on her subject (e.g., even though *Applied Science & Technology Index* does cover "Indians of North America," the reader may be quite satisfied with what she finds in only *Social Sciences Index* and *Humanities Index*). Nevertheless, I think it is important for researchers to realize how many indexes outside their own discipline may cover articles within their area of interest—for, given that you must "draw the line" somewhere in bringing an inquiry to a close, it is preferable to be able to *choose a stopping point while knowing what the options are for continuing* rather than to *have to stop because you have run out of alternatives.*

A knowledge of which indexes tend to use LC subject headings will thus greatly extend the range of options that most people will consider, and for this reason a familiarity with the Wilson and Information Access indexes is especially valuable for basic library research.

Unfortunately, you must also remember that "a little knowledge is a dangerous thing." The basic indexes just mentioned are not the end of the line. Indeed, the specialized indexes may not be the end, either. The problem is that many researchers—and I include graduate students and professors especially—believe that the few or "basic" sources within their discipline that they are aware of are the *only* ones available, or that the same few are the *best* ones for all searches. Neither assumption is trustworthy. There will always be scores of access tools you've never heard of unless you are a full-time reference generalist—and even being a full professor by no means guarantees familiarity with the range of information resources in that field, let alone the amazing variety of sources in all other tangential fields. (Indeed, a number of studies have demonstrated that academics use indexes only sparingly, and that they usually arrive at the limits of their research when they have merely followed up footnotes in known sources, used their personal collections, and browsed a few areas of the bookstacks.[4])

Librarians frequently notice the problem with *Readers' Guide to Periodical Literature*. Probably half the people who use it do so only because they are unaware of the existence of the more specialized indexes (and, too, they've been told that they "should know how to find things on their own" so they don't ask for guidance). The same problem occurs with each of the other indexes I've mentioned—and with others I could have mentioned. For example:

- A researcher in the social sciences will certainly want to know about the *Social Sciences Index* and will probably want to start there rather than in *Readers' Guide*. However, many other indexes in this broad field would be much better for many searches. The *Public Affairs Information Service Bulletin (P.A.I.S.)*, for instance, is much more comprehensive on matters of public policy and political and international affairs. Similarly, the most comprehensive index in psychology is not *Social Sciences Index* but *Psychological Abstracts*. (Both *P.A.I.S.* and *Psychological Abstracts* have corresponding computerized versions—although only for recent decades.) Some researchers will be better served by *Sociological Abstracts, Abstracts in Anthropology,* the *New York Times Index,* or the annual *Handbook of Latin American Studies*. And there are many more indexes (both print and computer) that may be of even greater use, depending on the search topic.

- *Humanities Index* is not always the best source for searches in its broad field. The *MLA International Bibliography* is the largest index to critical articles on literary works—but even it is decidedly inferior to a good published bibliography on an author. *Historical Abstracts* is the best ongoing index to sources on world history other than American; and *America: History and Life* is the best for American history; but the *Combined Retrospective Index to Journals in History 1838–1974* may be better than either in some cases. And then there are other specialized humanistic sources, such as *Philosopher's Index, Catholic Periodical and Literature Index, Religion Index*, and many more.

- *Applied Science and Technology Index* is not as comprehensive in its broad area as *Engineering Index* nor as specialized in the aerospace field as *International Aerospace Abstracts.* Nor is *Biological and Agricultural Index* as comprehensive as *Biological Abstracts, Index Medicus,* or the National Agricultural Library's *Bibliography of Agriculture,* each of which is the best overall index, and database, in its field.

- *Business Periodicals Index* is not the end of the line in its area, either—the *Predicasts F & S Indexes (United States, Europe,* and *International),* the *Wall Street Journal Index, Business Index, Accountant's Index,* the *Journal of Economic Literature*, and the *National Trade Data Bank* (among many others) may well be better for many searches.

These lists could be extended considerably. There are easy ways to find out which specialized indexes and databases exist (see Chapter 16); but the ability to do research involves more than your having a knowledge of a few finding aids, no matter how comprehensive they are. What are most important are your initial *assumptions* about what is *likely* to exist. If you start out by assuming that only general indexes are available, then you are likely to formulate your questions only in general terms and to stop your research when you have used only the most superficial access tools. If you don't know in advance that you should look for the most specific (not general) subject headings, and if you don't know in advance something of the range of specific (not general) indexes available, then you will probably miss much more than you find and then give up searching too soon in the mistaken belief that *Readers' Guide* has covered everything.

A knowledge of at least the Wilson indexes in all the specialized subject areas, however, should get you past the roadblock of thinking only in general terms. If you know enough about a few specialized sources to seek them out in the first place, then right there you will be greatly increasing the efficiency of your research. Your basic assumption should be that if you want specific information, *it is more efficient to start by looking for the specific* and *then* broaden your search as necessary, *rather than to start with the broad and narrow down to the specific.* The information storage-retrieval-indexing system allows you to proceed in *either* direction, of course; but comparatively few researchers seem to realize this—most think of a search strategy only in the direction of general to specific. And yet you would get much better retrieval results by proceeding in the opposite direction. The problem with starting in general sources is that most people who find any information within them—even if it's not right on target—stop their searches at that point because they don't see further alternatives. "Narrowing a search," to most readers, means starting with a pool of sources at the general level and then narrowing their focus *within that initial general pool*; to experts, however, "narrowing" means *choosing a more specific pool to begin with*. The way most library and indexing categorizations are structured—as we saw with *LCSH*—the general pools *do not include the narrower ones;* but most people mistakenly assume that they do.

The point applies to subject headings in either the library's book catalog or the various journal indexes. If you think of "narrowing" your topic as first selecting a broad heading and then looking for more relevant titles *within that initial broad category,* you may well be on the wrong track (because of the principle of specific entry). Consider instead the other sense of "narrowing" and *choose a more specific subject heading to begin with.* (Remember that there are four formal mechanisms that will bring to your attention the narrower headings that you couldn't specify in advance. Use them.)

A question that often comes up regarding periodicals is that of finding where a particular journal is indexed—that is, which indexes will provide subject (or other) access to the one journal in which you are interested. A number of sources are particularly useful in supplying this information:

1. *Ulrich's International Periodicals Directory* (Bowker, annual). This is a list of more than 165,000 periodicals published all over the world; the entries are listed under more than 900 alphabetical subject headings, which facilitate finding which journals are currently being published in particular fields. Each entry provides bibliographic information on the journal and gives the address of the publisher and the price of a subscription; it also tells you which indexes cover that journal.

2. *The Serials Directory* (EBSCO, annual). Much like *Ulrich's,* this source lists more than 151,000 serial titles published worldwide; the listings are categorized by subject, and information is provided on which indexes or abstracts cover the individual titles.

3. *Magazines for Libraries*, by Bill Katz and Linda Sternberg Katz (Bowker, revised irregularly). Less comprehensive than either *Ulrich's* or the *Serials Directory,* this volume still has an advantage in that it provides paragraph annotations for all the 7,000 journals listed; it tells you which are the *best* journals in any subject field, whereas the other directories simply list them all.

4. *Standard Periodical Directory* (Oxbridge Communications, annual). This is the largest listing of magazines, journals, and serials published in the United States and Canada, covering more than 90,000 titles arranged in more than 250 subject categories.

5. *Indexed Periodicals: A Guide to 170 Years of Coverage in 33 Indexing Services,* by Joseph Marconi (Pierian Press, 1976). This is most

useful for finding index coverage for older periodicals; for current information, a combination of the other sources is preferable.

6. *Chicorel Index to Abstracting and Indexing Services* (Chicorel Index Series, vols. 11 and 11A; 2d ed., 1978). These *Chicorel* volumes are also useful for finding index coverage for older periodicals.

7. The *Journal Name Finder* database (File 414) in the Dialog computer system (see Chapter 11). You type in a particular journal title to see which of Dialog's approximately 500 databases provide indexing access to it. This source also tells you which database offers the highest coverage of articles from that journal.

All of these sources are useful in listing where a journal or serial is indexed, although some of them provide such information only spottily. It is important to remember that you have to use a combination of them—studies done by librarians have shown that none of the hard-copy sources is complete (or, in some cases, even correct) by itself.

A rapidly growing area in journal indexing is that of providing the full texts of the articles in keyword-searchable databases. *Project Muse* is one such development; it offers the full texts of scores of scholarly journals from Johns Hopkins University Press. Currently it offers only recent years, from 1995 forward; but it plans to provide coverage of earlier years, too, if enough libraries subscribe to make retrospective conversion economically viable. *JSTOR* (short for Journal STORage) is another full-text project, mounting keyword-searchable texts of about 100 journals covering many earlier decades; access is provided through a licensed Web site. Both *Project Muse* and *JSTOR* are services that libraries can subscribe to—they are too expensive for individual subscriptions at home terminals, and so you must go inside the walls of a real library to use them. Once there, however, they will enable you to search and read the articles they provide without point-of-use reading fees. The possible catch is that you may have to pay for making *printouts* from these databases at prices higher than regular photocopying; but this can vary from one library to another.

Many thousands of journals are simply not indexed anywhere; nevertheless, you may wish to be aware of their existence, since the information in them may still be of great value. To identify all of the journals being published in any subject area, use *Ulrich's* and the *Serials Directory,* supplemented by the *Standard Periodical Directory*. The combination of these three will give you a virtually complete roster of current journals, house publications, and magazines, with subscription information for each (and subject access by broad categories). A fourth source, the *Gale Directory of Publications and Broadcast Media,* provides the best listing of U.S. and Canadian newspapers and newsmagazines. (For additional sources on newspapers, see the Appendix to this book.)

To find out which periodicals are considered the best or the most important in their areas, used the combination of *Magazines for Libraries* and the *Journal Citation Reports* microfiche supplements of the ISI indexes (see Chapters 5 through 7).

It is important for researchers to realize that libraries catalog serials and journals differently from monographs. It is not efficient to create separate catalog records for each issue of every journal; a more sensible practice is to catalog the journal as a whole once, with one catalog number for the whole run, and then simply to check in each new issue or bound volume as it comes in. Because of the constant checking and claiming of missing issues that must go on, the serials record catalog is usually separate from the main catalog (for monographs) and is usually located right near the cataloging department. The main catalog itself, in either card or computer form, will record the titles of journals—but sometimes you will need more information than just this. You may also need to check the library's *holdings* of the journal you're interested in— that is, does the library own the particular *volume* or *year* that you want? Libraries will not own complete sets of all titles represented in their catalogs, and the catalog record for journals listed in the main catalog will usually *not* indicate the library's *holdings*. The date of publication given on this record will usually be that of Volume 1, whether or not the library actually owns Volume 1 or a complete set after it. (This date is simply for identification purposes, to distinguish between or among journals with the same title.) When you want to find whether a library has the journal volume indicated in a citation you've found, check the *serials record rather than the main catalog,* or you may waste a lot of time searching for "missing" or "not on shelf" volumes that the library never owned in the first place. (Reference librarians frequently encounter frustrated researchers engaged in just such searches.)

While computerization makes it theoretically possible for the library's main catalog to incorporate the information in its serials record, problems of cost and complexity have not been overcome in most libraries; and so the serials record information is still usually to be found only in a separate place in the library.

Another frustrating problem that researchers often have with serials is one that can usually be prevented with a bit of foresight. The entries in most of the journal indexes give you a bibliographic citation to the journal articles, but they usually abbreviate the titles of the journals. Each index *also* has a separate section that expands these abbreviations into the full wording of the complete title, and it is very important to write down these *full titles rather than abbreviations*. If all you have is an abbrevation, you may have trouble looking up the title in the library's catalogs (e.g., "Educ" can stand for "Education" or "Education*al*," which file differently; "Ann" can be "Ann*ual*" or "Ann*als*"; "Com" can be "Com*munity*" or "Com*merce*"; "Res" can be "Res*ources*" or "Res*earch*"; "Soc" can be "Soc*iety*" or "Soc*ial*"; etc.[5]). The articles and prepositions that are left out can also cause problems. One researcher looking for *Bull. Hist. Med.* assumed that it means *Bulletin of **H**istorical Medicine.* It doesn't—it's *Bulletin of **t**he History of Medicine.* Note from the boldface letters how far apart these two would be in word-by-word filing—in looking for the first form, the researcher was nowhere near the locale of the journal he really wanted. Similar problems occur in computer keyword searches; remember that computers give you only what you exactly specify, so if you type in *Historical* as the title keyword you will miss *History.*

A wise researcher, in copying a citation, will therefore *never abbreviate the title of a journal. **Never***. The few extra seconds it takes to look up the full title (from the list at the front of the index volume) may save you literally hours of verifying at a later date—especially if you are looking for an article in a library other than the one in which you wrote down the citation.

There are, however, reference sources that will provide the full titles of most journal abbreviations; and while they can solve many such problems, they won't solve all of them, so it's still better to avoid creating the problem in the first place. The best sources for expanding abbreviated or incomplete journal title references are these:

1. *Periodical Title Abbreviations* (Gale Research, irregular). Lists 159,000 abbreviations and their spelled-out forms.
2. *Acronyms, Initialisms & Abbreviations Dictionary* (Gale Research, annual). This multivolume set is not limited to journal abbrevations, but it does have some that are not in *Periodical Title Abbreviations*.
3. *World List of Scientific Periodicals* (Butterworth, 1963 & supplements). This venerable set is still very useful for spelling out the full titles of abbreviations for old scientific journals from around the world published from 1900 to the 1970s.

Another problem with serials has been mentioned in Chapter 2 but bears repeating here: There was a change in the cataloging rules as of January 1, 1981. Under the new rules a journal such as *Journal of the American Medical Association* is entered under just this title. Under the old rules, however, it would appear as *American Medical Association. Journal.* The old rule was that *if the name of the society or organization appears in the title,* then file under the first word of the *society name* and not under the first word (e.g., *Journal, Annals, Bulletin, Proceedings,* etc.) of the title. Note the important distinction, however: The old rule applied only if the name of an *organization* appeared in the title; thus a form such as *Journal of Medicine* would file "as is," but a form *Journal of the Medicine Society* would file as *Medicine Society. Journal.*

This distinction obviously caused—and continues to cause—much confusion, as it leads many researchers who look under the wrong entry form to conclude that a library does not own a particular serial when it actually is available. Compounding the problem is the fact that many journals that began publication decades ago are still coming in—and if they were originally cataloged under the old form, that record form may still appear in the library catalog, so you may need to look under the *old* form of entry (under the organization's name rather than under *Journal* or *Proceedings*) in order to obtain the call number for *current* years of the journal. The important points are simply that you need to be aware of both alternatives and that you shouldn't give up if the first form you look under doesn't work.

Notes

1. Subsequent information on the individual indexes is derived mainly from the H. W. Wilson Company *Catalog*, from the *Wilsondisc Quick Reference Guide,* and from *Indexing and Cataloging Services of the H. W. Wilson Company*.

2. The descriptions of IAC indexes that follow are largely derived from the company's own promotional brochures.

3. The same point can be made about specialized encyclopedias.

4. See my *Library Research Models* (Oxford University Press, 1993), Chapter 8, "The Principle of Least Effort."

5. A study by John Martin and Alan Gilchrist, *An Evaluation of British Scientific Journals* (ASLIB, 1968), found that in the *Science Citation Index* citing authors abbreviated *Proceedings of the Institute of Electrical Engineers* 24 different ways!

5

Keyword Searches

The Wilson and Information Access Company indexes discussed in the previous chapter, like the library's book catalog, are of the subject-heading or controlled-vocabulary type. The advantage of such an indexing method is that it solves the problem of synonyms (e.g., "Death penalty," "Capital punishment"), of foreign-language equivalents ("*peine de mort*," "*pena capitale*"), and of possible variant word orders ("Fraudulent advertising," "Advertising, fraudulent"). That is, because of the principle of uniform heading, all works that treat the same subject but refer to it by different words are grouped together under a single English-language term. This grouping or collocation function saves you the considerable trouble of having to look under a wide variety of terms for material on one subject.

But there are corresponding disadvantages to a controlled-vocabulary system. First, the grouping function is sometimes achieved at the expense of blurring fine distinctions between or among subjects. One reader, for example, was interested in the idea of "patients actively participating in the therapeutic process." The LC subject heading that includes material on this topic is "Patient compliance"—which is not quite the same thing as "active patient participation." Still, it is close enough that the catalogers apparently decided to use it rather than to create a new heading. Another example is provided by the researcher who wanted material on "Subfractional horsepower electric motors." I showed her the *LCSH* heading "Electric motors, Fractional horsepower," but she insisted that she wanted only *sub*fractional and *not* fractional. When we looked at the entries under the "Fractional" heading, however, we saw that it included works on subfractional motors.

Evidently the catalogers, seeing no separate heading in the list for "Sub-fractional," simply chose the closest heading that did exist. This often happens. *Distinctions that are important to subject specialists may not be perceived as important by library catalogers; and if you want to retrieve library materials you must use the terms chosen by the catalogers, not the subject specialists. LCSH* headings thus often include subject areas that are not precisely indicated by the terminology of the heading.

Second, a controlled-vocabulary system frequently cannot get too specific within one subject. This is particularly true of a book catalog, which seeks to summarize the content of works as a whole (i.e., the principle of scope-match specificity, rather than indexing individual parts, sections, chapters, or paragraphs of a book). Thus the researcher who was looking for material on the dental identification of Hitler's deputy Martin Bormann could find a general heading on "Bormann, Martin, 1900– " but not a precise one on "Dental identification of Martin Bormann." Similarly, a researcher looking for "Effects of wing design on reducing heat stress at supersonic speeds in military aircraft" will not find a controlled-vocabulary term that is nearly as precise as he would wish.

Third, controlled vocabularies are also by nature rather conservative and slow to change. The main reason for this is that a cataloger cannot simply insert a new term into the list without integrating it with the existing terms through a web of cross-references that must extend *from* the new word to the others, and *to* the new word from the others, with broader/narrower relationships defined in both directions. This takes considerable time and effort, so catalogers are cautious about acting too quickly—they find it is often advisable to wait until the new subject comes to standardize its own vocabulary first. So if your subject is in a new field, or is of recent development, its terms may not yet appear in the system. An example is provided by Leon Festinger's groundbreaking book *A Theory of Cognitive Dissonance* (Row & Peterson, 1957), which opened up a whole new field of psychology. It was not until ten years later that the precise term "Cognitive dissonance" became a fixed subject heading in the vocabulary of *Psychological Abstracts;* thus, for a time, the literature of a developing field was not easily accessible.

Fourth, the cross-reference structure of a controlled-vocabulary system may not be adequate to get you from the terms you know to the heading that is acceptable. For example, *Psychological Abstracts* has always indexed articles on the psychological problems of hostages released by terrorists; but a few years ago (prior to the greater multiplication of such incidents) its thesaurus of subject headings did not include cross-references from the word "Hostages" to the term "Crime victims," which was used instead.[1]

In spite of these disadvantages, however, researchers must also keep clearly in mind the enormous *advantages* of controlled-vocabulary sources. This is especially the case with catalogs that provide access to *book* collections. There is unfortunately a great deal of what might be called bibliographic snake oil being peddled in the literature of computers these days; some of it maintains that the *LCSH* system itself is no longer necessary in an age of computerized keyword retrieval. This is nonsense, of course; it can be maintained only by people who lack substantive experience in the use of real libraries. Searchers who use only keywords in computer searches to gain entry into a library's book collections are very likely to miss most of what the library has to offer them.

Specifically, in providing access to *book* collections, the *LCSH* system greatly improves access beyond keyword retrieval, in three major areas:

First, as noted, controlled-vocabulary subject headings round up works on a particular subject that have unpredictable keyword variants in their titles (or tables of contents)—and even round up, systematically, *foreign-language* titles just as readily as those in English. Lack of English-language subject control of foreign works would decimate the research potential of most major research libraries and deny to English-speaking scholars the knowledge that such works exist, as well as remove from researchers' ken their immediately useful bibliographies and illustrations. (One wonders if libraries truly wish to undercut serious multicultural scholarship by abdicating control of all of the world's cultural output within a single, easy-to-use system.) Even apart from controlling the world's literature in a single system, however, loss of vocabulary control would make much of the world's output of English-language books unfindable, except through sheer guesswork. (See the example in Chapter 2 of the many unpredictable keywords used in the titles of books on capital punishment. Most subjects of similar "mass" have comparably variant terminology.)

Second—a point entirely overlooked by keyword advocates, who evidently lack the experience of using anything except computer terminals—

the *LCSH* headings within the library's catalog do much more than just round up titles that are alphabetically scattered; they also round up, in the catalog, *classification numbers* for works on the same topic that are widely scattered in the bookstacks. (See the examples on "Indians of North America," "Drinking and traffic accidents," "Drug abuse," and "Children's dreams" in Chapter 3.) Any researcher who finds only a few *titles* by keyword searching may be led by their call numbers to only one area of the library's shelves when, in fact, there may be a dozen other class number areas he is overlooking because he hasn't found the right *subject heading*. The ability to *systematically* scan groups of related books *down to the individual page and paragraph level within a library's bookstacks* is a method of subject searching that is entirely overlooked by advocates of keyword searching of computerized catalog surrogates. The *depth* of subject access that is availabe to historians, biographers, journalists, and others within book collections would be entirely lost if only their catalog surrogates—rather than the full texts themselves—were searchable in a systematic manner. If the classified bookstack arrangement is to be maintained, however, it requires a functional *index* that will tell readers which different class numbers have books on which subjects. An *LCSH*-configured catalog functions as this index, whereas a catalog searchable only by unpredictable keywords could not round up either variant titles *or* variant class numbers for the same subject.

Third, a catalog structured by *LCSH* brings to researchers' attention a variety of *types* or *genres* of research sources that they would never think to specify in advance. The example of Jefferson's views on religious liberty, in Chapter 2, is directly relevant—in that case, it simply didn't occur to me to specify either quotation books or bibliographies as relevant types of literature for answering the question; but the precoordination of the form subdivisions ("—Quotations," "—Bibliography") brought these highly relevant options to my attention even when it hadn't occurred to me to look for them. This quality of "plenitude"—the system's predisposition to show researchers many more relevant sources than they are capable of articulating beforehand—is entirely lost in a keyword system, which gives readers *nothing but* what they precisely specify. And the larger a book collection, the more subjects it encompasses, and the more languages it contains, all the more necessary are the formal mechanisms of categorization and standardization, such as precoordinated subdivisions, that enable researchers to recognize options they cannot specify in advance. This fact is of immediate practical use to people who actually work in real libraries; it seems never to be noticed, however, by ivory-tower theorists who never venture beyond the computer terminals in their offices.[2]

The overall point here is that a vocabulary-controlled system has both advantages *and* disadvantages; to use it efficiently you have to be aware of its trade-offs. Such trade-offs will be present in *any* system of indexing, whether done by controlled-vocabulary terms, keywords, footnote citations, or related records (i.e., *shared* footnotes). The critical issue that library users need to be aware of—because it will determine whether they continue to *have* controlled catalogs and classified bookstacks—is that "control" advocates ultimately argue that libraries need *both* controlled and keyword access systems. Keyword advocates, on the other hand, usually argue that their indexing method can *replace* the controlled-terminology system in the catalog; and they either simply ignore the need for browsing/scanning access to scattered class areas in actual bookstacks, or they naïvely assert that all books—not just some of them—will "soon" be digitized for full text keyword searching, in spite of persistent copyright, economic, and preservation considerations.[3] Academics who buy into such snake oil assertions may soon find themselves without functioning real libraries, with classified bookstacks, to back up the computer workstations in their offices.

Keyword avenues of access are indeed necessary as supplements to controlled avenues because of the trade-offs in subject heading systems. The basic problems are these: What do you do when there is no subject heading that corresponds to what you want to find? Or what do you do when the cross-references are inadequate to lead you to the heading that does exist somewhere in the system?[4]

There are two conventional and commonsense methods of circumventing such limitations of controlled vocabularies: You can look for likely *titles* rather than subject headings, as they may be more precise (but browsing for these requires that you guess correctly their *first* word); and you can systematically scan materials arranged in a subject classification scheme. Both methods work for books, but they involve a lot of hit-and-miss searching. And for journal articles, most print-format indexes don't provide title access; nor are the articles themselves arranged in logical groupings on the shelves.

A more focused alternative is keyword searching, which enables you to search for *any* word appearing anywhere in relevant titles (not just in the first position)—or even in abstracts, if you are searching certain computer databases; or even in full texts, if you are searching an even smaller pool of other databases. Very important points are that keyword searching can be done in *both* print and computer sources and that the latter do *not* include all of the print sources.

Computerized catalogs now make their records of books keyword-searchable (assuming that the library's online catalog has the enabling software); and hundreds of other databases make journal article citations (often with abstracts) equally searchable by component words.

We have already seen that the several Wilson indexes are unusually important among controlled-vocabulary indexes. This importance comes from the fact that they cover all subject areas and that their editors continually seek input from librarians concerning which journals are in demand and are actually being subscribed to in libraries. Their CD-ROM versions (while covering fewer decades than the print versions) now make these same Wilson indexes keyword-searchable. The same files are also keyword-searchable through the OCLC FirstSearch service (see Chapter 11).

There are now hundreds of computer databases, both for bibliographic citations and (fewer) for full texts themselves, that will enable you to do keyword searches in all subject areas; for an overview of your options here, see Chapter 11. These electronic sources will usually be your first choices for this kind of searching.

Among the hundreds of indexes and databases covering journal articles, however, three are especially important. They exist in both paper and computer formats. They are:

1. *Science Citation Index*, or *SCI* (print, 1945– ; CD-ROM, 1981– ; CD-ROM version with abstracts, 1991– ; remote-access Dialog version, 1974–); quarterly with annual, five- and ten-year cumulations in print; single-year discs (only) in CD. This huge index covers more than 3,300 journals in all fields of science. Since 1991 the

Dialog version covers an additional 1,900 scientific and technical journals not indexed in the print or CD-ROM versions. (A magnetic tape version is also available for local mounting; it is equivalent to the Dialog version.) Note, however, that for the period 1945 to 1964 many fewer journals are indexed; coverage in the thousands extends only from the mid-1960s to the present. A further note: While citation searching (see Chapter 6) is possible from 1945 to date, the keyword index first appears in the print version in 1965. Also important is the fact that two different CD-ROM versions are available: a conventional subcription that provides keyword access to only titles of journal articles, and an expanded version that provides searchable words from full author-supplied abstracts as well. (No abstracts are included in the Dialog/magnetic tape version.) A further complexity: Since 1991, both CD and Dialog (but not print) versions provide searchable keywords not only from the articles' own titles but also from the titles of sources cited in their footnotes!

2. *Social Sciences Citation Index*, or *SSCI* (print, 1956– ; CD-ROM, 1981– ; CD-ROM with abstracts, 1991– ; Dialog/magnetic tape, 1972–); quarterly with various cumulations, including 10- and 5-year sets in print, and 5-year cumulations in CD. This index/database provides complete coverage of more than 1,400 journals in all fields of the social sciences, plus selective coverage of 3,300 others in the sciences (but not the humanities). As with the *SCI,* the only format that provides abstracts is one of the two CD-ROM versions. Also, since 1991, both CD and Dialog/magnetic tape formats enable you to search keywords not only from articles' titles but also from the titles of sources cited in their footnotes.

3. *Arts & Humanities Citation Index*, or *A&HCI* (print, 1975– ; CD-ROM, 1980– ; Dialog, 1980– ; magnetic tape, 1975–); quarterly with semiannual (formerly annual) cumulations, and one 5-year cumulation in print (1975–79); annual discs with one 10-year (1980–89) and one 20-year CD cumulation (1975–94). This source provides cover-to-cover indexing of about 1,150 journals in its broad fields, plus selective coverage of more than 5,000 science and social science journals insofar as they have humanities articles (e.g., papers on electronic music in the technical journals, or on bal-

let dancers' foot problems in medical journals). No version of this index provides abstracts. Keyword access is provided to title words from articles, often supplemented by editorial additions of words to those titles that are not sufficiently descriptive of the articles' contents (a problem more frequent in humanities than in other subject areas). The CD-ROM and online versions of the *A&HCI* enable you to search keywords from the *footnotes* of articles.

All three are published by the Institute for Scientific Information (ISI) in Philadelphia. Coverage of all three indexes is both multidisciplinary and international in scope; foreign-language titles, however, all always translated into English for keyword search purposes.

The value of these indexes is that *they provide two methods of circumventing the limitations of subject heading indexes,* through *keyword searching* and *citation searching,* both of which involve much less hit-and-miss scanning than the other alternatives. (Their CD-ROM versions, while covering fewer years, also provide a third alternative search method, related-record searching, to be discussed in Chapter 7.)

Each printed issue of an ISI index, whether quarterly, semiannual, annual, or multiyear cumulation, is itself a multivolume set consisting essentially of a Citation Index, a Source (author) Index, a Corporate Index (by institution), and a "Permuterm" Subject Index. The last of these is an alphabetical list of all significant or keywords from the titles of all journal articles covered by that issue, and arranged so that if you look up one word you can tell if any other word of interest appeared with it in the title of an article. (Note that some formats and years of these indexes include additional searchable keywords.) This allows for great precision in searching.

For example, one reader looking for articles on "managing sociotechnial change" had a problem with the conventional indexes because no subject heading reaches this concept efficiently—the "Management" term in *LCSH* covers too wide a field. However, with the *Social Sciences Citation Index* the reader could look up the precise word "sociotechnical" to see if it appears with the words "managing" or "management"—or "planning"—in the title of someone's journal article. It does—there are more than ten hits right on the button. Similarly, a researcher interested in

"Empowerment in theology" could look up the precise word "empowerment" in the *A&HCI* to see if it appears with the word "theology." Again, there are a half-dozen hits right on the button. And the reader who couldn't find articles on "hostages" in *Psychological Abstracts* simply had to look up that precise word in the *SSCI* to find more than a score of hits.

Keyword searches thus frequently allow much more precise retrieval than subject-heading searches; and as an alternative to the latter they involve much less hit-and-miss searching than does the technique of scanning full texts of books arranged in classified subject groups. With a keyword search you can zero in very quickly on the exact words you are looking for.

There is an important trade-off involved, however. The price you pay for such precise access is the loss of synonym control—that is, with keyword indexes you *do* have to think up all the variant ways in which a subject can be expressed. If, for example, you look up on the words "capital" and "punishment," you will miss all of the citations that use the terms "death penalty" or "execution" or "death row." And there will be *no cross-references* to lead you from one term to another, nor will there be any intellectual structure that clusters citations predictably under the narrowest terms. Similarly, in the print-format indexes you must be careful to look up variant singular, plural, and possessive forms of the same word (e.g., "child," "child's," "children," "children's"[5]). Such problems are solved for you in subject-heading indexes and databases—that is the peculiar strength of controlled vocabularies. Their weakness is that they often lack precise enough terms, or terms that are up-to-date; but here keyword sources have their peculiar strength. The advantages and disadvantages of the two types of indexes are thus neatly complementary; each is capable of "seeing" information that lies in blind spots to the other.

All researchers should at least be aware of the three basic ISI sources, for collectively they provide access to all subject areas through a keyword approach. Especially important, too, is their choice of which journals to index in the first place. The Institute for Scientific Information has elaborate methods of determining which journals are generating the most footnote citations in other journals; this provides a very clever way to discern which journals are the *most important* sources within their fields. The editors continually monitor, and then select for indexing coverage, those journals that are the most influential. Given that there are more than 150,000 magazines and journals being published worldwide—and that there are now *also* hundreds of indexing databases to choose from—the fact that these few indexes/databases are known to cover "the cream of the crop" of the scholarly journal literature is a very important consideration. These indexes give you *unusually good starting points* from among what can otherwise be too large and too confusing a range of possible sources. (This can be a particularly welcome relief for researchers who find themselves frustrated and overwhelmed by the complexities and unpredictabilities of Internet searching.)

There is, however, a trade-off here, too: Since the criterion of importance for ISI coverage is derived from numbers (and weightings) of footnote citations, the ISI indexes concentrate on journals that *have* footnotes to begin with—they do not "see" or cover important news or commentary magazines and journals whose articles customarily lack this scholarly apparatus. Many of the popular and influential "newsstand" publications are of this "nonfootnote" type; for coverage of them, you will be better served by the Wilson or Information Access indexes.

All researchers should thus be aware of the three basic ISI indexes, for together they provide access to all subject areas through a keyword approach. These three, however, are by no means the only sources offering keyword access to knowledge records. Virtually any computer database nowadays—whether CD-ROM, online, or Internet—is keyword-searchable.

One online service, available from Chadwyck-Healey, is particularly noteworthy; it is the *Periodicals Contents Index (PCI)*. This database is something you will likely find only in a large research library; it is too expensive for most smaller facilities to subscribe to. It is essentially a keyword index to citations to journal articles from 3,500 journals internationally, covering more than two centuries, from 1770 to 1990. It covers a multitude of languages, too, so you will have to think up keywords in all of them if you wish to exploit its international scope. It is available in CD-ROM format, and via the World Wide Web, and in the OCLC FirstSearch System. (The latter two, of course, are restricted to those who pay the stiff access fee.) In the CD version you have to search each of many discs separately; in the Web and FirstSearch versions you can search the entire database at once. In the Web version you can also call up the table of contents of any individual issue or issues of any particular journal or journals within the file. This is an amazing source for historical and cross-disciplinary research—but keep in mind that, like the ISI indexes, it does not have subject headings or any kind of vocabulary control. And unlike the ISI indexes, the *PCI* does not translate foreign language titles into English.

In addition to the various electronic sources, there are also a number of *printed* keyword indexes that tend to be overlooked. Some have partial computer equivalents, but their particular virtue lies in enabling you to search earlier years of coverage that are blind spots to most databases. Among these are the following:

Combined Retrospective Index to Journals in History 1838–1974 (print only)

Combined Retrospective Index to Journals in Political Science 1886–1974 (print only)

Combined Retrospective Index to Journals in Sociology 1895–1974 (print only)

Biological Abstracts (print, 1927– ; CD-ROM, 1985– ; Dialog, 1969–)

Comprehensive Dissertation Index (print format with title keywords-searchable, 1861–); CD-ROM and FirstSearch *Dissertation Abstracts* (also 1861– with additional keyword-searchable *abstracts* from July 1980–)

Government Reports Announcements & Index (paper, 1946–); *NTIS Title Index on Microfiche* (1964–); CD-ROM *NTIS Index* (1983–) (These are indexes to U.S. government-sponsored research reports.)

Monthly Catalog of U.S. Government Publications (keyword index in print format from 1980–); CD-ROM version called *Marcive*, (1976–); online *GPO* file in FirstSearch (1976–)

Title Keyword and Author Index to Psychoanalytic Journals, 1920–1990, 2d ed., edited by Paul W. Mosher (American Psychoanalytic Association, 1991)

Index to Social Sciences & Humanities Proceedings (print, 1979– ; CD-ROM, 1990–)

Index to Scientific & Technical Proceedings (print, 1978– ; CD-ROM, 1991–)

Index to Scientific Reviews (print only, 1974–)

Index to Scientific Book Contents (print only, 1985–)

CompuMath Citation Index (print, 1976–) (This covers 400 computer and mathematics journals, with selective coverage of articles from more than 6,500 journals in the science, social science, and arts/humanities fields. A CD-ROM version covering a rolling 5-year period also exists.)

Several other sources, print and electronic, provide keyword (or minimal vocabulary-controlled) access to early journal article citations:

- *Index to Pre-1900 English Language Canadian Cultural and Literary Magazines* is a CD-ROM covering 190 early Canadian serials.
- *Early American Index to Periodicals to 1860* is a microform set from Readex Microprint covering 350 periodicals from 1730 to about 1860. It is an index of uneven quality, having been compiled by nonprofessional indexers as a public works project during the Depression.
- *Poole's Index to Periodical Literature 1802–1881* and five *Supplements* to 1906 (Houghton, 1887–1908). Also, *Cumulative Author Index for Poole's Index to Periodical Literature, 1802–1906*, compiled by C. Edward Wall (Pierian Press, 1971).
- Bonnie R. Nelson's *A Guide to Published Library Catalogs* (Scarecrow, 1982) can be used to identify old book-format catalogs of special-library collections in different subject areas; these old catalogs sometimes serve as indexes to journal articles in their fields as well as catalogs of books.

What is more important than remembering a list of specific indexes or databases, however, is that you remember the *technique* of keyword searching with its advantages and disadvantages, as an alternative to subject-heading searches. And, just as with subject-heading indexes, each of these keyword sources covers many subjects beyond whatever area of concentration may be mentioned in its title. No matter what your subject, in other words, *several* keyword indexes and databases will cover it. You can always assume that this method of searching is available for pursuing an inquiry.

As I mentioned earlier, a reference librarian often finds that the first question to ask is whether a good subject heading exists that corresponds to a researcher's need; if there is one, then a whole class of sources can be brought to bear on the problem. But if there isn't, then we can readily shift gears and use another approach, which involves a distinctly different class of sources: keyword indexes. (The line is blurred, of course, with computer databases that can be used for either type of searching; but among printed indexes—which often have no computer equivalents—the distinction is more readily perceptible.)

Nor is this approach limited to journal indexes and databases. The keyword search capability is involved in many alternatives:

- Dictionaries
- Encyclopedias (especially those with a separate index volume)
- The *First Stop* cumulative index to 430 specialized encyclopedias (see Chapter 1)
- Index pages at the ends of monographs
- Full texts of books that are scannable for keywords when the books are arranged in classified subject groupings
- Printed keyword indexes such as those described above
- Computer databases (see Chapters 11 and 12)
- *The Encyclopedia of Associations* (keyword index)

All of these methods and sources allow you to get around the problem of not finding a good subject heading for what you want.

The three basic ISI indexes should be kept in mind especially by scholars who wish to pursue cross-disciplinary inquiries. Each of them covers a vast range of subjects and so brings to bear on any inquiry a huge range of journals from many disciplines. (Note, however, that the cross-disciplinary coverage of the *Science* and *Social Sciences* indexes was greater prior to 1991 than it is today. Up to that point, each of the three ISI indexes covered not only its "own" subjects but also those subjects insofar as they appeared in the other two ISI indexes as well. The *Arts & Humanities* index, however, continues to cover subjects not only in its 1,150 core journals but also in more than 5,000 science and social science journals— nominally the province of the other two indexes—insofar as they have humanities-related articles. The change in indexing coverage of the *Science* and *Social Sciences* indexes was brought about by the explosion of articles being written in those areas. The databases were just getting too big to be economically supported!)

The *Science Citation Index* covers journals, cover-to-cover, in all of the following fields:

Acoustics
Aerospace Engineering and
    Technology
Agricultural Economics and
    Policy
Agriculture
Agriculture, Dairy, and Animal
    Science
Agriculture, Soil Science
Allergy
Anatomy and Morphology
Andrology
Anesthesiology
Astronautics
Astronomy and Astrophysics
Behavioral Sciences
Biochemistry and Molecular
    Biology
Biology
Biophysics
Botany
Cancer
Cardiovascular System
Chemistry
Chemistry, Analytical
Chemistry, Applied
Chemistry, Inorganic and
    Nuclear
Chemistry, Organic

Chemistry, Physical
Computer Applications and
    Cybernetics
Computer Science
Construction and Building
    Technology
Crystallography
Cytology and Histology
Dentistry and Odontology
Dermatology and Venereal
    Diseases
Drugs and Addiction
Ecology
Education, Scientific Disci-
    plines
Electrochemistry
Embryology
Endocrinology and Metabolism
Energy and Fuels
Engineering
Engineering, Biomedical
Engineering, Chemical
Engineering, Civil
Engineering, Electrical and
    Electronic
Engineering, Mechanical
Entomology
Environmental Sciences
Ergonomics

Fisheries
Food Science and Technology
Forestry
Gastroenterology
Genetics and Heredity
Geography
Geology
Geosciences
Geriatrics and Gerontology
Hematology
History and Philosophy of
    Science
Horticulture
Hygiene and Public Health
Immunology
Information Science and
    Library Science
Instruments and
    Instrumentation
Limnology
Marine and Freshwater Biology
Materials Science
Materials Science, Ceramics
Materials Science, Paper and
    Wood
Mathematics
Mathematics, Applied
Mathematics, Miscellaneous
Mechanics
Medical Laboratory Technology
Medicine, General and Internal
Medicine, Research and
    Experimental
Metallurgy and Mining
Meteorology and Atmospheric
    Sciences

Microbiology
Microscopy
Mineralogy
Multidisciplinary Sciences
Mycology
Neurosciences
Nuclear Science and
    Technology
Nutrition and Dietetics
Obstetrics and Gynecology
Oncology
Operations Research and
    Management Science
Ophthalmology
Optics
Ornithology
Orthopedics
Otorhinolaryngology
Paleontology
Parasitology
Pathology
Pediatrics
Pharmacology and Pharmacy
Photographic Technology
Physics
Physics, Applied
Physics, Atomic, Molecular, and
    Chemical
Physics, Condensed Matter
Physics, Fluids and Plasmas
Physics, Mathematical
Physics, Miscellaneous
Physics, Nuclear
Physics, Particles and Fields
Physiology
Plant Sciences

Polymer Science
Psychiatry
Psychology
Radiology and Nuclear
   Medicine
Respiratory System
Rheumatology
Spectroscopy
Statistics and Probability

Surgery
Telecommunications
Toxicology
Urology and Nephrology
Veterinary Medicine
Virology
Water Resources
Zoology

A rather impressive list![6] The fact to note is that journals in *all* these disciplines are brought to bear simultaneously on any problem being researched with the *Science Citation Index*.

Similarly, the *Social Sciences Citation Index* covers all of the following fields:

Anthropology
Archaeology
Area Studies
Business
Business, Finance
Communication
Criminology and Penology
Demography
Drugs and Addiction
Economics
Education and Educational
   Research
Education, Special
Environmental Studies
Ergonomics
Ethnic Studies
Family Studies
Geography
Geriatrics and Gerontology
Health Policy and Services

History
History and Philosophy of
   Science
History of Social Sciences
Hygiene and Public Health
Industrial Relations and Labor
Information Science and
   Library Science
International Relations
Language and Linguistics
Law
Management
Nursing
Philosophy
Planning and Development
Political Science
Psychiatry
Psychology
Psychology, Applied
Psychology, Clinical

Psychology, Developmental
Psychology, Educational
Psychology, Experimental
Psychology, Mathematical
Psychology, Social
Public Administration
Public Health
Rehabilitation
Social Issues
Social Sciences, Biomedical

Social Sciences, Interdisciplinary
Social Sciences, Mathematical Methods
Social Work
Sociology
Substance Abuse
Transportation
Urban Studies
Women's Studies

And the *Arts & Humanities Citation Index* brings to bear on any topic journals in all the following fields:

Archaeology
Architecture
Art
Arts and Humanities, General
Asian Studies
Classics
Dance
Film, Radio, Television
Folklore
History

Language
Linguistics
Literary Reviews
Literature
Music
Oriental Studies
Philosophy
Poetry
Religion
Theater

Students of classics or literature, particularly, should keep this index in mind as a supplement to both *L'Année Philologique* and the *MLA International Bibliography*. One professor of classics, for example, was interested in researching the voyages of the ancient explorer Pytheas. In using the *A&HCI* he found some very useful articles that had not been covered by *L'Année Philologique*—the major index of classical journals— because the *A&HCI* selectively covers geography journals, too, insofar as they have humanities subjects; and Pytheas's voyages were indeed discussed in these journals, which lay "beyond" the coverage of conventional classics sources.[7]

Collectively, the ISI indexes and databases summon the resources of more than 6,000 journals in all fields for use on any subject that may interest you.

This chapter has been concerned with the keyword search capabilities of the ISI indexes; the next two will consider their citation search and related record capabilities.

Notes

1. From 1982 to 1987 "Hostages" was used as a cross-reference term; in 1988 it became a descriptor itself.

2. There are actually dozens of advantages of *LCSH* control of a book collection beyond the three specified here. See my *Library Research Models* (Oxford University Press, 1993), pp. 121–26.

3. *Library Research Models*, pp. 131–40.

4. When using *LCSH* one must recall that there are ways other than using the BT, RT, and NT references alone to get from the term you think of to the best *LCSH* heading. Alphabetically adjacent headings, headings discovered through tracings on relevant records, and narrower headings discovered through scanning subdivisions in the catalog itself (rather than in the *LCSH* list) should all be considered functionally as parts of the cross-reference system that are just as important as the formally defined references.

5. Word truncation capabilities solve this problem in the computerized versions.

6. This list and the two that follow are taken from the prefatory material of the ISI indexes themselves and from ISI brochures.

7. Similarly, the coverage of the Chadwyck-Healey *Periodicals Contents Index* database is omnidisciplinary. One historian of slavery found in it, for example, an article with specific data on the cost of transporting a slave from Baltimore to New Orleans; she hadn't found such information elsewhere because the article appeared in an obscure economics journal rather than in a history journal. But the *PCI* covers both fields simultaneously.

6

Citation Searches

We have seen that the techniques of controlled-vocabulary searching, systematic browsing and scanning, and keyword searching each have advantages and disadvantages. There is still another method of doing a subject search that is potentially applicable in any field: citation searching. And it, too, has peculiar strengths and limitations.

In citation searching you must start with a known source that is relevant to your topic. It may be a book, a journal article, a conference paper, a dissertation, a technical report—it can be any kind of knowledge record, and it can have been published last year or centuries ago. It doesn't matter. What a citation search will tell you is whether someone has written a subsequent journal article that cites that source in a footnote, as a follow-up discussion of it, or at least reference to it. The assumption is that a later work that cites an earlier one is probably talking about the same subject, and this usually proves to be the case.

The same three ISI indexes that were discussed in connection with keyword searches are also the basic sources for citation searching:

1. *Science Citation Index* (print, 1945– ; CD-ROM, 1981– ; Dialog, 1974–)
2. *Social Sciences Citation Index* (print, 1956– ; CD-ROM, 1981– ; Dialog, 1972–)
3. *Arts & Humanities Citation Index* (print, 1975– ; CD-ROM, 1980– ; Dialog, 1980–)

Note that there are qualifications of the information on these dates and formats (see Chapter 5).

Suppose, for instance, that you are using the 1990 set (or disc) of the *SSCI*. If you already have a book or an article on your subject (whether published in 1989, 1920, or 1725), the 1990 *SSCI* will tell you if someone has written a journal article in 1990—in any of the 1,400 periodicals covered by the index—that cites that source in a footnote. (Note that books or monographs can be cit*ed* sources but not cit*ing*. The cit*ing* sources will always be journal articles.)

An example is provided by the reader who was interested in the Norse colonization of America before Columbus. He had already found one good scholarly article discussing the evidence; but on running it through the *SSCI* he found a subsequent article by another scholar who disagreed with the conclusions of the first. And this was followed by a rebuttal by the original writer. The combination of perspectives developed by this dialog brought up considerable information that did not appear in the first article by itself.

A more striking example of follow-up discussion is provided by Thomas Kuhn's classic book *The Structure of Scientific Revolutions,* originally published in 1962. (This is the work that introduced the concept of "paradigm shifts.") In 1990 alone this work was cited more than 120 times by the journals covered in the *Arts & Humanities Citation Index*, with more than 380 cites listed in the *SSCI* and an additional 50 in the *SCI* (the latter two indexes heavily overlap in picking up Kuhn citations).

The real advantage of citation searches should be apparent in relation to what has been said of the other methods: With citation searching you do not have to find the right subject heading or worry about the adequacy of cross-references, nor do you have to think up all relevant keywords and variant phrasings—*because there is no vocabulary involved at all.* Moreover, these searches are usually more directly efficient than the hit-or-miss results that browsing produces. All you have to do is look up the author of the source you already have, and underneath that person's name will be the notations of which other sources have cited him or her in their footnotes.

There are, of course, limitations as well: You must already have a good source to start with; and there is no guarantee that the best sources are linked by citations—it is quite possible that good works were produced entirely independently of each other. Sometimes, too, a good source will be cited by another in a context that is irrelevant to your interest. And the citation indexes cover articles written in only relatively recent decades (compared to the greater retrospective coverage of many subject heading and keyword indexes). Again, then, no one method of searching will find everything. Each is very likely to find something the others missed, but a combination of methods is needed for thoroughness.

A particularly useful "wrinkle" on citation searches is to cycle sources— that is, once you have found a first set of articles that cites your original source, you can then look to see who cited *them:* This will give you a second set; you can then see who cited this group, which will provide a third set, and so on. By pursuing this process as far as it will go you can sometimes develop an incredible amount of information on even the most obscure subjects.

While the ISI indexes are very useful in enabling you to follow the development of a debate or the progress of a scholarly discussion, they are also very useful when the various book review indexes fail—for there is still a chance that the book you're interested in may have been commented on, or referred to critically or favorably, in a journal article even if it hasn't been formally reviewed. The ISI indexes also provide the best way of finding a "review" of a journal article, as these are not covered by book review indexes. And they are especially useful for giving a new lease on life to the materials you locate through old bibliographies—if the latter refer you to somewhat dated articles, you can find out if someone has used them as background sources for a new look at the subject. It is particularly worthwhile to see if anyone has cited old state-of-the-art review articles (see Chapter 8).

These indexes sometimes play a part, too, in academic circles on questions of promotion or tenure, for departments wish to know not only whether a candidate has published, but also if he or she has been cited by other scholars in the field. (And this has led, predictably, to some scholars getting their friends to cite their works to artificially inflate the count.)

In addition to the three general indexes, the ISI also publishes several specialized citation indexes; all of these exist in CD-ROM format *only:*

- *Biochemistry & Biophysics Citation Index* (1992–), covering more than 3,000 publications
- *Biotechnology Citation Index* (1991–), covering more than 2,500 publications
- *Chemistry Citation Index* (1991–), covering more than 1,600 publications
- *Materials Science Citation Index* (1991–), covering more than 1,700 publications
- *Neurosciences Citation Index* (1991–), covering more than 2,800 publications

Each of these is published bimonthly, with annual cumulations. Each covers not only journal articles but also books and conference proceedings in its specialty. Keyword searching of title words, title words from footnotes, and component words from author abstracts is also possible in all five (as is author searching). Related-record searching can also be done in these CD-ROMs (see Chapter 7).

Several other citation indexes are published by Shepard's/McGraw-Hill in the legal field; for these, the cit*ed* materials include:

Cases in United States Supreme Court reports
Cases in federal reports (including administrative agency decisions and orders)
Cases in state courts
Cases in the National Reporter System
Opinions of the Attorneys General
United States Constitution
United States Code
United States Statutes at Large
United States Treaties and other international agreements
Code of Federal Regulations
Federal Court Rules
State Constitutions
State Codes
State Session Laws

Municipal Charters
Ordinances
State Court Rules
Jury Instructions
Restatements
Legal Periodicals
Standards of Criminal Justice
Patents
Trademarks
Copyrights

The cit*ing* materials include:

Cases in United States Supreme Court Reports
Cases in federal reports (including administrative agency decisions and
    orders)
Cases in the National Reporter System
Opinions of the Attorneys General
Articles in legal periodicals
Annotations in the American Law Reports[1]

Again, it is important that you remember the advantages and limitations of
the *technique,* and perhaps the three basic ISI indexes. The others can be
found with the help of reference librarians.

Several other points about the ISI indexes are worth noting:

1. They provide access to articles through the author's organizational
   affiliation—that is, you can look up any institution (such as a university department) and find out who within it has published a
   paper in any given year, through the use of the *Corporate Source
   Index* volumes within each ISI set.
2. The *Science Citation Index* and the *Social Sciences Citation Index*
   are each supplemented—if your library chooses to subscribe to
   it—by a publication called *Journal Citation Reports*. This annual
   listing is currently available on either CD-ROM or microfiche (the
   fiche goes back to 1989, paper prior to that). It presents elaborate

statistical data on which journals are being most frequently cited by other journals, both in general and within specialized fields. In other words, it provides rankings of how important a journal is, based on the amount of discussion it generates in other journals.

3. The *Arts & Humanities Citation Index*, unlike the other two, follows an editorial convention of "implicit citation"—that is, it will tell you in its *Citation* index section if a person, or a play, or a work of art, etc., is *even mentioned in the text of a journal article*, even if the person or thing is not formally cited in footnote format. Such internal references "count" as footnotes for indexing purposes. The *A&HCI* thus provides a truly remarkable *depth* of indexing—far beyond just title keywords—to articles within its subject fields.

4. ISI offers a service whereby for a fee you can order a copy of any journal article covered by one of their indexes, in case you cannot find one in a library. It's called "The Genuine Article" service; its can be reached at 800-336-4474, extension 1145; or at <www.isinet. com>.

5. Cross-disciplinary inquiries can be pursued through the citation-search method in a way that will give results unlike those achieved through subject-heading or keyword search methods—that is, sometimes you will find that a given source on a particular subject is unexpectedly cited by journals in completely different fields. Eugene Garfield, in his book *Citation Indexing: Its Theory and Application in Science, Technology, and Humanities* (John Wiley & Sons, 1979), mentions a spectacular example: "From 1961 to 1969 a citation for one of the classic papers published by Albert Einstein in *Annallen der Physik* in 1906 is linked [by the *Science Citation Index*] to papers from the *Journal of Dairy Sciences, Journal of the Chemical Society, Journal of Polymer Science, Journal of Pharmacy and Pharmacology, Comparative Biochemistry and Physiology, Journal of General Physiology, International Journal of Engineering Science, Journal of Materials, Journal of the Water Pollution Control Federation, American Ceramic Society Bulletin, Journal of the Acoustical Society of America, Chemical Engineering Science, Industrial and Engineering Chemistry Process Design and Development, Journal of Colloid and Interface Science, Journal*

of Fluid Mechanics, Journal of Lubrication Technology, Journal of Molecular Biology, Journal of Food Science, Journal of Biological Chemistry, Journal of Sedimentary Petrology, Review of Scientific Instruments, and the *Journal of the Electrochemical Society."*

And with all this, we are still not done with the ISI indexes.

Note

1. The above lists are from the booklet *How to Use Shepard's Citations* (Shepard's/McGraw-Hill, 1980).

7

Related-Record Searches

The CD-ROM versions of the three basic ISI indexes enable you to do yet another type of subject searching that is different from either controlled-vocabulary, keyword, citation, or browsing/scanning searches. Related-record searching, as it is called, is available *only* via the CD format of these indexes—not through the paper copies, and not through the online Dialog or OCLC FirstSearch versions.

With related-record searching, as with citation searching, you must start with a known source. The difference here is that in citation searching your starting-point source can come from anywhere and from any time period; with a related-record search, however, you must first find a good source within the ISI CD-ROM disc you happen to be using. In other words, you have to start the process with either a regular keyword, author, or citation search. Once you've found a good starting point, you press the "R" button on the keyboard, and the related-record search software will find *any other articles within the same CD disc that have any footnotes in common with your starting-point article.*

In most cases the CDs you will be searching are single-year discs. This is always the case with the *Science Citation Index* (1980–) database, which has no multiyear CD cumulations. The *Social Sciences Citation Index* on CD (1981–) has five-year cumulations, followed by annuals; and the *Arts & Humanities* CD has two multiyear CD discs, 1980–89 and 1975–94, followed by annuals.

The virtue of related-record searching is that it will bring to your attention articles written within the same year (or 5-, 10-, or 20-year cumulation) that are "playing in the same intellectual ballpark"—but the "ballpark" is *defined by shared footnotes rather than by shared title keywords*. And the related-records will be presented to you in ranked order according to the number of footnotes shared. (Thus the list may start with a citation to one article having five shared notes, followed by five citations to articles having three in common, then to a dozen others having a single shared footnote.)

Articles that have many footnotes in common are probably talking about the same subject. The fascinating thing about related records, though, is that even though they have many shared footnotes, they may have entirely different title words—terms that you would never be able to specify in advance. For example, if you are interested in the subject of medical or biological information systems, you could start the process by typing in those keywords: "(medic* or biolog*) and information"—the * symbol being used for truncation. This will give you a set of starting-point articles with titles such as these:

Expanding the Concept of Medical Information
Society and Medicine—Bridging the Information Gap
Diffusion of Information in Medical Care

Pushing the "R" button at this point will then give you articles that do not have all of the keywords you specified, such as:

Students Can Learn Medicine with Computers
The Information Needs of Family Physicians
Status and Progress of Hospital Information Systems

Note that in these titles the word "Computers" appears when only "Information" had been specified; and "Physicians" and "Hospitals" appear when only "Medic*" or "Biolog*" had been called for explicitly.

Other titles that show up in such a related-record search have *no* keywords in common with those originally specified:

The Future of Biomedical Communication
Computers as Clinician—An Update

An Intelligent Computer-Assisted-Instruction System Designed for Rural Health-Workers in Developing Countries

Physicians' Use of Computer Software in Answering Clinical Questions

If it did not occur to you to search "Biomedical," "Clinician," or "Health" (in addition to "Medic*" or "Biolog*"), and "Communication" and "Computer" (in addition to "Information"), you would have missed these citations entirely in a keyword search. But a related-record search finds them because these articles have *footnotes in common* with the titles whose keywords you started with.

Related-record searches are thus another way to get around the problem of synonyms and variant phrases. They effectively bypass the problem by searching for *points of commonality other than title words* within articles talking about the same subject—so you don't have to think up all of the possible variant phrases yourself. They present you with a set of options within which you can simply *recognize* relevant titles whose keywords you couldn't specify in advance.

This is an extremely useful search technique, especially since the conventional controlled-vocabulary indexes to journal articles, such as the Wilson indexes, don't cover as many thousands of journals as the ISI indexes do; and the specialized indexes that do cover more journals within particular fields (e.g., *Psychological Abstracts*, or *PsycINFO* in CD-ROM) lack the cross-disciplinary breadth of the ISIs. Moreover, journal articles are harder to "control" to begin with via subject headings because so many new things show up so quickly, and often fade away just as fast, that new topics appearing within periodicals sometimes never come to standardize their own terminology. Related-record searching gives you a kind of *categorization* that keyword searching cannot match.

It is useful to think of this kind of searching in relation to the blind spots of other search methods. Suppose, for example, that you've found a good starting-point article in the 1991 disc of any of the ISI indexes. There are three things you can do to develop further information from it:

1. When you call up the actual article in your library, you can look at its footnotes. This is simply a matter of common sense. Remember,

however, that footnote chasing always leads you *backward in time*, to *previous* sources.

2. You can do a citation search from that starting point. Citation searching always leads you *forward in time*, to *subsequent* journal articles.

3. You can do a related-record search. Related-record searching leads you, essentially, *sideways in time*, to articles that appear *in the same year* (or, technically, in the same disc) as the article you start with.

While most researchers pursue footnote chasing as a matter of course, the same students routinely overlook both citation and related-record searching, which often can be equally as useful.

As with the other search techniques we've looked at so far, however, this one, too, has limitations as well as strengths. The major one is that the "pool" of citations within which you can do related-record searching is rather shallow. With subject-heading or keyword indexes and databases, or with published bibliographies (see Chapter 9), you can search for sources that are hundreds of years old, and you can look for formats—such as *books,* or government documents, conference papers, dissertations, diaries, manuscripts, etc.—other than just journal articles. Related-record searching gives you *only* journal articles—and only *recent* ones at that. Note, too, that the ISI CDs index only "academic" journals that have footnotes to begin with—so they overlook most "newsstand"-type magazines that lack this scholarly apparatus. They do indeed "see" things that are in blind spots to conventional indexes and bibliographies; but the others see things that are in blind spots to them.

In addition to its three basic indexes, the ISI also produces several specialized CD-ROMs within particular scientific fields (listed in Chapter 6); and these, too, enable you to do related-record searching.

Note further that related-record searching is not available through the Internet; it can be done only on CD-ROMs that are situated in real libraries. Researchers who confine themselves to the Information Superhighway are missing not only a wealth of printed sources that are not digitized but also a variety of important digital sources that cannot be tapped into remotely.

There is no equivalent for related-record searching in paper copy indexes. The closest thing available in print format can be found in ISI's

CompuMath Citation Index (1976–). This has, in addition to keyword, author, and citation-search capabilities, an extra index by "Research Front Specialty." Essentially the editors have identified, through various sophisticated computer analyses, a variety of footnote clusters—groups of articles that tend to be cited together—that are referred to repeatedly within the computer science and mathematics journals. They pull out these footnote clusters, give them names, and then enable you to find all of the articles that use them. It's sort of like related-record searching, only backward—you are given a menu of clusters of footnote-related articles as your starting point rather than as your end product. ("Research Front" searching can also be done in the ISI's *Index to Scientific Reviews;* see Chapter 8.)

A repeated theme of this book is that no one way of searching does everything. (And here I would emphasize that keyword searching by itself is *particularly* problematic.) You simply have to be aware of the trade-offs among the several search techniques so that your overall strategy can balance their various strengths and weaknesses against each other. Remember, though, that what you *cannot* do with one way of searching, you *can* do with another.

8

Higher-Level Overviews: Review Articles

Researchers are especially well advised to look for a particular type or subset of journal articles called review articles. These are not at all the same as book reviews and should not be confused with them. Review articles are a "type of literature" unto themselves (see Chapter 16) in which the author tries systematically to read all the relevant literature on a subject, sometimes also to interview the experts in the field, and then to organize, synthesize, and critically evaluate the range of information. His or her goal is to provide a state-of-the-art assessment of knowledge in the particular field and sometimes to indicate areas that need further research. A review article is somewhat like an encyclopedia article in trying to present an overview of a subject, but there are two important differences: (1) a review article is often written for specialists rather than laypeople and so may assume familiarity with technical jargon; and (2) its bibliography will usually be exhaustive rather than selective or merely introductory.

In other words, if you are doing serious research and can find a review article on your subject, you're in great shape. There are several sources to check.

Index to Scientific Reviews or ***ISR*** (semiannual, 1974– ; paper only, no CD-ROM version). An author, corporate-body, and keyword index to review-type articles in more than 3,000 journals in about 150 disciplines in the fields of science, biology, medicine, behavioral sciences, chemistry, physics, computer sciences, and technology. It also indexes these articles by "Research Front Specialties," which means that the indexers identify clusters of shared footnotes, give names to the clusters, and identify all articles citing them. The assigned names are themselves keyword-searchable; and each article within a "Research Front" is also designated by a number that can be used to identify the other citations within that group. (This is similar to related-record searching; see Chapter 7.)

***Annual Review of . . .* (series).**   Various publishers (especially Annual Reviews, Inc.) produce different series of review articles in many fields. They have titles such as *Annual Review of Anthropology; of Astronomy and Astrophysics; of Biochemistry; of Energy and the Environment; of Information Science; of Materials Science; of Military Research and Development; of Medicine; of Physical Chemistry; of Psychology; of Sociology.* A good overview of these publications is Tony Stankus's *Special Format Serials and Issues: Annual Review of —, Advances in —, Symposia on —, Methods in —* (Haworth Press, 1996).

Computer searches.   The computer databases (both remotely accessible online and locally accessible CD-ROM versions) that correspond to the ISI *Citation* indexes can be searched in such a way that review articles are retrieved instantly. In the Dialog system, the searcher simply keys in the appropriate keywords and then adds the specification "dt = rev?" (document type equals review); in the CDs, the searcher first chooses the "limit" option (<Alt-L>), then selects "Review" from the menu, and then types in the desired keywords. Many other databases in specialized fields have a similar "document type" feature that allows instant retrieval of review article citations. The use of this feature is not difficult; the problem is that you have to be aware that it's there to begin with. This method of locating review articles is the fastest.

Paper copy ISI Indexes *(Science Citation Index, Social Sciences Citation Index, Arts & Humanities Citation Index).*   If your library doesn't have access to the CD or online versions, the paper copies can be used instead. Searches via keywords will tell you which articles have been written on your subject; to find out if any of them is a review article, note how many footnotes the article has. The *SCI* will tell you how many footnotes each has; the *SSCI* and *A&HCI* will show you by listing them. Journal articles with large numbers of footnotes tend to be review articles.

Bibliographic Index (H. W. Wilson, 1937–).   If your library doesn't own *ISR,* it may still have this basic Wilson index, which is a subject guide to published bibliographies, including those at the ends of books and journal articles. About 2,800 periodicals are covered. Its criterion for including a bibliography is that it must contain at least 50 citations, so this *Index* is useful for finding review articles, since any journal article that has at least 50 citations is likely to be a review.

Library Literature (H. W. Wilson; print, 1921– ; CD-ROM and First-Search, 1984–).   This index covers more than 200 periodicals in the field of library science. It is useful for finding review-type articles because reference librarians often publish for each other annotated bibliographies or bibliographic essays that discuss all the best sources or finding aids on particular subjects (e.g., on women in religion; on novels set in academia; etc.). And they are sometimes not picked up by *Bibliographic Index* because fewer than 50 sources are discussed. Unfortunately, nobody *except* reference librarians uses this source for this purpose; but it deserves a wider audience because the articles it points to are first-rate starting points for research.

Modern Language Association and G. K. Hall Monographs.   Review articles in the humanities are harder to find sytematically than those in the physical sciences and social sciences, for they tend to be published as essays within books rather than as articles within journals. There are some in English literature, however, that interested students should know about. Most of them are published by the MLA and include: *The English Romantic Poets: A Review of Research and Criticism,* 3d rev. ed., ed. Frank Jordan (1972); *Victorian Prose: A Guide to Research,* ed. David J. DeLaura (1973); *Victorian Fiction: A Guide to Research,* ed. George H. Ford (1978); *The Victorian Poets: A Guide to Research,* ed. Frederic E. Faverty (Harvard University Press, 1968); and *Anglo-Irish Literature: A Review of Research,* ed. Richard J. Finneran (1976). Each of these devotes a whole chapter to each of the major writers of the respective period, trying to synthesize all the scholarship that has been done. (Note that these are for specialists—they are not the best sources to which an undergraduate should turn for criticisms of particular literary works [see Appendix—Literary Criticism section].) G. K. Hall publishes a more extensive collection of guides, called the Reference Guides to Literature Series. There are scores of titles in it, most providing an overview article and a comprehensive bibliography of critical articles about a particular author in British or American literature. They are always cataloged under the heading "[Author's name]—Bibliography" in library catalogs. They also appear in *Bibliographic Index*.

The *Syntopicon* Index.   This comprises Volumes 1 and 2 of the set *Great Books of the Western World,* 2d ed., 60 vols. (Encyclopaedia Britannica, 1990). It provides 102 review articles on philosophical subjects. The essays have been reprinted in a single volume as *The Great Ideas* (Macmillan, 1992). For a shortcut, either version can be used with Mortimer Adler and Charles Van Doren's *Great Treasury of Western Thought* (Bowker, 1977), which provides in one volume long quotations of the actual texts of many of the philosophical and literary works that are referred to in the review articles.

Institute for Philosophical Research Monographs.   This institute, · founded by Mortimer Adler to expand on the reviews done in the *Syntopicon,* has produced several articles and full-length books that summarize the history of thought on various important ideas. Among these publications are:

- *The Idea of Freedom* by Mortimer Adler, 2 vols. (Doubleday, 1958–61). This massive 1,443-page study is skillfully digested by Charles Van Doren in "The Idea of Freedom," Parts One and Two, in *The Great Ideas Today* (1972), pp. 300–392, and (1973), pp. 232–300.
- *The Idea of Justice* by Otto Bird (Frederick A. Praeger, 1968). This book-length study is summarized in Bird's "The Idea of Justice," *The Great Ideas Today* (1974), pp. 166–209.
- *The Idea of Happiness* by V. J. McGill (Praeger, 1967); summarized by McGill in "The Idea of Happiness," *The Great Ideas Today* (1967),

pp. 272–308, and updated in Deal W. Hudson's "Contemporary Views of Happiness," *The Great Ideas Today* (1992), pp. 170–216.

- *The Idea of Love* by Robert G. Hazo (Praeger, 1967).
- *The Idea of Progress* by Charles Van Doren (Praeger, 1967).
- "The Idea of Religion," Parts One and Two, by John Edward Sullivan, O.P., in *The Great Ideas Today* (1977), pp. 204–76, and (1978), pp. 218–312.
- "The Idea of Equality" by Mortimer Adler in *The Great Ideas Today* (1968), pp. 302–50.
- "On the Idea of Beauty" by Donald Merriell in *The Great Ideas Today* (1979), pp. 184–222.

Each of these studies spells out very articulately what might be called "the range of options" of thought that has been done on these most important topics. Especially recommended are the extraordinarily insightful overviews *Freedom* by Van Doren (following Adler), *Justice* by Bird, and "Religion" by Sullivan.

Other sources that can often provide review-type information are the following:

- *Congressional hearings.* These are frequently overlooked by academic researchers, but they are a gold mine. Congressional investigations and oversight reviews extend into an amazing range of subject areas in the social sciences and sciences. (One estimate is that an average of 20 hearings are held every day.) And when Congress wants to find the best information on the current state of any situation, it generally gets it, for it calls the best experts available to testify. Moreover, hearings usually bring out all points of view on the subject at hand (although, of course, they *can* be manipulated for political purposes); and, further, Congress has the power of subpoena, a most useful investigative tool generally unavailable to other researchers. The best index to hearings since 1970 is the *CIS U.S. Congressional Index;* the same publisher has also produced other indexes covering hearings all the way back to the beginnings of Congress. (These CIS indexes are also available in CD-ROM format.) Microfiche sets of the hearings themselves, keyed to the index citations, are also available.

- *Congressional committee prints* and *CRS reports*. In addition to being able to draw on hearings for information, Congress can use the Congressional Research Service (CRS) of the Library of Congress, which often produces book-length "state of the situation" reports on public policy issues. Many of these are published as committee prints. The *CIS U.S. Congressional Index* picks up those since 1970; and the *CIS U.S. Congressional Committee Prints Index: From the Earliest Times through 1969* covers the rest. Libraries that own the indexes may also own corresponding microfiche sets of the prints. Another source for CRS publications is the *Congressional Research Service Index* (University Publications of America, quarterly with annual cumulations), which is keyed to a microfiche set of the studies. (The older title of this index is *Major Studies & Issue Briefs of the Congressional Research Service*, also keyed to microfiche; its first two volumes cover the years 1916 to 1989 in one cumulation.) This index is also available as the *Congressional Research Service Index on CD-ROM*, which annually cumulates the entire index back to 1916.
- *Doctoral dissertations*. These are sometimes useful for review-type surveys, especially in areas of the humanities and social sciences—although the sciences are covered, too—that don't get picked up by the *ISR* or the *Annual Review*-type series. Frequently writers will begin their dissertations with a survey of the literature of a field, to present a background and context for their own contribution to it. The best index is *Dissertation Abstracts* on CD-ROM; another computer version, with a less sophisticated search software, is available through OCLC FirstSearch.
- *Talking to knowledgeable people*. The human resources that lie outside a library's walls are often the best sources for overviews of a subject, as they can not only provide answers but also alert you to questions you didn't think of on your own (see Chapter 14).

Review articles located through any of the above sources can often be updated by running them through the citation indexes to see if there has been any subsequent discussion of them.

To sum up the last five chapters on journal articles, several points are especially important:

- Subject heading access to journals is provided by the Wilson and Information Access Company indexes and databases—and by scores of others. The Wilson and Information Access sources tend to use *Library of Congress Subject Headings* (although not strictly).
- Keyword searching allows you to find material that cannot be found through subject heading searches (with the trade-off that you lose *categorization* of sources in exchange for precision in searching).
- Citation searching is another valuable technique that will turn up still other material. The basic keyword and citation indexes are the three ISI indexes (and corresponding databases); but many others of both kinds exist as well.
- Related-record searching is yet another way to do subject searchers, and it will produce results that cannot be duplicated by the other techniques. It is available only on the ISI indexes in CD-ROM format.
- Review articles, like encyclopedia articles, are often excellent starting points for research.

9

Published Bibliographies

One of the best ways to start a research project is through subject bibliographies, which can be either published or computer generated (the latter will be discussed in Chapters 11 and 12). The published variety are especially important because they offer several advantages over their computerized cousins: They are compiled by experienced scholars who can judge the relevance and importance of items; they often include nuggets that can be found only by serendipity and persistent searching in obscure sources not covered by databases; and they may include types of material and dates of coverage that are blind spots to computers. In some cases they approach the goal of offering "everything" available (up to a certain year) much closer than computers can; and in others they may provide a selective distillation of only the best material to consider, chosen in light of an expert compiler's deep appreciation of a subject.

A bibliography can give you much more extensive and specific information than a library catalog; it can save you a great deal of browsing time by rounding up in one place citations to works that are widely scattered in bookstacks; and it can list journal articles on a subject all in one place, so you don't have to repeat the same search through several different databases or many annual printed volumes. It may also pick up "fugitive" sources such as dissertations, theses, pamphlets, and government documents that are not covered by most databases. Further, it can alert you to the existence of relevant works that are not held by your local library but may still be available to you through interlibrary loan.

One of the most useful features of a published bibliography is that it will often enable you to do a simple "Boolean combination" search in records that are too old to be picked up by computer databases. This type of inquiry involves looking for two different subjects at the same time; and with databases such things are very easy to do. For example, I once helped a student who wanted to find a comparison of the educational philosophies of Aristotle and John Dewey. A search of a few databases with the command "select Aristotle and Dewey" turned up a list of recent works discussing both men. However, through a published bibliography we could do a similar search for older material not in the online files. Very simply, we consulted Milton Thomas's *John Dewey: A Centennial Bibliography* (University of Chicago Press, 1962; 370 pages); this is an exhaustive list of studies about Dewey. In looking at its index, under "Aristotle," we were immediately led to a number of works that discussed the two, some of which had not appeared on the printout.

Similarly, another student looking for information on "religion in Ethiopia" first tried various CD-ROM databases and found only about two dozen citations—and many of them turned out to have the right words in the wrong context. In searching for a published bibliography, however, we found Paulos Milkias's *Ethiopia: A Comprehensive Bibliography* (G. K. Hall, 1989); it has a 47-page section "Religion," specifically on that country's religion, and listed more than 1,300 directly relevant citations.

Now, it is true that most readers will not want to *end* their search with well over 1,000 citations; but the important point is that most researchers do indeed want to *start* their inquiries by looking at the best possible initial retrieval pool of sources, from which they will *then* make a more limited selection. The trick is find the best pool to start with—and the Milkias bibliography fitted that description much better than a few indifferently retrieved articles chosen mechanically by a computer that had no informed overview of the subject it was searching.

Remember, then, that published bibliographies enable you to find starting points that are often much better than those provided by computer printouts—and that the published sources *also* enable you to do Boolean combinations. You simply look for a bibliography on one subject (Dewey, Ethiopia) and then look for the second subject (Aristotle, Religion) in its index.

One problem that keeps coming up in research is that there is often no subject heading in a library catalog that is a good match for one's particu-

lar interest. Traditionally, libraries have offered two major avenues for circumventing this difficulty: systematic scanning of the subject-grouped
books themselves in the classification scheme, and detailed subject bibliographies. The latter allow for very easy scanning of titles, and sometimes
of annotations as well, that are free of the constraints of an artificial, controlled vocabulary. The newer approaches (through keywords, footnote
citations, related records, and "postcoordinate" combinations via computer) are the result of relatively recent advances in the technology of
indexing; but they have merely supplemented rather than replaced the traditional methods. (This is an important distinction that is sometimes lost
even on librarians, who, these days, are often trying to improve their "status" by ignoring any sources that are not electronic.) Published bibliographies will never be replaced by machine searches because, as mentioned
before, they often reach materials that dedicated scholars can find but that
lie beyond the reach of databases. (And the copyright law is simply not
going to change to allow their work to be "scanned in" routinely—indeed,
in most cases the high-quality published bibliographies won't be scanned
into the Internet *at all*.) Further, a printout is generated only in response to
specific words being typed in, whereas a published list is compiled
according to the ideas in a human mind without rigid verbal criteria of
exclusion. Published bibliographies, in other words, can often present perspectives on the literature of a subject that cannot be duplicated by
machine searches. And the published lists will continue to be valuable in
any event because they provide the best access to records dating to the
period before the advent of database coverage.

The main advantage of a bibliography is that it can save you the trouble
of reinventing the wheel—of doing the laborious spadework of identifying relevant sources. The disadvantage is that its compiler will almost
never tell you how he or she compiled it or what sources were used—you
won't know what you've missed, in other words. (The fact that a bibliography gets commercially published by a reputable publisher to begin with,
however, is usually an indication of some editorial quality control.)
Researchers pursuing a subject in depth can never rely on any one source
to be completely exhaustive; in-depth research always requires a combination of various approaches and sources. And even in those cases when
depth or exhaustiveness is not the goal, a published bibliography may be

still much preferable to a computer printout in defining the best initial pool of sources from which to make a narrower selection to start with.

There are two big problems that researchers routinely have in *finding* bibliographies. The first is that, in either Library of Congress or Dewey Decimal classification schemes, *bibliographies on a particular subject are usually not shelved with the regular books on that subject.* In the LC scheme, for example, books on "Indians of North America" tend to get call numbers within the range E51–99 (Pre-Columbian America and Indians of North America). Bibliographies on Indians of North America, however, get classed in Z1209–10—which will probably put them on an entirely different floor in the library. The reason for this is that rounding up all subject bibliographies in one place (at the end of the class scheme, in Z call numbers) gives them an aggregate power that would be dissipated if they were scattered among the regular B through V classes. Having all—or most, anyway—of the bibliographies on American history right next to each other in Z1200 through Z1363 enables researchers to recognize many other search options that would never occur to them if the bibliographies were dispersed (e.g., bibliographies listing American county histories are in this area, too; and many of them provide angles for researching Native American topics). Having all of the published bibliographies, on all subjects, next to each other in Z1200 through Z8999 gives them a cumulative capacity to serve as a kind of index to the rest of the classification scheme, much like the index volume at the end of an encylopedia.

There is an analogous situation in the Dewey Decimal system; there, however, the bibliographies are usually grouped together at the front of the system, in class 016, rather than at the end. Thus, while a regular book on civil engineering would be classed in 624, a published bibliography on the subject would be shelved in 016.624—again, such a number probably puts the bibliographies on an entirely different floor in the library. (Note that individual libraries do not *have* to shelve their bibliographies in either the Z or the 016 areas; they can choose to class them directly into the various subject areas. To do this costs more money, however, since most of the "copy cataloging" that is available for them to use from various computer networks will offer them already established Z and 016 call numbers. Having to create their own, different numbers in all of the various classes is more expensive than simply accepting what's already available. So most libraries will indeed separate the bibliographies from the monographs, and you simply have to be aware of the separation.)

The first problem in finding bibliographies, then, is this: They are usually not shelved with the regular books on a subject, and so if you browse only that subject area for your topic you will be missing all of the published bibliographies. And there will be no "dummy" cards on the bookshelves to tell you that they are shelved in an entirely different area.

How, then, do you find them? This brings up the second problem. You can find the bibliographies in a library collection by looking for the subdivision "—Bibliography" attached to the LC subject heading for your topic. The problem here, as indicated in Chapter 2, is that most people fail to find the right LC term or terms to begin with. The most common mistake is to search under general rather than specific headings. The result is that you won't find the subdivision "—Bibliography" if you're not looking for the right *heading* that it's a subdivision *of*.

So most researchers overlook the published bibliographies *twice*—they don't find them in the catalog because they look under the wrong LC headings, and they also miss them in the bookstacks because they don't realize the bibliographies are physically shelved in a separate area of their own. (Curiously, "Bibliographic Instruction" classes taught by librarians almost routinely fail to alert researchers to these difficulties.)

The primary solution to this problem is to find the right LC subject headings to begin with. Actually, there are several ways to find out if a published bibliography exists on a subject. Researchers should keep in mind the following:

The Library Catalog.   Four forms of subject headings in the Library of Congress system are relevant. After you have determined the proper *LCSH* word or phrase for your topic (or the one that comes closest) through the various methods discussed in Chaper 2, plug it into the following forms:

[Subject heading]—Bibliography
[Subject heading]—[Geographic subdivision]—Bibliography
Bibliography—Bibliography—[Subject heading]

MONITOR (IRONCLAD)

E473
.2   **Hoehling, Adolph A**
.H57   Thunder at Hampton Roads / by A. A. Hoehling. — Engle-
            wood Cliffs, N.J. : Prentice-Hall, c1976.

            xvi, 231 p., [8] leaves of plates : ill. ; 24 cm.

➤   Bibliography: p. 221-[226]
            Includes index.
            ISBN 0-13-920652-3 : $9.95

            1. Hampton Roads, Battle of, 1862.   2. Monitor (Ironclad)   3. Shipwrecks
            —North Carolina—Hatteras, Cape.   4. Hatteras, Cape—History.   5. Underwa-
            ter archaeology.   I. Title.

            E473.2.H57   973.7′52   76-18261
                                                                     MARC

            Library of Congress   76   MCat

Fig. 6

Additionally, a library catalog record (whether card or digital) will usually
note the presence of a bibliography at the end of a book. And such a note
can appear on any catalog record under any subject heading. So even if
you don't find the form "[Subject heading]—Bibliography" you may still
be able to pick out bibliographies of several pages' length under other
headings (without the specific subdivision) if you look for this note field
(Figure 6). If your library's online catalog has a sufficiently sophisticated
software, it is also possible to create a set of records under any subject
heading and then *limit* that set to only those records that note the presence
of these "back of the book" bibliographies.

The Z1201–Z8999 (or 016 in Dewey) stack areas.   It would be a good
idea for you to just browse around these areas to get a sense of what's
there. In the LC system there is a further structure to the arrangement of
Z-class subject bibliographies:

Z1201–Z4890   Geographically localized subject
                               bibliographies (by continent,
                               country, state, county, etc.)
                               arranged in the order of North

America, South America,
Europe, Asia, Africa, Australia,
and Oceania, with narrower
localized subdivisions within
each continent

Z5000–Z7999   Subject bibliographies (usually
lacking geographical limitations
or focus, arranged alphabetically
by subject)

Z8000–Z8999   Personal bibliographies (on
individual people, usually
literary authors or historical
figures), arranged alphabetically
by the surname of the subject

The personal bibliographies on individual authors are usually the best sources to start with when you are looking for literary criticism of particular stories, plays, or poems. A full-size published bibliography on a particular author—there are hundreds of them—will usually give you a *much better overview* of the range of criticism available on any particular work than any database search (such as the *MLA* computer file).

Note that the tripartite structuring of this arrangement will cause some scattering. Thus, bibliographies on American drama will be classed in Z1231.D7 (in the North America grouping), whereas those on English drama will appear in Z2014.D7 (within Europe); and those on drama in general—without a particular geographic focus—will appear in Z5781–85, which lies within the "D" alphabetical range for subjects in the middle group. And bibliographies on individual dramatists will appear in the Z8000s, as Ibsen in Z8431 and Shakespeare in Z8811–13.

Similarly, bibliographies on philosophy in general will appear in the "P" section of the alphabetical sequence (Z7125–30), but a bibliography on a particular philosopher, such as Socrates, will appear in Z8824.34. It's very hard to see this scattering when you're simply looking directly at the bookshelves; but if you understand the structure of the arrangement before you plunge in, you can use the collections much more efficiently. Remember in particular that all bibliographies on individual people are segregated in the Z8000s.

Bibliographic Index (H. W. Wilson, paper three times per year with annual cumulations, 1937– ; no computer version as of this writing). This is a very useful source, as it lists not only bibliographies that are separately published, but also those that appear at the ends of books and journal articles. Those that are included contain at least 50 citations, in English and foreign languages. The editors currently examine about 2,800 periodicals in addition to books and annual publications, so its coverage is excellent. It uses LC subject headings for its category terms.

A word to the wise, however: Since this index covers more than a half century of publishing, it may list many bibliographies on your subject without indicating their quality. To prevent information overload it may be best, therefore, to first ask for help at the reference desk. I once helped a student who wanted to find a bibliography on "Jacksonian democracy," but she didn't ask for this—she just asked for *Bibliographic Index*. When I found out what she really wanted, however, I could refer her directly to the *Harvard Guide to American History* and the *Library of Congress Guide to the Study of the United States of America*, both of which provide excellent lists of books on this subject—lists determined by standards of quality, not quantity of citations. Often a librarian can short-circuit a potentially lengthy search in this way—but you won't know unless you ask for help in the first place.

Encyclopedia Articles. The bibliographies at the ends of these are often very good for listing the standard or most highly recommended works on a subject; but they are usually very brief, and do not include specialized or narrowly focused works (e.g., they would not be good for someone looking for material on "Social Darwinism in Hardy"). A good trick for identifying a short list of "best" books is to compare the bibliographies from two different encyclopedia articles on the same subject. I recommend using the *Encyclopaedia Britannica* as one of the sets, since its bibliographies are usually evaluative—i.e., the *Britannica* writers don't just list sources; they give a running commentary on their quality in a short bibliographical essay at the end of the subject article. To find another encyclopedia to use in comparison, look at *First Stop: The Master Index to Subject Encyclopedias* by Joe Ryan (Oryx Press, 1989). This is a cumulative index to 430 *specialized* encyclopedias. If the bibliography from the specialized encyclopedia mentions the same titles recommended by the *Britannica,* you can be sure you've found some very good starting points. (For example, I was once interested in reading a book about Confucius; but I wanted to read only *one*, and I didn't know which of the many available titles to choose. So I compared the bibliography from the "Confucius" article in the *Encyclopedia of Philosophy* to that in the *Britannica;* both recommended H. G. Creel's *Confucius: The Man and the Myth* [reprinted as *Confucius and the Chinese Way]*, so that's the one I read.)

Review Articles.   These have excellent and lengthy bibliographies, and can be located by the approaches discussed in Chapter 8.

U.S. Government Printing Office *Subject Bibliographies Series.*   The U.S. federal government publishes material on an astonishing variety of subjects, and the more than 150 subject bibliographies published (and updated irregularly) by the GPO are a good shortcut to what's available; collectively these lists catalog more than 12,000 different books, periodicals, pamphlets, and posters. A free list of all topics covered by the bibliographies can be obtained from the GPO (Superintendent of Documents, U.S. Government Printing Office, Washington, DC 20402); the same subject bibliographies are also available on the Web at <www.gpo.gov> by selecting the "Information for Sale" option and then browsing "by Topic." The subjects covered, among others, include:

Annual Reports
Art and Artists
Birds
Census Publications
Civil War
Directories
Educational Statistics
Environmental Protection

Films and Audiovisual Information
Foreign Country Studies
Grants and Awards
Graphic Arts
High School Debate Topic
Languages
Maps and Atlases
Military History
Naval History
Occupational Outlook Handbook
Patents and Trademarks
Posters and Prints
Procurement
Radiation
Small Business
Student Financial Aid
Telecommunications
Veterans
Women

Subject Guide to Books in Print and **Book Review Digest.** The former is a good shortcut that reference librarians use to find the most recent books on any subject. The subject index to *Paperbound Books in Print* and the *Subject Guide to Forthcoming Books* are also useful for identifying the most recent material. (The caveat to be observed here is that recency is not necessarily synonymous with quality.) To get a sense of the *quality* of recent books, use the subject index that appears at the end of recent volumes of *Book Review Digest*. This source not only lists recent books, by subject; it also gives several excerpts from *evaluative reviews* of the books. It does not cover as many titles as the larger *Subject Guide to Books in Print*, however. (Think of the subject guide to *Book Review Digest* as another shortcut to finding quality books—like the other shortcut of comparing the bibliographies of two different encyclopedia articles.)

Theodore Besterman's *World Bibliography of Bibliographies* (4th ed., 5 vols.; Societas Bibliographica, 1965–66). This venerable source can be very useful for research in older literature. It is arranged by subject, listing thousands of published bibliographies. Volume 5 is a detailed index. An update is provided by Alice F. Toomey's *World Bibliography of Bibliographies, 1964–1974* (2 vols., Rowman and Littlefield, 1977). As useful as the *World Bibliography* is on occasion, it is the observation of reference librarians that whenever a graduate student asks for "Besterman" without *also* asking for Toomey and the *Bibliographic Index,* then that student is probably being taught by a professor who is simply teaching from his or her own antiquated graduate notes.

Bonnie R. Nelson's *Guide to Published Library Catalogs*   (Scarecrow, 1982). There are hundreds of libraries that have specialized in acquiring materials in particular subject fields. More that 400 of these have published their catalogs in book format, and each is a gold mine of sources in its area because such catalogs sometimes provide in-depth indexing of individual journal articles, research reports, and chapters of books. This level of information—especially the indexing of pre-twentieth-century journal articles—does not get indexed by the library catalogs that are searchable via OCLC's FirstSearch service (see Chapter 11). Nelson's *Guide* is the best list of what's available; she decribes each catalog in detail and provides a good subject index. (I wish that some enterprising scholar would take the time to update this most useful listing of printed catalogs.)

Library Literature   (H. W. Wilson Company; paper format, 1921– , bimonthly with annual cumulations; CD-ROM from December 1984– , updated quarterly; also available through OCLC FirstSearch, 1984–). This is a subject index to more than 200 library journals. It is surprisingly useful for bibliographies in *all* subject areas, however, because reference librarians use these journals to communicate with each other and to publish annotated lists of sources on things they get asked about. (For example, one of the sources, *Reference Services Review,* has published excellent annotated bibliographies on how to get grant money, on field guides to birds, on the impact of plastic on the environment, and on Afro-American movies.) And many of these articles are overlooked by *Bibliographic Index* because they contain fewer than 50 sources.

Serial Bibliographies.   These are regularly published bibliographies covering particular topics, usually appearing in specialized journals. Three good sources for identifying serial bibliographies are Richard Gray's *Serial Bibliographies in the Humanities and Social Sciences* (Pierian Press, 1969), William Wortman's *Guide to Serial Bibliographies for Modern Literatures,* 2d ed., (Modern Language Association, 1995), and David Henige's *Serial Bibliographies and Abstracts in History* (Greenwood Press, 1986). *Bibliographic Index* is also useful for identifying the serials.

Related to the bibliography is another form of research aid, called the "guide to the literature." This is ideally more than just a list of sources (with or without annotations); it frequently provides a running evaluative commentary on the literature of a subject, with full paragraphs in connected exposition. The better ones will discuss not only the finding aids and research techniques that are appropriate to the discipline, but also the basic and advanced works essential to the content of the field of study. They seek to provide a structure of perception for the field—which is more than a bibliography provides.

Some guides are more successful than others in achieving this ideal. *Research Guide to Philosophy,* by Terence N. Tice and Thomas P. Slavens (American Library Association, 1983), is a good example of what can be done. It provides overviews of the literature of philosophy from two different perspectives, by time period and by particular subject subfield (epistemology, aesthetics, moral philosophy, etc.). Within each chapter it identifies the major works that have established the boundaries of the discussion, with running commentaries on what the issues are, what the various positions are within them, and who the important writers are. Other guides, such as Harold Kolb's *Field Guide for the Study of American Literature*, are little more than annotated lists of books. The word "Guide" in the title is no guarantee that the book is more than a bibliography of finding aids.

The following brief list of titles will suggest some of the variety of specialized guides—of varying quality—that are available:

The Reader's Advisor (This is a multivolume set, updated irregularly, listing recommended works in British & American Literature, World

Literature, Social Sciences, History, The Arts, Philosophy, Religion, Science, Technology, Medicine, and Reference. Indexes are by Name, Title, and Subject. It is often especially useful in identifying the best collected set of an author's writings.)

A Brief Guide to Sources of Scientific and Technical Information

Fieldwork in the Library: A Guide to Anthropology and Related Area Studies

Guide to English and American Literature

Guide to Information Sources in the Botanical Sciences

Guide to Sources for Agricultural and Biological Research

Guide to the Literature of Art History

Guide to the Literature of the Life Sciences

Guide to the Study of the United States of America (and supplement)

Guide to the Zoological Literature

Harvard Guide to American History

The Historian's Handbook

How to Find Out in Philosophy and Psychology

Information Sources in Engineering

Information Sources in Law

Information Sources in Physics

Information Sources in Science and Technology

Information Sources in the Environment

Information Sources in the Life Sciences

The Information Sources of Political Science

Introduction to Library Research in French Literature

Literary Research Guide

A Reader's Guide to the Social Sciences

Research and Reference Guide to French Studies

Research Guide to Musicology

Research Guide to Religious Studies

Research Guide to the History of Western Art

Scientific and Technical Information Sources

Sources of Information in the Social Sciences

The Use of Biological Literature

The Use of Chemical Literature

The Use of Medical Literature

Usually such works can be found in the library catalog or in *Subject Guide to Books in Print* under the form already mentioned: "[Subject heading]—Bibliography." The best overall list of these guides is Martin Sable's *Research Guides to the Humanities, Social Sciences, Sciences and Technology* (Pierian Press, 1986). Although it is dated, the various research guides themselves are often of most use in identifying noncomputer sources useful for searching older literature.

For general lists of what to read for self-education, a number of "great books" lists are available. In addition to the sets of the *Harvard Classics* (various printings) and the *Great Books of the Western World,* 2d ed., 60 vols. (Encyclopaedia Britannica, 1990), analogous rosters may be found in Charles Van Doren's *The Joy of Reading* (Harmony Books, 1985), Clifton Fadiman's *New Lifetime Reading Plan*, 4th ed. (HarperCollins, 1997), Mortimer Adler's *Reforming Education* (Macmillan, 1988), pp. 318–50, and Harold Bloom's *The Western Canon* (Harcourt Brace, 1994), pp. 531–67. An older "great books" list is Asa Don Dickson's *The World's Best Books, Homer to Hemingway: 3000 Books of 3000 Years, 1050 B.C. to 1950 A.D., Selected on the Basis of a Consensus of Expert Opinion* (Wilson, 1953); Dickson assembled it by collating scores of previous lists of classics.

There is also a CD-ROM product, irregularly revised and expanded, called *Library of the Future,* which reproduces full texts of classic works (although limited to copyright-free editions and translations that are sometimes substandard [see Chapter 11]).

I mentioned that published bibliographies are often the best means of gaining access to literature too old to be in databases; they are *especially* useful for getting into pre-twentieth-century literature, that is, material written prior to the existence of even the printed indexes—let alone the computer sources—that we also take for granted today. (Even the large *Periodicals Contents Index* [see Chapter 5] does not make published bibliographies obsolete.)

It is particularly useful to look for published bibliographies *in addition to* computer-generated lists. (Most researchers stop with the latter.) The bibliographies will almost always turn up valuable sources—*recent as well as old*—missed by the printouts. And it is important to *actively search* for such bibliographies, especially since they are usually overlooked for the two reasons given above. Almost every researcher has had the experience of using a bibliography that appears at the end of a book or article; but it is comparatively rare—at least from this reference librarian's perspective—for researchers to *start out* by looking for a published bibliography, as opposed to simply using one that happens to come their way as a by-product of something else they've done. A hallmark of the experts is that they actively look for such lists, especially in the early stages of their investigations. The best researchers regard the aggregate of published bibliographies as collectively forming an avenue of access to sources that is *quite different from, and not superseded by,* the alternative avenue provided by computer-generated bibliographies. You will be a much more efficient scholar if you do not confuse the two.

10

The Differences Between Real and Virtual Libraries

Computer searches offer a myriad of research opportunities, leading variously to bibliographic citations, full texts of some documents, locations of desired items, current information, and direct contacts with people who are knowledgeable in particular subjects. Many published overviews of computer sources, however, must be taken with a grain of salt; imaginative projections of virtual libraries containing "everything" in electronic form frequently boil down to bait-and-switch claims entailing radically diminished understandings of just what the "everything" *is* that constitutes the universe of available sources. Assertions that "everything" is—or "soon" will be—accessible electronically often entail a dismaying ignorance of the abundance of material that is not, and never will be, included in any virtual library.

When all of the hoopla settles down and the truly remarkable advantages of computer sources are viewed realistically, it will be seen that the importance of real libraries—those having actual walls and shelves with printed books, journals, microforms, maps, and so on—lies precisely in their capacity to allow free access to a wide range of both copyrighted and public domain sources that will never be found on the Information Superhighway, due to both legal and economic realities. Rather than being primarily "on-ramps" to the highway—hookups from the more convenient sites of home and office will probably be as common as VCRs or cable TV links in a few years—real libraries will continue to be most valuable as destinations that the highway can only point to without actually entering beyond the vestibule/catalog. (The highway, of course, does enter many other resources more fully—but most of them are sources that would never have been selected by a library to begin with.) Several specific differences between real libraries and virtual libraries need to be kept in mind.

Copyright Restrictions

Real libraries offer free access to the full texts of thousands, even millions, of copyrighted books. The Internet, on the other hand, is comparatively barren of such texts. (For convenience I am using the terms "Information Superhighway" and "Internet" interchangeably.) For example, one of the largest full-text sources on the Net is called Project Gutenberg; it is striving to mount electronically searchable full texts of 10,000 books by the year 2001. In contrast, the Library of Congress's book collection grows by about 10,000 volumes *every two weeks*. Not only is the electronic virtual library not catching up to the print world, it is in fact falling farther and farther behind every day. Moreover, the Library of Congress has *532 miles* of bookshelves for works already in its retrospective collections; and not even the most rabid virtual library proponents, when pressed, will claim that even a thousandth of this material will ever be digitized. (They seldom *are* pressed on this point!) In a sense, every book that is published is the equivalent, in its information content, of a "nonelectronic Web site"—and thousands of new "sites" are produced in such paper formats every single day, without appearing on the Net.

One could say that the Internet is filling a niche of its own within the universe of knowledge sources—a niche that overlaps but does not cover the one filled by printed books.

Real libraries also offer free access to copyrighted journal articles. Although there are many full-text databases of periodical articles available, and also document-delivery services that will enable readers, for a fee, to buy copies of articles, these services—unless heavily subsidized or site-licensed within real libraries to avoid passing direct costs on to individual users—are expensive enough to discourage easy access or routine use by most researchers outside real libraries. Their point-of-use costs are especially discouraging to those who are simply curious about a topic, as opposed to readers who have an economic stake in finding definite information. The result is that copyrighted articles that are technically "available" online "from anywhere at any time" wind up effectively outside the reach of most who would actually read them if they were available in print format for free and immediate consultation within real libraries. (The provision of access to electronic full-text journals, as in *Project Muse* or *JSTOR* [see Chapter 4], is subject to the same conditions: If ordinary citizens readers want *free* access, they have to go inside real library walls to search these databases; they cannot freely tap into them from anywhere.)

An additional problem is that the universe of electronically available journals is only a fraction of what is actually being published in printed form. The NEXIS database—which costs about $4.00 *per minute* when searched in its entirety—offers about a thousand periodicals; and document delivery services such as Faxon Finder and CARL UnCover (see Chapter 11) offer about 17,000 serial titles and charge about $10 to $13 for each article. The Library of Congress, by contrast, has more than 400,000 serial publications in its holdings, of which about 65,000 are live subscriptions. Moreover, two standard directories of periodicals, *Ulrich's International Periodicals Directory* (Bowker) and *The Serials Directory* (EBSCO), each list more than 150,000 titles currently being published worldwide. Again, to view the electronic services as offering "everything" is thus to radically dumb down one's understanding of what "everything" means to begin with, especially in comparison with what a real research library can offer.

The bottom line is that copyright restrictions will never disappear from the Information Superhighway. Neither U.S. nor international law is simply going to change to allow free access to "everything." Some virtual library enthusiasts regard copyright protection as a problem that will eventually be "solved." This is nonsense. Copyright is not the problem. *Piracy* is the problem. Copyright is the *solution*. That fundamental relationship will not go away.[1]

Given that fact, there must always be restrictions on copyrighted texts. And in the electronic world there can be only two kinds of those: Either you can restrict *what* is made available to begin with—which means that you can freely mount only copyright-free texts, and these, collectively, are *much* less than "everything"; or you can restrict *who* has access—which means that only people who can pay stiff fees or high subscription costs will be able to get into much of the "virtual library." The only middle ground in the electronic world lies in large organizations subsidizing costs for their members—some university libraries, for example, subsidize computerized document delivery charges for faculty members. But membership in such a group, with restricted passwords, is actually just another form of the *who* restriction.

There are two big implications for researchers. The first is that there will always be a major difference between bibliographic citation databases and full-text files. It does not violate anyone's ownership rights to simply cite their publication, or even to provide a brief abstract of it; and so the bibliographic citation databases will always be much broader in their coverage than the text files. They are more superficial—a citation is much less informative than the actual text it points to—but much wider in scope. The text files are correspondingly much deeper but also much narrower in what they include. This is an inevitable trade-off.[2]

The second major implication is that one must go *outside the Information Superhighway* to escape its inevitable *what* and *who* restrictions—but this is *precisely* what can be done in *real* libraries. The full texts of every book and every journal there can indeed be freely read by anyone who comes in the door—and the libraries are not bound to offer only public-domain material, to restrict who can come in, or to charge patrons any direct (and prohibitive) per-minute costs at all for their use of copyrighted items in the collection. One could say that overcoming the *what* and *who* restrictions of virtual libraries thus entails a *where* limitation—that is, a restriction to a library place that actually has walls. This particular limitation, however, is mitigated by the lending practices of most real libraries—much of their material can be loaned or checked out for use elsewhere, and in those other locations can be used at any time of the day or night—and also by the fact that there are so many real libraries and that they are so geographically dispersed in so many communities.

There are going to be trade-offs of some kind no matter what the information universe of the future looks like. The point here is that may futurists nowadays criticize real libraries for restricting access to only those people who can come to a certain place; and this *where* limitation, they assert, is not a problem in a "library without walls." This networked electronic "solution," however, is itself a trade-off—and a *massive* trade-off at that. What advocates of virtual libraries naïvely overlook is the fact that as soon as you eliminate the localized walls you inevitably and unavoidably create other restrictions of *what* and *who*. This is the danger of advocating the Information Superhighway as *replacing* rather than merely *supplementing* real libraries. Such advocacy, in ignoring the very real and unavoidable trade-offs among *what*, *who*, and *where* restrictions, can ultimately result, with the loss of real libraries-as-places, in much less material being made freely available to researchers.

The mere existence of information does not assure its use—reality checks such as *price* considerations (and *format* changes [see below]) need to be factored into naïve claims of electronic "accessibility." In other words, researchers in the real world can, and will, find a great deal of information in a *library* that they could not find in an online *bookstore*—even though many of the same sources could be found in either. Fee access is simply not the same thing as free access—especially for students—and the result of exchanging the latter for the former will inevitably be a diminution rather than an expansion of the range of sources that actually get *used*.

Quality Control

Another major area of difference between the Net and real libraries is the often-discussed lack of quality control in the former. Sources that make their way into real libraries generally have to go through a series of winnowing processes. Books, for example, have to surmount the hurdle of finding a publisher who makes judgments that they are worth publishing to begin with—judgments that have real economic consequences for the survival of the publishing house. They then must must go through an editing, and sometimes a fact-checking and even legal review process.

Many libraries, especially local public branches, are reluctant, given their limited budgets, to purchase new works that they know nothing about; and so many volumes that wind up on library shelves must also go through the further process of being reviewed in journals before libraries will consider them. (Alternatively, library purchases are also sometimes made on a "blanket order" basis from reputable supply houses—but the reputation of such suppliers won't last long if they don't establish criteria of quality themselves in the lots they send on to their customers.)

Authors of journal articles, too, must overcome various hurdles of submission, review, and editing to achieve publication. Further, the journals that publish them do not automatically get selected by libraries; those that are subscribed to are often screened according to whether they are indexed by commercial services such as the Wilson or the ISI indexes—which have their own measures of quality for determining which titles they will cover. Choices made by librarians in the expenditure of limited funds for either books or journals are also subject to oversight by local boards or faculty committees. These choices do not always assure that the "best" material will always be available—in a world of trade-offs such an ideal is never achievable—but they do go a long way toward weeding out mountains of material that are clearly *not* the best, and whose cluttering presence would otherwise seriously impede the efficiency of the research process.

The Internet, in contrast, circumvents all these hurdles, filters, and reviews; the niche it is most notably exploiting—one that real libraries cannot afford to enter—is that of offering to any author a wide audience for anything that he or she wishes to say, whether or not it is sensible, accurate, documented, true, up-to-date, hateful, obscene, or even coherent. Anyone can put up his own home page on the World Wide Web; there is *no filtering process*. Moreover, the quality of discussion on many listservs—even moderated ones—is often at the level of "Well, *my* impression is . . ." or "IMHO (in my humble opinion) . . ."—such impressions often being based on whims, ideologies, or preconceptions rather than evidence. Moreover, disagreements about facts often descend, in the electronic environment, all too quickly to "flaming." Of course, this means that there are millions of sources on the Net that you can't get in printed formats in a library. Precisely. But that statement is actually more of a compliment to real libraries than a criticism of them.

The contents of the Information Superhighway and of real libraries inevitably have some overlap, of course. If we think of traditional libraries as offering various types of literature—monographs, scholarly journals, popular magazines, encyclopedias, almanacs, directories, catalogs, timetables, and so on (see Chapter 16)—it is evident that the Net is overlapping, even superseding, some forms much more than others; it is especially good for current information that does not require extended (i.e., book-length) analysis. In traditional terms, this means it is wonderful for finding information that otherwise would have to be searched for in reference literature such as almanacs, directories, catalogs, and timetables. It overlaps encyclopedias and popular magazines in some respects, too—with the qualification that, again, Net sources may or may not have undergone any editorial review or fact-checking. While scholarly journals, which do guarantee some review, are beginning to appear in electronic forms, most of these sources are severely restricted by site licenses. This means, effectively, that they aren't really on the Information Superhighway to begin with because you cannot get into them "from anywhere at any time"; you need to go inside a real library to use the specific terminals to which they are licensed. And even if their site limitation extends to a whole campus, you still have to be within the limits of a certain *place* to gain access to them.

In spite of the overlap, especially in the area of current, noncopyrighted information, the Net and real libraries are still filling niches that have substantial differences. Each does something the other cannot; and neither replaces the other.

Format Differences and Their Significance

Real libraries offer access to all kinds of books—those in the public domain as well as copyrighted—in a *format* that people actually feel comfortable with. One of the key assumptions of information science is that the intellectual content of a written work remains the same even when it is "freed" from its original format of presentation—that is, the "content" of a printed book remains the same even when its format is changed to microfilm or digital screen display. While this assumption is true, several decades of experience with screen-display formats indicate that it is also naïve—that is, while, in a sense, it is wholly true, it is nevertheless not the whole of the truth. The assumption, by itself, overlooks the additional truth that changing the format of presentation also changes *access* to the contents; and formats that tend to make the sustained reading of lengthy texts more difficult also tend to discourage the use and "absorption" of such lengthy texts in the first place.

Most people simply do not like having to do sustained reading of book-length texts on electronic screen displays—*fictional* representations of such activity in *Star Trek* and *2001: A Space Odyssey* notwithstanding. Moreover, the cost and inconvenience of reading a printout of a book-length text made on a ream of unbound sheets seriously undercuts the naïve assumption that electronically "available" books will actually be *read* in either screen or unbound-ream format. (Assertions that bound copies can be generated to order always overlook the prohibitive point-of-use cost of such operations.[3])

I am not saying that such reading cannot be done at all; I am simply pointing out the neglected fact that increasing the level of inconvenience in reading book-length texts will ultimately decrease the level of their use.[4] This is especially true if alternative formats of shorter length (and with color, sound, graphics, and motion, all of which are more congenial to computer displays) are immediately available at one's desk, and one would have to travel elsewhere for convenient access to books (i.e., free access to print formats). People who claim that all books will be available online—usually implying thereby that real libraries will become unnecessary—seem very seldom to have actually read any book-length works themselves in the electronic format they would so readily impose on other people.

Of course, computerized texts do indeed offer keyword search capabilities that printed formats do not; but doing such electronic searches of a text for *information* is simply not the same as doing sustained reading of the book for *understanding*. The latter requires a reading and a grasp of the work as a whole; and no amount of keyword searching will provide this. The two levels of access—indeed, of *thinking*—are simply not the same;[5] and even if the content of a book is identical in printed and electronic formats, the *access* will be different because the different *formats* facilitate (or impede) inquiries at different intellectual levels.

The computer format, in other words, is not neutral—when it aims to present full texts for sustained reading (as opposed to keyword searching), it has a definite bias toward shorter (article-length) rather than longer (book-length) texts because of the discomfort its format causes with the latter.[6] The facile claim of information science that the format of a work can be changed without altering its content—the key assumption that forms the basis for claims that books and real libraries are becoming irrelevant and outdated—needs to be critically evaluated, and supplemented by the additional understanding that changing the format also changes both the *convenience* and, to some extent at least, the *intellectual level* of access. Those formats that increase the inconvenience or drudgery of access will also bring about a reduction in actual use;[7] those that require greater efforts at prior specification by the user, as opposed to simple recognition, will lessen the efficiency of searching; and those that make it more difficult to grasp a lengthy expository or narrative work as a whole will lessen understanding.

Cataloging

Real libraries *sort and categorize* their knowledge records and then *standardize* and *link* the category labels. The creation of such artificially defined *groups* of resources enables readers to *recognize* relevant individual items within sets—items whose keywords they could never have specified in advance. The various search engines available for Web searching, in contrast, are all essentially keyword-search devices. They may use sophisticated methods to display results by weighting or ranking hits according to frequency counts or word proximity measures; but they are limited in that their automated spiders and crawlers can find to begin with only the natural language words that happen to appear on the sources they scan—they cannot find synonyms and variant phrases for the same idea. (The few automated algorithms that correlate synonyms with each other, as in the Excite search engine [<www.excite.com>], are inconsistent and haphazard at best; machines simply cannot notice relationships that human catalogers can spot.)

As of this writing some attempts are being made to categorize Internet and Web resources—that is, to add artificially created, standardized category terms that will create retrievable points of commonality among records with otherwise disparate keywords; but the Web sources are proliferating faster than the cataloging can keep up with. One particularly interesting attempt to control the Net using *LC Subject Headings* and Dewey Decimal classes is called NetFirst, from OCLC. It catalogs Web pages, FTP sites, gopher servers, discussion groups, and electronic publications.[8]

Libraries may subscribe to this service for a fee; it is available as part of the OCLC FirstSearch system. The point is simply that while the Information Superhighway does indeed contain wonderful resources, many of them cannot be found because access to them is so much a matter of guesswork—unlike the systematic access available to sources in real libraries.

Ranges of Electronic Resources in Real Libraries

Real libraries can offer researchers free access to *a much greater array of electronic sources themselves* than they could ever get from the Internet. Hundreds of CD-ROM and FirstSearch/Eureka-type databases (see Chapter 11) that can be tapped into without direct charges to the user can be found in real libraries with walls, whereas the Information Superhighway equivalents that are available at home or office via modem—if they are available at all—have either stiff per-use charges attached at the point of use, or subscription costs that put them way beyond the reach of individuals.

Researchers who venture onto the Internet, especially those who are looking for the "library" sources that are indeed available online (whether free or for fee), need most of all to have some sense of the range of full-text information that is not there to begin with. It is especially important to remember that the depth of information contained in *bibliographic citations* to texts, or in *catalog records* for books, is simply not the same as that in the full texts themselves. And the free, in-depth scanning access to page- and paragraph-level information contained *in books* on library shelves, in all subject areas, made possible by subject-classified shelving (see Chapter 3), is not even remotely duplicated in most subject areas by the component word searching that can be done in the much tinier pools of electronic texts.

All of this is to say that you should not assume that "everything" is available in electronic virtual libraries.[9] If you're going to be a good researcher, you need to perceive the larger context of resources of which the Internet is only a part. Don't make the mistake of equating NEXIS with classified bookshelves; of assuming that access to journal articles or full texts is confined only to the recent years covered by most databases; of disregarding the millions of sources available in microformats; or of believing that the

"National Digital Library" is equivalent to a real library rather than just a pool of a very few copyright-free special collections of noncurrent sources.

What is so strange about the bait-and-switch claims of "everything" being available on the Information Superhighway, to the extent that it can "replace" real research libraries, is that the Net sources offer so many genuine and substantive advantages to researchers that they do not *need* to be misrepresented as covering "everything"—as though anything short of that made them worthless. Like all other tools (such as printed books or microforms), the Internet fills particular niches within the total universe of available sources. But confusing the part with the whole will greatly diminish your effectiveness as a researcher, as it will blind you to vast arrays of free options within real libraries that ought to be part of your arsenal.

Notes

1. It is noteworthy that the cyberprophets who so facilely predict the replacement of real libaries with electronic virtual libraries are themselves making their predictions *in printed books,* and that these books uniformly carry a notice on the verso of their title pages to the effect that "No part of this book may be reproduced in any form by any electronic or mechanical means (including photocopying, recording, or information storage and retrieval) without permission in writing from the publisher." In other words, if anyone wants to read *these* books for free, he or she will have to go to a real library to do it because the disparagers of real libraries—those who predict "everything" will be available electronically—will not allow their own works to appear in the digital form of which they are so enamored! Shouldn't we regard what these authors actually do themselves, as spelled out on their title-page versos, as more telling than what they merely say?

2. It is sometimes asserted that since copyright protections cannot be effectively enforced on the Internet—and there is some truth to this—the notion of copyright itself will be become obsolete. This conclusion, however, is a non sequitur. What will probably happen, instead, will be a continuation of what is already happening right now: Those who do not care to guard their intellectual property rights will freely contribute to the Internet; and those authors and publishers who do wish to protect their rights *will avoid putting their works on the Information Superhighway in the first place.* This simple solution is much more

sensible than doing away with copyright altogether; and its practicality is already being exemplified routinely in the actions of even those writers themselves whose books predict the end of copyright.

3. An analogous service exists today for ordering copies on demand of doctoral dissertations. University Microfilms International (UMI) will sell a bound paper copy of any American dissertation—but it will cost you $57.50 for a paperback copy, or $69.50 for a hardcover. This kind of on-demand publishing obviously discourages anyone but the most determined researchers. (In contrast, the UMI dissertation collection at the Library of Congress—the only complete set of dissertations in the country that is *freely* available to anyone who visits—is the most heavily used microfilm collection in the whole Library. People will read dissertations avidly—even in microformats—*when they do not have to pay for the privilege*.)

4. On the Principle of Least Effort in information-seeking behavior, see my *Library Research Models* (New York: Oxford University Press, 1993), pp. 91–101, 221–42.

5. See the hierarchy of levels outlined in the Preface to this book.

6. See Michael Gorman and Walt Crawford's *Future Libraries: Dreams, Madness, and Reality* (Chicago: American Library Association, 1995), especially the technical section "Resolution" within the larger section "Reading: Still Best on Paper," pp. 17–23.

7. See Chapter 8 in my *Library Research Models*.

8. A clearinghouse for other Web sites that attempt to organize Net resources by means of standard classification systems or controlled vocabularies can be viewed at <www.public.iastate.edu/~CYBERSTACKS/CTW.htm>.

9. Another difference between real and virtual libraries lies in the area of long-term preservation of material. In additional to the ephemeral institutional support (or lack thereof) for most Web sites, the more fundamental problem remains that electronic formats cannot, in general, be viewed as the means to solve preservation problems when it is in their very nature to cause the problems in the first place. This is more an area for library administrators to deal with, however; and since the focus of the present book is on the concerns of researchers, I regard preservation issues as somewhat out of scope here—with the obvious recognition that, of course, material that isn't preserved cannot be found or used. Interested readers may consult *Library Research Models*, pp. 137–39.

11

Computer Searches: Types of Sources

The range of sources available electronically includes scores of thousands of individual databases, files, home pages, and contacts; and the field is changing so rapidly that anything written at any time about it will need serious revision within a year. Basically, only a fool would try to present a coherent overview of the whole thing. I will begin, then, with a sketch of different types of computer sources.

Bibliographic Citation Databases

There are both "free" and "fee" sources in this category. By "free" I mean, here and elsewhere, sources that do not require direct costs to be paid by individual researchers at the point of use; subscription or access charges for these sources are usually born by institutions supported by tax monies or tuition. Such sources are especially distinguishable from "fee" services in that they provide no point-of-use cost barriers to unlimited access by individuals. (In line with the observations in the previous chapter on *who, what,* and *where* trade-offs, there will be a *where* restriction on most of these databases: You will be able to use them only within real libraries, with walls—not in just any location that has a computer and a modem.)

The free sources are of several types:

Online Public Access Catalogs (OPACs). These are library "card catalogs" in electronic format. Your local library will probably have such a catalog; and thousands more can be searched for free on the Internet. Usually these will cover primarily the book holdings of the library without providing access to individual journal articles. Nonbook formats (films, posters, sound recordings, etc.) owned by the library may be included, or may be in separate files. An annual published volume called *OPAC Directory* (Information Today) lists which catalogs are remotely searchable.

CD-ROM databases.   There are hundreds of these available; any individual library may offer access to dozens. They are commercially produced indexes, usually providing citations to journal articles; but CD-ROMs covering other formats such as dissertations, government documents, technical and educational reports, investment analyses, and so on, also exist. Many are derived from previously existing printed indexes (e.g., *Humanities Index, Biography Index*), and most cover only recent years (often from the 1970s or the 1980s forward), whereas the print versions may go back for many decades. In the earlier years of the electronic revolution in libraries, computer access to journal article citations was available only on a fee basis. CD-ROMs now make available for free the kinds of searches you used to have to pay for, through commercial services such as Dialog (see below). Note, however, that hundreds more bibliographic citation databases are still available only for a fee than are accessible for free on CD-ROMs. The latter do not make Dialog (or other comparable) searches obsolete, because the CD-ROMs simply do not offer as many bibliographic citation files to choose from. There are also a variety of full-text sources available on CDs (see below). An annual directory from Gale Research, *CD-ROMs in Print*, lists the range of options.

OCLC FirstSearch databases.   The Online Computer Library Center, more commonly known simply as OCLC, is an organization that offers libraries the opportunity to connect to more than sixty bibliographic citation and directory databases (and some full-text sources) on its computer in Ohio; more files will be added in the future. Usually they are comparable to CD-ROM databases, that is, providing access primarily to bibliographic citations of periodical articles, and only for recent years. Access to some other formats (e.g., conference papers, government documents, newspapers, dissertations) is also provided. The advantage to libraries is that this kind of remote access frees them from the costs of acquiring and maintaining the hardware needed to mount CD-ROMs locally, and also simplifies the complexities of subscribing to many individual discs that need to be continually updated. Not all libraries subscribing to the First-Search service will offer all of the databases within it; some may subscribe to only a handful of its dozens of files. All of the computerized Wilson indexes (see Chapter 4) are offered here.

The most important file within FirstSearch is called WorldCat; it is primarily a book database that in effect combines the OPACs of about 25,000 libraries all over the world and lets you search them simultaneously. It includes records for more than 30 million books, periodicals, sound recordings, videos, music scores, and manuscripts. Libraries in more than 60 countries participate (but the large majority of them are in the United States). If you wish to look for books available outside your own library, it is usually more sensible to search WorldCat than to bother with searching the OPACs of individual libraries, one at a time, via the Internet.

While FirstSearch offers library managers a number of economic and administrative advantages, it presents end users with both advantages and disadvantages when compared to the CD-ROM alternative. One advantage is that FirstSearch databases usually offer document delivery capabilities—they tell you how to buy copies of articles, in either print or electronic formats (and via fax) that may not be in your local library. A disadvantage is that the FirstSearch software is different from that of the CD-ROM versions of the same databases; and the FirstSearch version is usually less complex. This means that even though the content of the various databases may be identical, you will not have the same *access* to it—you may not be able to do all of the kinds of searches in FirstSearch that you could do in the CD-ROM versions. For example, the *Arts & Humanities Citation Index* is available both in CD-ROM and via FirstSearch—but the FirstSearch version does not allow you to do related-record searching (see Chapter 7).

RLG Eureka databases. Like OCLC, the Research Libraries Group (RLG) offers a service that enables libraries to tap into a variety of remote databases, including the Research Libraries Information Network's RLIN BIB file, a catalog of the combined holdings of more than 250 very large research libraries (somewhat comparable to the WorldCat database in OCLC), plus dozens of "CitaDel" files covering journal articles, newspapers, government documents, and so on; both the BIB and the CitaDel files are searchable through a common software known as Eureka. The RLIN BIB file contains more than 25 million titles in all formats—books, periodicals, maps, photographs, sound recordings, scores, films, and so on. Document delivery capabilities, for a fee, are also part of this system. Since OCLC and RLG are competitors, each offers a number of databases that the other lacks; the point to remember is that while the two services are comparable, they are not "the same." For example, as of this writing, the *MLA International Bibliography* is exclusive to FirstSearch, while *Anthropological Literature* appears only in CitaDel. The *English Short Title* catalog, recording almost all English-language printed material produced from 1473 to 1900, is also unique to the RLG system. There are always trade-offs of coverage in using one system rather than the other.

CARL UnCover and Faxon Finder databases.   These two companies provide similar services, although without much overlap in coverage. Each company scans into its database the tables of contents from each issue of about 17,000 journals since 1988 (UnCover) or 12,500 since 1990 (Faxon). These databases, like those of OCLC and RLIN, are available on a subscription basis; libraries that offer them, however, will not pass on direct costs to individual users.

The Faxon service is stronger in covering research-oriented journals, and its indexing extends to editorials, letters to the editor, obituaries, and so on; the UnCover indexing is largely limited to titles of substantive articles.

Both services offer document delivery capabilities that can supply, for a fee, the full-texts of any articles located. Fees will vary per article, but $7 to $15 for each seems to be a rule-of-thumb range. (Some universities may subsidize the service, reducing the costs to their own faculty or students still further.)

In addition to the "free" sources of bibliographic citations, there are a number of fee-based database providers that will charge you directly, at the point of use, for each search. The "fee" services for which you have to pay *directly* for bibliographic-citation searches can come from several sources:

Dialog searches.   Dialog Information Services, a subsidiary of Knight-Ridder, is a company that offers more than 400 different databases that can be dialed-up remotely and searched for a fee. Although there are other companies in competition with it that offer different or overlapping databases (e.g., Orbit • Questel, offering about 80 files; DIMDI, offering about 80; and Knight-Ridder's DataStar, with more than 300), Dialog is clearly the 600-pound gorilla in this area. The others are mainly used in specialized corporate, legal, medical, and scientific libraries. (For a list of which databases are available in each service, consult the annual *Gale Directory of Databases*.) Many of the Dialog files offer the option of printing full-texts of articles in addition to simple bibliographic citations, or citations with abstracts.

Searches can be done in almost any subject area, and the terms can be tailored to even the narrowest subjects. Costs will vary depending on how much time is spent in any database, how many hits are retrieved, and in what format they are printed (citation, citation + abstract, full text). There may also be a surcharge levied by the individual library. Because of this, you will usually want to have Dialog searches done for you by a trained intermediary, such as a librarian, who won't waste the time or money you would expend figuring out how the system works. Those who are not affiliated with a university can obtain searches through private research companies, through some local public libraries, or possibly through joining a university library's "Friends of the Library" organization.

The librarian or other searcher must select in advance which of the 400+ databases she wishes to search for your subject. There are, however, a few "umbrella" databases in the system that will tell her which databases will provide the most hits for any given search terms. The *Dialindex* (File 411) database enables the operator to look for specified words in either all of the Dialog files (SET FILES ALL), or in a variety of "supercategories":

    ALLBUSINESS
    ALLGENERAL
    ALLLAW
    ALLGOVERNMENT
    ALLNEW
    ALLREFERENCE

ALLSCIENCE
ALLSOCIAL
ALLHUMANITIES
ALLTEXT

Results can be shown in ranked order by the number of hits that lie in each database. (Once the databases have been scoped out by *Dialindex*, each one then has to be searched individually in order to retrieve the actual citations.) The advantage of *Dialindex* lies in bringing to your attention files with hits that would otherwise not have occurred to you to search. Other umbrella databases are *Journal Name Finder* (File 414), which tells you where any given journal is indexed within the Dialog system; *Company Name Finder* (File 416); and *Product Name Finder* (File 413). (Other systems like Dialog have comparable overall indexes like *Dialindex*; in the DataStar system, for example, the umbrella index-database is called CROS.)

People who request computer searches are well advised to be aware that many databases are in a one-to-one correspondence with a conventional printed index. The *Philosophers' Index* computer file, for example, contains exactly the same information that can be found in the printed index of the same name. The largest education database, called *ERIC,* contains the same information as the printed version; similarly, *Historical Abstracts* corresponds to its printed form, *America: History and Life* to its, and so on. The reason for this is that the computer companies acquire the magnetic tapes from which the printed indexes are originally generated and mount them in a way that allows for direct searching. In many cases, then, researchers who inquire about online services find that they really do not need them, and that a half hour spent with the print indexes is quite sufficient. (Not all searches require keyword access to abstracts or complicated Boolean combinations of several terms. Print-format indexes also offer two definite advantages: They are easier to scan or browse, and this often enables researchers to recognize citations whose keywords they would not have thought to specify in advance in a computer search; and print indexes often provide cross-references, especially to important narrower search terms, that are either omitted or harder to see in their online counterparts.)

Often there are significant differences between the bibliographic citation databases and the print indexes. The hard-copy version of *Biological*

Abstracts, for example, covers from 1927 to date; but only the years from 1969 to the present are in the database. Similarly, the print index *Public Affairs Information Service (PAIS)* covers from 1915 to date—and has a cumulative printed subject index for the years 1915–74—but only the years from 1976 are loaded in the computer. *Psychological Abstracts* is searchable as *PsycINFO* from 1967 onward; but the hard-copy version extends back to 1927. There is also a *Cumulative Subject Index to Psychological Abstracts* in print format, covering from 1927 to 1983; and a printed *Cumulative Author Index to Psychological Index 1894–1935 and Psychological Abstracts, 1927–1958* (with *Supplements* through 1983). For years prior to 1967, these indexes are not searchable by computer.

There may be other differences as well. You can search titles and abstracts of doctoral dissertations via computer from June 1980 to date; but prior to that time you can search only their titles and not their abstracts, which were not put into the database. To read the abstracts of the earlier works, you must use the printed *Dissertation Abstracts.* Similarly, even though the *Biological Abstracts* database covers from 1969 to date, none of the entries from 1969 through June 1976 includes an abstract.

The scope of coverage (as well as the dates) and the methods of searching allowed may also vary among print and online *and* CD-ROM versions of the "same" index. Since May 1980 the *PsycINFO* database has included *more* material (mainly doctoral dissertations) than is found in the printed *Psychological Abstracts* version. And the Dialog files corresponding to the *Science* and *Social Sciences Citation Indexes,* depending on which year you consider, have either more or less than their printed counterparts. Further, their CD-ROM versions offer an entirely different way of doing subject searches that cannot be done in either the print or the Dialog versions. I've already described some of these differences above, in Chapter 5, especially the extra coverage found in the Dialog and CD versions not available in the printed formats. But earlier years of the print indexes have some coverage not in either computer form, even when the years in question overlap:

- The hard-copy *Science Citation Index* (1945–) covers conference proceedings and multiauthored books and *Festschriften* (indexed at the chapter or essay level) for five years, 1977–81, in addition to its coverage of journal articles and "Annual Review"-type publications. But the corresponding Dialog *Scisearch* database (1974–) includes only the latter forms—not the conference proceedings or multiauthored books. But as of 1982 there is nothing in the print version that is not also covered in the computer format (neither covering the proceedings or multiauthored books); there is now, however, a great deal covered by the Dialog and CD versions not to be found in the print format (see Chapter 5).

- The hard-copy *Social Sciences Citation Index* (1956–) covers multiauthored anthologies indexed at the chapter or essay level, in addition to journals, for the years 1979 to 1982. It also covers conference proceedings for the years 1979 to 1981. The Dialog *Social Scisearch* database (1972–) and the CD version (1981–), however, cover only journals; but in recent years they both cover material not available in the print format (see Chapter 5).

Full-Text Databases

Again, there are both "free" and "fee" sources in this category; and again, by "free" I mean those sources that are subsidized so you do not have to pay direct, per-search costs. Among the free sources are the following:

CD-ROM sources. These tend to contain copyright-free books or documents, which usually means the books will be more than 75 years old, and the documents will be government published. One large "book" CD is called the *Library of the Future* (World Library, Inc.), revised irregularly; it contains a kind of "great books" library of more than 1,500 titles by authors such as Aristophanes, Aristotle, Chaucer, Confucius, Plutarch, Poe, Shakespeare, and so on. A somewhat comparable CD is called *Great Literature* (Bureau of Electronic Publishing, 1992); it contains about 1,000 full texts. (One problem with these products is that they frequently fail to identify the original publisher or the date of the particular edition or translation of a work they have keyed or scanned in; this makes it very difficult to cite these sources. A further concern is that any translations included are there not because they are the best available, but simply because they are old enough to be copyright-free.) The primary virtues of such collections is that they enable you to do component word searching of so many texts simultaneously; this is useful for finding quotations or half-remembered passages, and for some kinds of linguistic studies. It is very tedious to try to *read* full books in this format, however. (For a sampling of other CD full-text sources, see Chapter 15, and the "Business and Economics" section of the Appendix.) A good overview listing is the *CD-ROM Book Index: An International Guide to Fulltext Books on CD-ROM*, by Ann Niles (Meckler, 1993).

Many U.S. federal government reports, especially of a statistical nature, are now being published in CD format. These include such titles as *Census of Agriculture, American Housing Survey, Congressional Districts of the U.S., Statistical Abstract of the United States,* and *County Business Patterns*. Many of these will be available to you in local depository libraries (see Chapter 15).

Internet full-text sources.   The Internet (or the World Wide Web subset of it) can lead you to thousands of copyright-free book texts, government documents, directories, home pages, and current newsletters and electronic journals (usually of nonprofit organizations). Its full-text sources are "free" to the extent that you can get on the Internet to begin with, of course; if you have a university, government, or corporate affiliation then you won't have to pay for basic access yourself. Otherwise a variety of commercial services such as America Online or CompuServ offer connection for a monthly fee. One of the largest full-text sites on the Web is Project Gutenberg, at <www.prairienet.org/pg/pg_home.html>; it plans to key in texts of 10,000 copyright-free books by the year 2001. Another, comparable Web site is the English Server at <http://english-server.hss.cmu.edu>.

A good overall listing of the book texts that can be found at various different sites is called the *Alex* catalog at <gopher://rsl.ox.ac.uk:70/11/lib-corn/hunter>; this enables you to search for individual titles or authors that are available in Project Gutenberg, as well as texts mounted by Wiretap, the Eris system at Virginia Tech, the On-Line Book Initiative, the online portion of the Oxford Text Archive, and the English Server at Carnegie Mellon University. More sites will be included in the future. *Alex* does not list online journals or serials; a good source for them is the printed *Direc-*

tory of Electronic Journals, Newsletters, and Academic Discussion Lists, published annually by the Association of Research Libraries' Office of Scientific and Academic Publishing.

Some Internet full-text sources are not "free" in that you cannot tap into them from anywhere at any time (from home or office)—but may be "free" in the sense of being available without charge within the walls of your library. *Project Muse* and *JSTOR,* for example, are databases offering full-text-searchable journal articles (see Chapter 4). They are site-licensed services, however, which means that if your library subscribes to them, you can search them without any direct charges; but you'll have to be inside the library to do the search.

Most full-text material in computer form is not free. The more prominent fee-based providers include:

NEXIS and LEXIS databases.   These are huge full-text sources that enable you to search for individual words or phrases within the texts of thousands of sources. NEXIS offers more than 1,000 periodicals and newsletters, plus newspapers, wire service reports, telephone books, property records, corporate filings, company and industry reports, statistical sources, and directories. LEXIS offers the full texts of laws and statutes, judicial rulings, legal decisions, administrative determinations, law review articles, legal reference publications, and other law-related documents covering the United States, individual states, the United Kingdom, and many other countries.

It is very expensive to search these files. There are cost-saving ways to segment one's search to avoid the expense of scanning everything simultaneously, and use of these is usually advisable.

Dow Jones News/Retrieval.   This full-text service is geared to business and investment sources. It offers the full text of *The Wall Street Journal,* SEC filings on more than 10,000 companies, and thousands of research reports from analysts at brokerage firms. It is also very expensive.

Dialog databases.   The Dialog system actually offers more online full texts of journals than does NEXIS; but in Dialog you cannot easily search all of them simultaneously, as you can in NEXIS. Dialog offers more than

3,000 journals, newsletters, newswires, directories, encyclopedias, market research reports, and so on; and, of course, the list is growing. When you have done a search in one of the bibliographic citation databases, when you get to the point of printing out the list, you will sometimes have the option of printing out the full texts of articles rather than just their citations. You can also search the full texts directly in a variety of segments called OneSearch categories. These include:

FIRST (up-to-date newswires)
MAGTEXT (full texts of general-interest magazines)
MARKETFULL (market research reports)
MEDTEXT (medical journals)
PAPERS (U.S. newspapers)
PAPERSEU (European newspapers)
NEWSWIRE (all newswires, including back files)
PATFULL (U.S. patents)

These files are geared toward business, scientific, and legal firms that can afford high prices for current information; most individual or student researchers will not want to venture into these waters. This system, like NEXIS, is a mini-"virtual library" that is routinely available only to the rich; it cannot replace the printed sources that real libraries subscribe to and make freely available to anyone who is curious to read them. (I once discovered, in the nick of time, that making a printout in "Format 15" of Dialog's File 519, *D & B Duns Financial Records Plus*, costs $102 *per minute*.)

A good directory of full-text sources is *Fulltext Sources Online* (Bibliodata, semiannual); it covers periodicals, newspapers, newsletters, newswires, and TV/radio transcripts. You can look up a particular title and it will tell you which online service provides access, and for how many years retrospectively. The *Gale Directory of Databases* (Gale Research, semiannual) also lists full-text sources; in addition, Gale publishes the annual *CyberHound's Guide to Internet Databases*. The best overall sources to the Internet, however, are its various site directories and search engines (see below).

Internet and World Wide Web Sources

The Internet is a sprawling array of electronically available sources from all over the world, and the World Wide Web is a subset of it that allows sound, graphic, and video formats, as well as texts, to be communicated. For the average researcher its major advantages lie in its capacity to link him or her to current information that is equivalent, or analogous, to that found in reference literature such as directories, almanacs, encyclopedias, timetables, schedules, commercial catalogs, phone books, and city directories. Beyond these, the Web extends as well into electronic equivalents of broadsides, promotional literature, advertisements, government documents (which tend to be copyright-free), nonprofit research reports, museum exhibition catalogs, and articles analogous to those in popular magazines. Many thousands of older, copyright-free books are also searchable; but, as noted elsewhere, their online format tends to favor searches for reference and informational purposes rather than sequential reading for understanding.

Beyond its analogies to printed sources, the Net can link you in real time directly to people and organizations that are knowledgeable in various subject areas. The term "experts" needs some qualification, however; like-minded people who can be found on particular listservs or in various focused discussion groups may indeed have subject interests in common but may or may not have real expertise. Since there are at least as many idiots out there as experts, commonsense rules of critical evaluation should not be overlooked simply because an "answer" to a question has come from someone on the Internet. To the extent that you phrase a listserv inquiry to ask for specific factual information rather than opinions, you will get the expert—and genuinely useful—answers more readily.

The Internet offers four main services: electronic mail and discussion lists (Mail), remote log-ins (Telnet), connections with graphical or sound components (Web access), and file transfer capabilities (FTP).

The Mail, or e-mail, component allows for direct person-to-person message exchanges and also listserv access. Listservs are discussion groups devoted to a particular topic (from Jane Austen to Zoology) that enable participants to send messages to, or ask questions of, the entire group simultaneously. You can request that answers be sent directly to your own e-mail account rather than to the whole group. Through listservs you can query large numbers of experts whose individual names you don't know beforehand. For example, I once asked the members of a listserv on railroads if anyone knew the origin of a particular slogan about railroad history, that "Railroads got into trouble because they thought they were in the railroad business rather than in the transportation business." Of the four responses I received, three were simply incorrect, and led me for several days into the wrong areas of my library's print collections to check out the leads I'd been given. The fourth response—somewhat late in appearing—gave me a correct answer I could verify immediately in a print source.

A good print-format overview of sources is the *ARL Directory of Electronic Journals, Newsletters, and Academic Discussion Lists,* revised irregularly and published by the Association of Research Libraries in Washington, D.C.

The Telnet aspect of the Net is more and more being replaced by the World Wide Web. The purpose of Telnet is to allow you to log in to a variety of remote computers, including hundreds of online public-access catalogs (OPACs) of individual libraries worldwide, and thousands of directories of individual agencies, institutions, and companies. Text files and electronic journals or newsletters are also frequently mounted on remote computers for reading purposes via Telnet. (A good way to think of Telnet is that it means simply "Go to a remote site and look at what's there.") Since the Web component of the Internet is proving much more popular because of its graphic and audio (as well as text-transfer) capabilities, most Telnet sites are being transformed into Web sites. Web versions also allow easier "point and click" search commands. The Web and Telnet domains are not identical, however; each part of the Net has things not in the other. But the future belongs to the Web.

The File Transfer Protocol (FTP) component of the Net enables your computer to contact another computer, log on anonymously (i.e., without any special password), and search for text files, graphics or pictures, video images or sounds, or computer software programs, and then not just read, look at, or listen to whatever you find, but also transfer an actual copy of the located file or files back to your home computer.

The World Wide Web is the subset of the Internet that includes graphics, sound, motion pictures, and color displays in addition to straight textual material. It is searchable by site directories or search engines (see Chapter 12). An interesting registry that lists Web sites that have adopted standard classification schemes or controlled vocabularies to organize Internet resources is Gerry McKiernan's *Beyond Bookmarks* at URL <www.public.iastate.edu/~CYBERSTACKS/CTW.htm>.

Although there are thousands of guides to the Internet, the best way to start is to have a friend show you the ropes. The printed books—including this one—just can't answer the most basic questions about how to get into the system to begin with, or what, specifically, to do when you have trouble. Moreover—a point I almost despair on while writing this section—anything you read in any book on the Internet may become rapidly dated by new and unanticipated developments. While a guidebook may be useful, at some point you still have to have a knowledgeable person sit next to you.

Points to Remember About Computer Sources

1. There are inevitable trade-offs between what you can get for free via the Information Superhighway/Internet and what you can get for free in a real library with walls. For access to copyrighted works, you can get many more bibliographic citations online than full texts. Copyright limitations will never go away, and *what, who*, and *where* restrictions are unavoidable. Real libraries, with walls, offer not only printed sources that are not, and never will be, digitized; they also offer, on a no-fee basis, more electronic resources than you can afford to subscribe to from your home or office.

2. The same trade-offs discussed so far among methods of searching apply to computerized sources just as much as to print formats. Keyword searching is not going to give you "everything." It is not the equivalent of controlled vocabulary searching. And neither of these is comparable to either citation searching or related-record searching. Scanning the full texts *of most books,* down to individual page and paragraph levels, can be done systematically only outside the electronic world of computers, via classified shelving in real

libraries. The copyright restrictions that keep most full texts off computers do not keep them off library shelves; and this affects the *method* available to you for searching them (i.e., scanning texts on shelves rather than keyword searching in computers).

The peculiar strengths of the *methods* of computer searching—a consideration that is distinct from the *contents* of the various databases—will be discussed in the next chapter.

12

Computer Searches: Types of Searches

Searching a computer database offers several advantages over searching the same pool of information in a corresponding print index:

1. In addition to searching controlled-vocabulary subject headings, the computer can search for keywords within titles or even abstracts. This is an extremely important advantage when no good subject heading exists for your topic, and especially in those files for which the print version allows access only through a controlled-vocabulary system. For example, a few years ago the *Psychological Abstracts* thesaurus did not have a term "Burnout" as either a heading or a cross-reference; but a computer search under the term as a keyword produced a printout of more than two hundred items. The descriptor fields on the citations, which are analogous to subject tracings on catalog records for books, indicated that the articles were indexed under several different subject terms in the print index (e.g., "Employee attitudes," "Occupational adjustment," "Occupational aspirations," "Occupational stress"). Here a keyword search was clearly more efficient than that afforded by controlled-vocabulary headings.

Academic researchers in the fields of language, literature, folklore, and linguistics should especially note that the Modern Language Association's *MLA Bibliography* is searchable online in the FirstSearch system, although only from 1963 to date. The print version, which extends back to 1921, is notoriously difficult to search for subjects (prior to a reformatting that took place in 1981) other than particular authors and their works. The computer version, however, provides keyword access to any terms within the titles of books or articles.

2. In some databases the machine can also do other types of searches that are not possible with printed indexes, such as searching by document type. In the *Science Citation Index,* the *Social Sciences Citation Index*, and the *Arts & Humanities Citation Index* databases (in Dialog or on CD-ROM), for example, you can search directly for state-of-the-art review articles (see Chapters 8 and 16). And many of the other databases that are more comprehensive in specialized fields (e.g., *PsycINFO, ERIC, MEDLINE*) have similar features that can pull out review articles, software reviews, hardware reviews, editorials, letters to the editor, teaching guides, tests and questionnaires, curriculum guides, and so on.

3. Another major advantage of a computer search is its ability to look for two or more subjects at the same time. For example, if you are interested in "Fungal diseases in conifers in Canadian forests," in a printed index you would have to look under at least three different headings (fungal diseases, conifers, Canada) separately, and then weed out all articles that don't appear under each of the three. But the computer can search all three subjects simultaneously and give you only the citations that meet all three specifications.

This combining or crossing capability is particularly useful where each separate idea is itself expressible in several variant phrasings. For example, one researcher was interested in articles on "Computer-assisted instructional techniques in the field of geography." In looking through the subject heading list for the major database in the field of education, called *ERIC,* he found that several descriptors were useful to express each of the two ideas he wanted to combine:

Programmed instruction	Geography
Learning laboratories	Physical geography
Programmed instructional materials	World geography
Computer-assisted instruction	Geography instruction
	Geographic concepts

A search of the corresponding printed *ERIC* indexes under all nine headings would have been very time consuming. The computer, however, could search for all four of the first-column terms at once, and all five of the second column, and then cross the two sets against each other, printing only those citations that "hit" at least one descriptor from each column simultaneously. Had he so desired, the searcher could have introduced a third column, further specifying the output to only those citations indexed under the descriptors "Secondary schools," "Secondary education," "Secondary school curriculum," and so on. A further specification could have produced a final set composed only of those relevant articles published in the past five years.

The computer accomplishes this process of combining and screening through operations of "Boolean logic,"[1] which can be illustrated in Figure 7. If Circle A represents the set of citations retrieved by terms expressing one subject idea (either controlled-vocabulary descriptors or keywords or both), and Circle B represents another subject, then the area of overlap in Figure 7a represents those citations that deal with both subjects. Other circles or limiting factors can be introduced for further specification. And other types of combinations are possible, as shown in Figures 7b and 7c.

Figure 7c represents a problem that you need to be particularly wary of when you are doing a computer combination; it should not be confused with 7a or 7b. For example, suppose you want articles on "Dog food *and* cat food"; in this case, if Circle A represents "Dog food" and B is "Cat food," the *and* operator between them will give you the shaded area in Figure 7a. Now suppose you want either "Dog food *or* Cat food." The *or* operator between the two terms will give you the shaded area in Figure 7b. Finally, suppose you specify "Dog food *not* Cat food." The *not* operator here will give you *only the shaded area of Circle A—not the entire Circle A*—represented in Figure 7c. The area where the circles overlap contains citations that talk about *both* dog and cat food—but by saying you wish to eliminate any that include cat food (*all* of Circle B), you have unwittingly eliminated some entries within Circle A that *also* talk about dog food. Be careful about using *not* as a combining term, in other words—you may be eliminating more than you want to.

One type of question that comes up repeatedly can be rather easily answered by a particular Boolean combination of elements. If you have a student assignment to write a paper based on "primary sources," these materials can be easily located by first finding the *LCSH* term for the subject area of your interest (e.g., *United States—History—Civil War, 1861–1865*) and then combining it with a second set made up of these

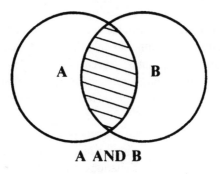

A AND B

a.

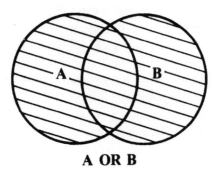

A OR B

b.

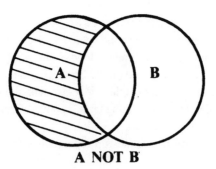

A NOT B

c.

Fig. 7

three elements: *Diaries* **or** *Personal narratives* **or** *Sources*. These three are actually subdivisions of headings rather than headings themselves; but that makes no difference to a computer. Their combination rounds up primary-source material very efficiently. (This is something of an oversimplification; see the section "Primary Sources" in the Appendix.)

4. Computer searches can look for individual elements that are shared by multiple controlled-vocabulary terms. In the *Library of Congress Subject Headings* list, for example, there are eight full pages of headings that start with the element "Afro"; these include such terms as the following:

Afro-American actors
        architecture
        beauty operators
        diplomats
        families
        historians
        leadership
        painting
        parents
        preaching
        quilts
        radio stations
        students
        veterans
        whalers
        wit and humor
        women
        women composers
Afro-Americans—Biography
        —Civil rights
        —Folklore
        —History
        —Legal status
        —Religion
Afro-Americans and mass media
        as consumers

> in business
> in the newspaper industry
> in veterinary medicine

There are more than 270 different subject headings in *LCSH* that start with the "Afro" element. (Note, by the way, the advantage of having these headings in the form "Afro-American" rather than "African-American." If the basic heading were in the latter form, rounding up all its variants by having to select "African" rather than "Afro" would automatically and unavoidably create a much larger set including irrelevant works on the African continent in addition to the desired, smaller, subset specifically on Blacks in America.) Similarly, there are 7 pages of headings that start with the word "Television"; among them are the following:

Television advertising and children
Television and politics
Television and women
Television comedy writers
Television in education
Television in elementary education
Television in politics
Television news anchors
Television programs for children
Television programs for women

While there are thus many separate headings with either "Afro" or "Television" in them, there are also precoordinated headings that combine the two concepts:

Afro-Americans in television
Afro-Americans in television broadcasting

The point is that the component word search capability of the computer can find additional relevant records that are not included under these precoordinated headings by, in effect, simultaneously crossing *all* of the various "Afro" subject headings against *all* of the various "Television" headings. In the Library of Congress's LOCB database of book records since 1968, for example, the command would be "Find s Afro and s Television" (the "s" tells the computer to search the subject fields of all records for these component words).

The result is noteworthy: In addition to retrieving all of the records to be found under the precoordinated headings, this command also turns up records with titles such as *The Oprah Winfrey Story: Speaking Her Mind: An Authorized Biography* and *Suzanne de Passe: Motown's Boss Lady.* The subject tracings on the former record show that *two* headings were retrieved:

Afro-Americans—Biography
Television personalities

Similarly, on the second record, two headings were found:

Afro-Americans—Biography
Television producers and directors

These records, in other words, would have been missed if the researcher had used only the precoordinated phrases listed in *LCSH*. In a sense, this technique of searching for individual elements *within* subject strings is a fifth way to find the right *LCSH* terms for a topic, over and above the four listed previously in Chapter 2. Note, however, that this is not simply a keyword search of transcribed words from titles or from any other elements within the books themselves. Rather, it is a keyword search of artificially created terms—subject headings—that were *added to* the catalog record by librarians (rather than transcribed from the title page or other elements). The controlled-vocabulary terms had to be there to begin with for these records to be found, because their title words do not contain words designating either the "Afro" or the "Television" subject content.

Searching for individual words that appear in many different subject headings is very useful whenever there are such large clusters of related headings. ("Business," "Indians," and "Women" are other component words that each appear within scores of different *LCSH* terms.)

5. Computers can also search for "invisible" coded elements on catalog or index records, and limit large sets by them. They are invisible because

they do not appear, as subject tracings do, in fields that can be easily displayed by some software programs. They enable you to limit by year of imprint (before or after any specified date), by presence of a bibliography or of illustrations, by intellectual level (juvenile or not juvenile), by the geographic area code of the subject of the book, or by the country of the book's publication. Whether these elements can be exploited in your local public or university library's catalog is a matter of its software—and, surprisingly, in spite of the existence of these elements on catalog records, they are frequently not searchable. The reason is simply that many library administrators these days, in trying to cut cataloging costs, have convinced themselves that simple keyword searching, which provides "some" access quickly, is "enough" access for researchers; and since most patrons have no idea how much they are missing when they search *only* keywords, the fact that no complaints reach administrative ears is enough to justify them in ignoring both the catalog elements and the software to exploit them that would make for systematic and complete, rather than just "some," access to the library's books.

Regardless of local software conditions, readers with access to the Internet may at least exploit the post-1967 records in the catalog of the Library of Congress, whose elements and software do allow searches—at least as of this writing—via coded elements. The URL is <lcweb.loc. gov>; ultimately you want to follow a path into "Library of Congress Catalogs" as far as "multiple file searching options" to the option of searching LOCB (a combination of three database segments that include all book records since 1968, or earlier records modified after 1968); note, however, that LOCB does not include the unedited PREM or PREMARC records, which are the bulk of the pre-1968 files.

For example, one researcher needed a list of English-language translations of Southeast Asian literatures. The *LCSH* subdivision "—Translations into English" is routinely attached to all translated books, no matter what their country of origin; and a search for this element alone rounds up more than 9,000 translated books from all over the world (see Figure 8). This initial set can then be limited by geographical area codes:

limit 1/gac = a-v.   geographic area code = asia - vietnam
          a-cb.   = asia - cambodia

a-th.	= asia - thailand
a-io.	= asia - indonesia
a-ph.	= asia - philippines
a-ls.	= asia - laos
a-si.	= asia - singapore

These specifications limit the initial large set to 41 books, with titles such as *Voices from the Thai Countryside: The Short Stories of Samruan Singh,* that are right on the button.

Had the specification been simply "limit 1/gac e a." then translations from *all* of Asia, including but not limited to the above countries, would have been retrieved. There is thus a "roll up" feature in the geographic area codes such that larger area designations *include* smaller areas—unlike geographic subdivisions in the *LCSH* subject heading system.

In *LCSH,* the heading "Television—United States" would *not include* state areas such as "Television—California" (because of the principle of specific entry). Creating a set of all books on television in the United States, including each state, would thus involve, in the subject heading system, the separate selection and combination of dozens of distinct headings—one for the United States generally, combined with one for each state. With the codes, however, the broad set "Television" can be limited to the whole United States inclusive of smaller areas, as in Figure 9.

There, the "limit 2/gac e n-us." command (and the period after the "us" is essential for truncation to smaller areas) would thus include any further subdivisions such as:

gac = n-us-al	geographic area code = n.amer. - us - alabama
n-us-ca	= n.amer. - us - california
n-us-pa	= n.amer. - us - pennsylvania

```
***** SEARCH HISTORY *****                      SETS 1 - 2 OF 2
SET  1      9,169: RETR SUBJ/TRANSLATIONS INTO ENGLISH
SET  2        41: LIMT   1/GAC = A-V.,A-CB.,A-TH.,A-IO.,A-PH.,A-LS.,A-SI.
READY FOR NEW COMMAND:
```

Fig. 8

```
***** SEARCH HISTORY *****                    SETS 1 - 3 OF 3
SET  1          30: RETR SUBJ/TELEVISION--UNITED STATES
SET  2       1,398: RETR SUBJ/TELEVISION
SET  3         171: LIMT    2/GAC E N-US.
READY FOR NEW COMMAND:
```

Fig. 9

Thus, when you limit by geographic area code rather than by place sub-division within *LCSH*, each state *is* "included" within the "us." code (provided that you put the period after "us." Should you wish to specify a limitation to the state level, each is designated by its two-letter postal code. (The one exception is Nebraska: n-us-nb.)

Note that the geographic area codes usually start at the *continent* level and are then further subdivided by countries and states. The broadest designations are:

gac =	n.	geographic area code	=	north america
	s.		=	south america
	cl.		=	latin america
	e.		=	europe
	a.		=	asia
	f.		=	africa
	u-at.		=	australia
	po.		=	(pacific) oceania
	d.		=	developing countries
	xd.		=	the Western Hemisphere

Again, remember always to end the sequence with a period (e.g., limit 1/gac e d.); this will assure inclusion of any smaller subdivisions to the right of the last element specified. Other helpful geographic area codes are:

a-cc	=	China
a-ja	=	Japan
a-su	=	Saudi Arabia
e-fr	=	France

e-gw	=	Germany
e-it	=	Italy
e-uk	=	Great Britain
e-ur-ru	=	Russia
n-mx	=	Mexico
n-usp	=	West (United States)

Area codes are assigned to reflect the geographic area of the *subject* of the book—regardless of where the book itself is published. (Thus a book published in the United States on the subject of Africa will have an "f" code assigned to it.) The list of these codes is published in *USMARC Code List for Geographic Areas* (Library of Congress, Network Development and MARC Standards Office; revised irregularly). The geographic area codes also appear, like tracings, on catalog records in the Library of Congress database (see Figure 10); but the same record displayed in some other library's system may conceal this field. (Records displayed in the OCLC WorldCat and RLIN BIB databases do not display this field; nor does their software [as of this writing] allow you to limit by it.)

As useful as the geographic area codes are, most limitations are done simply by language and by date of publication. The forms to use in these cases are "limit [set #]/lng = eng"—the language being indicated by the first three letters of its name. More than one language can also be specified: "limit [set #]/lng = eng,fre,ger" will save English, French, and German books while excluding all others. Dates are specified by *year of imprint*: "limit [set #]/yri eg 1990" will save books published whose imprint date is equal to or greater than 1990; one can also specify "yri e 1990" (for books in that year alone) or "yri el 1990" (for years of imprint equal to or less than 1990). A list of the "limit" options (lacking geographic area codes, however) in the LC book database can be called up by typing the word "help" and following the menu.

It is noteworthy that most large British libraries are now using cataloging records copied from LC, and contributing records of their own to the OCLC system using *Library of Congress Subject Headings*. Good Web sites now let researchers around the world tap into the catalogs of these British facilities:

```
Rossinelli, Michel.
  La liberte de la radio-television en droit compare / Michel Rossinelli.
Paris : Publisud, c1991.  v, 221, xvi p. ; 23 cm.

LC CALL NUMBER: K4325.4 .R67 1991

SUBJECTS:
  Radio--Law and legislation--Europe.
  Television--Law and legislation--Europe.
  Freedom of speech--Europe.
  Radio--Law and legislation--United States.
  Television--Law and legislation--United States.
  Freedom of speech--United States.

SERIES TITLES (Indexed under SERI option):
  Collection Droit public et institutions politiques, 0993-6637

NOTES:
  Includes bibliographical references (p. vi-xvi).
PAGE 1 OF 2. READY FOR NEW COMMAND OR PAGE #(FOR NXT PG, XMIT):

4B█                Aa              BO--LCHOST     R 22 C 65          12:17  3/13/97
91-156136 (continued):
GEOG. AREA CODE:  e------ n-us---   ◄━━━━━━━━
ISBN: 2866005232
CATALOGING SOURCE:  DLC DLC
LCCN:  91-156136


90-622202                          ITEM 37 OF 142 IN SET 4     (BKS3)

Pennsylvania production guide : a guide to Pennsylvania film and video
resources.  1989 ed.  Harrisburg, PA (Room 455, Forum Building, Harrisburg 17
120) : Pennsylvania Film Bureau, Department of Commerce, 1989.  132 p. : ill. ;
28 cm.

LC CALL NUMBER: PN1998.A1 P33 1988

SUBJECTS:
  Motion pictures--Pennsylvania--Production and direction--Directories.
  Television--Pennsylvania--Production and direction--Directories.

OTHER NAMES:
  Pennsylvania Film Bureau.

NOTES:
  Kept up to date by supplement.

GEOG. AREA CODE:  n-us-pa   ◄━━━━━━━━
```

Fig. 10

- <http://opac97.bl.uk> leads to the British Library's online public access catalog, as does <http://portico.bl.uk/gabriel/en/countries/uk-opac-en.html>.
- <http://copac.ac.uk/copac/> leads to the combined university catalogs of Cambridge, Edinburgh, Glasgow, Leeds, and Oxford.

(One caveat to keep in mind is that coding from non-LC sources may not always be as full as that from LC itself.)

A site that will enable you to enter the online catalogs of dozens of libraries throught Europe is <http://portico.bl.uk/gabriel/en/countries>.

Let me give a few more examples of interesting search techniques that computers make possible.

A reader who wanted information on "changing paradigms in the concept of property" found that the *Social SciSearch* CD-ROM provides some unexpected ways to get at this topic. One approach, of course, is simply to search for the keywords "Property" and "Paradigm*" ("*" being the truncation symbol); and this does produce relevant hits such as articles entitled "Information, Incentives, and Property Rights—The Emergence of an Alternative Paradigm" and "Symposium—Toward a 3rd Intellectual Property Paradigm." There are other ways to search this topic, however. Anyone who writes about paradigms in a scholarly journal probably cites, in a footnote, the book that put this term into prominence: Thomas Kuhn's *The Structure of Scientific Revolutions*. Similarly, a scholarly discussion of private property is likely to cite the classic work on that subject, John Locke's *Second Treatise on Civil Government*. When footnotes are introduced as searchable elements, a researcher then has a larger variety of elements that can be combined:

A. the word "property" itself appearing in the title of an article
B. a footnote referring to John Locke's work on property
C. the word "paradigm*" appearing in the title of an article
D. a footnote referring to Kuhn's book on paradigms.

One can thus combine "(**A** or **B**) and (**C** or **D**)" to find a number of relevant articles that do not have both keywords in their titles. The article titled "The Concept of Property in Private and Constitutional Law - The Ideology of the Scientific Turn in Legal Analysis," for instance, has the word "Property" in its title, but not "Paradigm." The latter concept is "included" however, because this article cites Kuhn's work in a footnote.

Similarly, the article "Paradigms as Ideologies—Liberal vs. Marxian Economics" does not have "Property" in its title; but it does have a footnote citing Locke's *Second Treatise*. And the articles "A Consent Theory of Contract" and "The Constitution and the Nature of Law" have neither relevant keyword in their titles; but each article cites both Kuhn and Locke in its footnotes. (And a related-record search [see Chapter 7] on some of these titles will lead to an additional relevant article, "Property Rights and Economic Theory—A Survey of Recent Literature.")

The ability to search footnote citations, and to combine them with either keywords or other footnote references, is an option that few researchers think of; but it can provide extraordinary results, and if you want to be an expert searcher you should be consciously aware of this possibility as a search technique.

Search capabilities on the Internet change so rapidly that only a rather broad overview of types of searching is possible; any detailed instructions will be outdated very quickly. The most popular kinds of Net searches are those done in the World Wide Web subset of the system; and within the Web there are a variety of different site directories (compiled and categorized by human beings) and search engines (using automatic "spiders" or "crawlers" that simply search out keywords). Site directories include:

Lycos <www.lycos.com>
InfoSeek <www.infoseek.com>
Yahoo <www.yahoo.com>

Search engines include:

HotBot <www.hotbot.com>
Webcrawler <www.webcrawler.com>
Excite <www.excite.com>
AltaVista <www.altavista.digital.com>

Both site directories and search engines allow keyword searches. As of this writing there is an additional site that enables you to search most of these directories and engines simultaneously; it is mounted at the University of Kansas: ProFusion <http://topaz.designlab.ukans.edu/profusion/>.

In general, it is useful to think of two broad types of searches that can be done in the Web: hierarchical, and what I'll call "direct stab" searches.

Hierarchical searches require choices to be made from initial menus of broad subject categories, followed by a series of additional choices from narrower and narrower menus, until the desired bit of information is located. The problem here is that if, at any point, you choose a wrong menu option at any of the various levels of specificity, you may find yourself thereafter in a line of descent that ultimately misses the specific information you want; and you won't always be able to tell at which level of menu choices you got off the right track. The plus side, however, is that in following various arrays of options from general to specific, you can sometimes recognize "side" choices that would not have occurred to you to look at but that may be of interest in their own right.

An example is my attempt to find the official text of the Dayton Peace Accords, intended to bring peace to war-torn Bosnia. I tried both "direct stab" and hierarchical methods, just to see what would happen. The "direct stab" approach initially ran into a common problem: I first typed "Dayton Peace Accords" as the keywords to be searched (in Lycos), since this was how the reader phrased her inquiry to me. The word "Accords," however, turned out not to be present; and only when I simplified the search to "Dayton Peace" did it work.

The hierarchical search, starting with the Lycos home page, went as follows:

Sites by Subject
  Government
    International Government **(dead end)**
  The World
    Countries and Continents
  Europe
    Bosnia and Herzegovina
      Bosnia Home Page at CalTech
        Newsstand **(dead end)**
        Maps, Status Quo, Factbook and Ethnicity
          Dayton Peace Agreement Official Texts

Note that I wound up making what proved to be the wrong choice at two levels of the menu, resulting in dead ends, at which points I had to back up to a higher level and choose another descending path. This is the problem with the hierarchical searching of menus—the best series of choices leading to the goal you ultimately want is not always obvious, and the trial and error involved in finding it may be time consuming and frustrating.

"Direct stabbing" is usually preferable in searching the Web, in that it bypasses the often confusing hierarchy of many levels of subject menus and goes directly—one hopes—to what you want. And it will enable you to employ Boolean combinations in your searches. There are disadvantages, however: The biggest problem is that the Internet and World Wide Web search engine systems basically work with keywords rather than controlled vocabularies. Some of the more sophisticated engines will add bells and whistles such as automatic truncation, word proximity searching, weighting or ranking of results by word frequencies (sometimes in relation to document length), and so on; but none of this overcomes the problem that they are manipulating, to begin with, only the natural language words that happen to appear within the sources they look at.[2] Without *cataloging* and *classification* of the various sites, there are no artificially created points of commonality—that is, standardized subject headings or class numbers created by human catalogers and attached by them to records that would otherwise not have shared elements. It is only such elements, which are added to rather than transcribed from records, that enable you to retrieve together subject-related sources that happen to express their common subject in different words or phrases. You can sometimes recognize such variants through hierarchical searching—but you will miss the hierarchical categorizations entirely when you use the "direct stabbing" method. Here, as in every other kind of information retrieval technique, there are simply unavoidable trade-offs you need to be aware of.

Regarding computer searches in general, you must be especially wary of bad, superficial, or naïve advice. Students are sometimes told, for example, that "the only way to combine two things together is with computers; you can't do this kind of searching with 'old-fashioned' print sources." This is nonsense. There are any number of print or card-format sources that enable you to combine two (or even more) search elements together and thereby to reach sources that do not exist on computers; the options here include the following:

1. The *Permuterm Subject Index* volumes of the ISI indexes, which enable you to search for combinations of any two keywords appearing in the titles of journal articles (and also to search earlier years that are not available in the computer versions). Indeed, the print format version of these indexes has a definite advantage over the Dialog and CD-ROM formats: When you start with the first word of your combination, the print version enables you to *recognize* options for the second element that you couldn't specify in advance. For example, if you want articles on "Russian or Soviet musicology," in using the *Arts & Humanities Citation Index* you will first look up the words "Russia" or "Russian" or "Soviet," and then look at the column of other words appearing underneath each to see if the word "musicology" is present—and it is. However, in scanning these columns for the desired second word, you will notice that the variant term "ethnomusicology" *also* appears; and it leads to additional sources. This is the kind of keyword variant that is very easy to overlook when you have to specify your terms in advance for a search of the Dialog, FirstSearch, or CD-ROM versions of the *A&HCI*.

2. *Precoordinated subject headings in conventional indexes and catalogs.* With a computer you can take two or more subjects that have not already been combined and cross them against each other to determine if there is any area of overlap; this is known as postcoordination of subjects. A *pre*coordinated heading, on the other hand, is one that in effect has already done such a combination for you; it already expresses in one phrase or word "string" the overlap of two or more subjects, so you don't have to put them together yourself through postcoordinating computer manipulations. Examples of such precoordinate headings in the *Library of Congress Subject Headings* system are:

Women in aeronautics
Sports for children
Theatre in propaganda
Minorities in medicine—United States—Mathematical models
Education and heredity
Doping in sports
Architecture and energy conservation—Canada—Awards
Erotic proverbs, Yiddish

Church work with cowgirls

Hallucinogenic drugs and religious experiences in art—Mexico—
    Zacatecas (State)

Odors in the Bible

Smallpox in animals

Miniature swine as laboratory animals

Television and children—South Africa

3. *Standard subdivisions limiting headings in conventional indexes and catalogs.* Rather than expressing a relationship of one subject to another, standard subdivisions were originally used to distinguish the various aspects *within* one subject. This distinction is usually nonexistent in actual cataloging practice, however; the only real difference here is that "standard" or "free-floating" subdivisions attached to a heading in a library's catalog are often not recorded in the *LCSH* red books. Examples of subdivided headings are the following:

United States—History—Civil War, 1861–1865—Regimental histories

World War, 1939–1945—Underground movements—France

Juvenile delinquency—Case studies

Corporations—Charitable contributions

Hospitals—Job descriptions

Hardware—Marketing

Potatoes—Social aspects

Mexican-American agricultural laborers—United States—Bibliography

Cancer—Psychological aspects

Bird droppings—Pictorial works

Toilet training—Germany—Folklore

Flatulence—Humor

There are hundreds of thousands of actual and potential precoordinated headings in any catalog or index that uses the *LCSH* vocabulary system; some other controlled vocabularies have analogous capabilities. Reference librarians are trained to literally *think in these terms*. To the extent that you understand the possibilities and probabilities that there may be a precoordinated heading for your subjects, you can in effect do Boolean combinations without a computer. This is an especially important skill to have if you need to do research in material too old to be in a database that allows for postcoordination. Indeed, with a system of precoordinate terms you can sometimes *surpass* computer combinations—a point that highlights two mistakes that are often made by overzealous computer buffs.

The first mistake is to think that combinations of subjects can be found *only* with computers, as though it never occurred to anyone before about 1968 to want to put two or more ideas together. The standard subdivisions in the *LCSH* system, however, allow for surprising range and flexibility in this regard (as do the other techniques of noncomputer combinations discussed in this section).

The second mistake is to regard the continued maintenance of precoordinated vocabulary strings as merely a carryover from a manual age of indexing, and to assert that it is no longer necessary in an age of postcoordinate technologies. The mistake here consists in seeing only one, rather than two, functions of precoordinate strings. The first thing such strings do is to subdivide large files; the various subdivisions under "Jefferson, Thomas—" given in Chapter 2 are an example. The second thing they do, however, is to enable researchers to *recognize* the second (or third or *n*th) element that needs to be combined, *from an array of options that otherwise would never occur to the searcher.* (Again, see the Jefferson example.)

This point is so important that a second example is appropriate. I once had to help a classics professor find out how ancient writers transcribed animal sounds. One of the approaches that worked was simply to look through all of the subdivisions of the heading "Greek language—"; one of these turned out to be "Greek language—Onomatopoeic words," which led to a dictionary that, among other things, gave transcriptions of animal sounds. While it can be said that a postcoordinate search of these two elements would have produced the same result, the problem is that it did not occur either to the professor or to me to use "Onomatopoeic words" *as* the second element until I saw it displayed in front of me in an array of precoordinated search options. The larger the file, the more such helps are needed by fallible human researchers in real search situations.

4. *Bibliographies with indexes.* This is a very useful way of crossing ideas against each other. For example, a scholar looking for material comparing the philosophy of Sartre with that of Christianity could turn to Francis H.

Lapointe's *Jean-Paul Sartre and His Critics: An Annotated Bibliography (1938–1980)*. He could then simply turn to its index to see which of the studies is listed under "Christianity." (There are eleven.) Similarly, a researcher looking for material discussing both Samuel Beckett and Alberto Giacometti turned to Cathleen Andonian's 754-page *Samuel Beckett: A Reference Guide* (G. K. Hall, 1989) and simply looked for "Giacometti" in its index, to find four articles. (*ArtAbstracts* within FirstSearch gave only two with the same combination, and *MLA Bibliography* gave three.)

The trick, then, is simply to find a bibliography on the first element of the combination and then to look for the second in its index.

5. *Shelf scanning of full texts.* It is possible to "combine" two subjects by judicious use of a library's classified bookstacks. The example of "traveling libraries in lighthouses" mentioned in Chapter 3 is relevant. In this case, after exhausting all of the computer databases I could think of, with no luck, I went directly to the bookstacks to the group of texts on "Lighthouse service" (VK1000–1025) and quickly looked through all the volumes on those several shelves, scanning for "libraries" as an index entry or a text work within the books. And I found fifteen directly relevant sources. The trick here, then, is similar to that with published bibliographies: first find the *classification area* of the bookstacks for the first subject; then look for the second subject within that limited range of shelves. This scanning technique, too, enables you to cross subjects that cannot be brought together by computer searches.

Such are the more important noncomputer methods of doing *Boolean combinations*. It is also advisable to remember that there are noncomputer ways of doing *keyword searches,* of both the full texts of books themselves and of entries in a variety of reference sources. The way to do keyword searches of books, outside of databases, is that just mentioned above, through shelf scanning of full texts within limited areas of a library's classified bookstacks.

For keyword searching of reference sources, two particular options should always be kept in mind:

- *Quotation books.* Most libraries will have a special area in their reference collections that groups together dozens or scores of books of quotations. Most of these compilations will have keyword indexes.

- *First Stop: The Master Index to Subject Encyclopedias* (Oryx Press, 1989). This was mentioned in Chapter 1; it is a remarkable keyword index to 430 specialized encyclopedias in all subject areas. It also covers similar sources, such as the Oxford Companion and Cambridge Guide series. To be included, the articles indexed must be at least 250 words in length and have a bibliography.

Thus, while the great advantages of computer searches lie in their abilities to do Boolean combinations and keyword searching, neither of these advantages is *exclusive* to computer databases.

The versatility of computer searching is so dazzling that a large number of researchers—and also *librarians*—are failing to note or heed its limitations. And, contrary to the popular saying, what you don't know *can* hurt you. I have seen this problem repeatedly, particularly with graduate students who want to do a literature review in preparation for writing a dissertation. One student, for example, told me she'd heard that "there was a way to have all your research done for you automatically," and she wanted to know how to have that done. (She was thinking of Dialog-type searches.) When I tried to explain to her how computer searches work, and that they have certain limitations as to what they can provide, she did not want to listen. She wanted a printout that would give her everything, period, and didn't care to hear otherwise. She finally said she'd "settle" for the computer search anyway, as she was "sure" it would give her enough for her dissertation (!), and, besides, she had a job and therefore "didn't have the time to do any other research." (This attitude is by no means atypical.) Never mind that she was missing single-author books, or relevant chapters or discussions within books, on her subject; never mind that she was missing journal articles written before the 1970s; never mind that she was searching only a few keywords from only the titles of dissertations written before 1980. Her casual assumption, as found in so many students, was that only "the most recent" material is worth reading, and that the computer would give her "everything" she needed.

What is just as bad is that professors who direct doctoral dissertations *allow* computer searches to pass for complete literature reviews—for the professors are usually just about as naive about their limitations as the students are.

What this amounts to can only be described as cultural lobotomy on a grand scale. When a significant percentage of our most educated people (prospective Ph.D.s) relies almost exclusively on computer or Internet searches for "in-depth" research, then we are fostering the growth of an intellectual system with very shallow roots. Since so much of the written memory of humanity before the 1970s is not in the computer in the first place—or is only superficially or nonsystematically indexed—it is likely to be ignored by immature scholars if it isn't as easily retrievable as the most recent material. The older material—especially older journal articles—"does not compute"; and to many graduate students this tends as a practical matter to mean "therefore it is not important." A moment's reflection will indicate that the computers are no better than the material that is loaded into them; and yet a surprising number of researchers expect them to be omniscient.

I suspect that one major reason for this situation lies in the fact that professors continue to tell their students, "You're no scholar if you can't find what you need by yourself." Librarians who teach "bibliographic instruction" classes often leave behind a similarly crippling message. The result is that inadequately prepared students—who don't even know how to find the right subject headings in a library catalog—feel that there is a stigma attached to them whenever they ask for help. The problem is compounded by those who teach instruction classes that talk only about CD-ROM and World Wide Web sources; such classes often fail to teach students the radical differences between controlled-vocabulary vs. keyword searching—sometimes not even mentioning the library's basic book catalog or *Library of Congress Subject Headings*. Remember, in this connection, that simply typing in whatever keywords occur to you will cause you to miss all of the following:

- The cross-reference structure that will lead you to the crucial narrower terms you need to find
- The alphabetically adjacent narrower terms displayed in the printed *LCSH* red books, which can alert you to many unanticipated aspects of your subject
- The displays of subdivisions of a heading within the computer catalog, which, spelled out in a "browse" format, will also enable you to recognize many search options you could never specify in advance

Students in such classes "learn" that mere keyword searching of only a few databases "in their subject area" will give them "everything"—all the while not realizing that they are missing most of what's available if they fail to find the right subject headings, that there are *several* efficient techniques of searching beyond mere keyword inquiries, and that a *very* wide variety of cross-disciplinary sources and published bibliographies on their subject have never even been mentioned.

In spite of the range of qualifications, the *appropriate* use of computers is a boon of incalculable value to researchers. Two questions that must arise, then, are "How can I find out which databases exist?" and "How can I find out what limitations there are in their coverage?" Three directories are especially important in providing this information:

- *Gale Directory of Databases* (Gale Research), semiannual. This set is a consolidation of three other directories, *Computer-Readable Databases, Directory of Online Databases,* and *Directory of Portable Databases.* It describes more than 11,000 publicly available databases, including all of the files available on services such as Dialog and LEXIS-NEXIS, as well as CD-ROMs and electronic bulletin boards.

- *CyberHound's Guide to Internet Databases* (Gale Research), annual. This work lists, indexes, and describes about 3,000 U.S. and international databases available via the Net. It does not, however, cover listservs, discussion groups, USENET groups, or online public access library catalogs.

- *CD-ROMS in Print* (Gale Research, annual). This decribes more than 9,000 titles.

Sources on the Internet are covered by any number of directories; as of this writing they include titles such as *The Internet Yellow Pages* and *The Internet Directory.* There will undoubtedly be much turbulence in this area, with new titles appearing and disappearing rapidly. Consult your library; and remember, too, that the Internet provides a wide variety of its own online indexes and directories and that these sources will always be more up-to-date than the printed directories.

Notes

1. So named after George Boole (1815–64), a British mathematician and logician who developed an analogy between the operations of logic and those of ordinary algebra.

2. An additional problem with keyword searching on the World Wide Web is that a company called Iron Mountain Global Information Systems (IMGIS) has "bought" the rights to certain keywords from the leading search services (or "engines"). This mean that any searches on these specific words will always bring IMGIS's client companies into the "top ten" list of hit sites retrieved by any searches for those words. Such "top" rankings, in other words, may have nothing to do with actual word frequency counts or with any expert's judgment of quality. The search engines you use to search the Web are not neutral, in other words—many are slanted by cash payments to emphasize certain commercial or political interests. See David Corn, "Anatomy of a Netscam: Why Your Internet Search May Not Be As Honest As You Think," *Washington Post* (July 7, 1996), p. C5.

13

Locating Material in Other Libraries

If your own library does not own the material you need, or if you just want to know what is available elsewhere on your subject, you will want to look into the holdings of other libraries. There are three steps involved:

1. Determining which specific sources exist on your topic
2. Determining where copies of these can be found
3. Determining which libraries have special collections on your subject, for further research or browsing

Determining Which Specific Sources Exist on Your Topic

The best place to start is usually your own local public or university library. By means of the variety of search options discussed so far—subject heading, keyword, and citation searches in either databases or print sources; systematic browsing of classified bookstacks; related-record searches in CD-ROMs; use of encyclopedias, review articles, and published bibliographies (including footnotes within discovered sources); and Boolean combinations of search elements—you will be able to identify a number of book, journal, and other sources relevant to your topic, some of which may not be held by your local library.

Beyond these general search techniques, however, there are other sources for identifying books. These include *Book Review Digest* (with its subject index) and *Subject Guide to Books in Print* and its British equivalent, *Whitaker's Books in Print;* and, for older works, the PREMARC database, the *Cumulative Book Index*, the *Bibliography of American Imprints to 1901*, and the *BPR Annual Cumulative.* Most of these use the *Library of Congress Subject Headings* list for their basic vocabulary control of subject terms (although, as explained below, there are major problems with PREMARC's consistency).

Given the avalanche of books available, most people will want to focus or limit their searches to a few works, at least initially. Two ways to do this are to limit by either quality of material or recency of publication.

There are two good shortcuts to finding the *best* books on a subject. One is to check several relevant encyclopedia articles to see if their selective bibliographies mention the same works. *First Stop* (see Chapter 1) is particularly useful in identifying which encyclopedias have pertinent articles. (It is especially recommended to compare a bibliography from a specialized encyclopedia with one from a *Britannica* article; the latter set provides critical annotations to the entries in its bibliographies, which the other encyclopedias do not.) The purpose of an encyclopedia article is to give you a basic orientation to its subject, so its bibliography will usually try to list only the most important works. And writers of encyclopedia articles usually are experts in their fields, so by comparing the views of two or more experts on what the important books are, you can often short-circuit some otherwise lengthy research.

The second shortcut is to use *Book Review Digest* (H. W. Wilson, 1905– ; CD-ROM and FirstSearch versions, 1983–). This monthly publication has annual cumulations that form a permanent set; it covers reviews appearing in 80 American, British, and Canadian journals to about 6,000 books every year. The important things about *BRD* are that it provides digests or extended quotations from several evaluative reviews of each book so you can assess its critical reception from several viewpoints; and that it has a subject index (which is often overlooked). If you start with this index, you can quickly find citations to relevant books *and* an assessment of their quality. And you can do this kind of searching for both recent and older sources. It is sometimes advisable to consult *BRD* in addition to the encyclopedia bibliographies, especially if these are somewhat dated.

Subject Guide to Books in Print (Bowker, 1957–) is an annual set listing those works published in the United States that are currently available in bookstores or by mail. It quotes prices; and a companion volume, titled simply *Publishers,* provides addresses and phone numbers (including toll-free numbers). *Subject Guide* provides an efficient way to identify the most recent books on a subject. Its LC headings are rather broad (i.e., it makes little use of the standard subdivisions to limit topics), so you will have to do some scanning for specific works. There are companion volumes you will also want to check: *Books in Print Supplement, Subject Guide to Forthcoming Books,* and *Paperbound Books in Print* (which has its own subject index). All libraries will own all of these volumes, and will usually have them right next to each other in the reference department. A comparable British set is the annual *Whitaker's Books in Print.*

If you wish to do searches that are broader in scope (not limited either to the best or the most recent books), the most convenient sources will be the WorldCat database in the OCLC FirstSearch system, or the RLIN BIB database (assuming your library subscribes to them). Each is the combined catalog of either hundreds or thousands of libraries (see Chapter 11); and each can be searched by subject, using either *LCSH* or keywords.

If your library does not have access to these files, it may nonetheless provide access to the Internet; if it does, you can then do searches in the large book catalogs of the British Library at <http://opac97bl.uk>, or the Library of Congress at <lcweb.loc.gov> (then choose "Command Search" and "Multiple File Searching").

There are two computerized "card catalogs" of the books in LC; one, called LOCB, covers works received and cataloged (or recataloged) since 1968, regardless of their dates of publication. It is generally complete and reliable. The second database, called PREMARC (or PREM), is the Library's first step toward getting the earlier book records into machine-readable form; but its coverage of the earlier books in the LC collection is spotty. You cannot trust it to give you a complete record of even the older books within LC, let alone a list of "everything" published before 1968.

PREMARC was produced by a private company that keyed in records from the Library's Shelflist Card Catalog, rather than from its Main Card Catalog. The Shelflist is an ongoing record of all books added to the collection with only one card (filed by call number) for each book. It includes no records of changed subject headings. Over the decades, as thousands of changes were made in *Library of Congress Subject Headings* terminology (from "Woman" to "Women," from "Aeroplanes" to "Airplanes"), these changes were made in LC's Main Card Catalog records but not in the Shelflist. Therefore the PREMARC records have all of the tens of thousands of outdated and superseded headings from all of the first nine editions of the *LCSH* list. These old headings are usually omitted from current editions, and they are not referred to by the cross-reference network—which has itself changed over the decades, without being recorded in PREMARC (which has no cross-references at all). For example, PRE-MARC has more than 2,000 records under the current heading "Women," but it also has more than *7,000* under the old heading "Woman." Similarly, there are more than 3,500 old books under the obsolete heading "Negroes" rather than under the current headings "Afro-Americans" and "Blacks."

The computer's capability to do keyword searching does not solve such problems. For example, a keyword search of "Airplanes" finds nearly 400 records but misses more than 5,000 that are retrievable only under the obsolete heading "Aeroplanes." PREMARC, in other words, does not abide by the important principle of uniform heading. It's sort of like the ruins of a Greek temple—there are fragments of order in it, but they no longer cohere—they aren't connected to each other systematically—and many of its pieces are now buried out of sight, underground. Furthermore, about 10 percent of the records that should be there are missing; and subtitles of books, contents notes, and series statements were usually not keyed in to begin with, so the records are "skeletal." Again, too, none of the hundreds of thousands of cross-references among the old records was entered. Also, the company that keyed in the more than 4.5 million records introduced literally millions of spelling errors—up until about 1990 there were 64 books under "Untied States"—all of which undermine keyword search capabilities.

The solution to all these problems at the Library of Congress itself has been its retention of the old Main Card Catalog, which is complete and does have consistent subject headings, using the ninth edition of *LCSH*. (While PREMARC uses the ninth edition, it *also* uses the eighth, seventh, sixth, fifth, fourth, third, second, and first.)[1] But the Main Card Catalog is not available online via the Internet. The primary online version for the pre-1968 records is PREMARC.[2] And you are *not* getting "everything" in the Library of Congress by searching this database; you are not even getting everything that is in its old card catalog.

Three other good sources exist if you wish to do searches for older books. The first is *Cumulative Book Index* (or *CBI*; H. W. Wilson, 1928–), which is a monthly publication with annual cumulations. Unlike *Books in Print,* which is limited to works published in the United States, *CBI* is an ongoing record of all English-language books published anywhere in the world. It lists each under author, title, and subject entries, all interfiled in one alphabetical sequence.

The second is *BPR Annual Cumulative,* which is the yearly hardbound cumulation of the monthly publication *American Book Publishing Record.* What is especially useful in this set is that it has some very large retrospective cumulations, covering 1876 to 1949 and 1950 to 1977. Afterward there are annual volumes. It is a list of books published in the United States, and it has some advantages over the *National Union Catalog* (see below), which has no subject index, and over retrospective sets of *Subject Guide to Books in Print*, which aren't cumulated and don't go back as far. *BPR* has other advantages: (1) It lists entries in subject groupings according to the Dewey Decimal Classification, which facilitates browsing; (2) it has a separate subject index that uses *LCSH* terms *with* the subdivisions that are usually omitted in *Subject Guide*, and these are very useful for fine-tuning a search or combining two or more subjects; and (3) its entries give the tracings for each book, which are very helpful in suggesting related subject headings.

The third is the *Bibliography of American Imprints to 1901* (92 volumes; K. G. Saur, 1993). This is a listing of about 400,000 books, pamphlets, leaflets, and broadsides (but not periodicals) published anywhere within the present borders of the United States from 1640 through the end of 1900. The main sequence is by Title (volumes 1–42); there are also indexes by Name (including authors, editors, compilers, translators, etc.; volumes 43–56), by Subject (volumes 57–71), by Place of Publication (volumes 72–82), and by Date (volumes 83–92). These index volumes are what make the set so useful; it's very hard to get lists like these out of computer databases.

When you are doing research with any of these sources, remember that they do not provide access to four additional types of sources that are especially valuable: special collections, microform collections, CD-ROM compilations, and government documents. (For locating special collections, see below in this chapter; for the others, see Chapter 15.) Nor do they cover magazine or journal articles, which can be identified through the various databases, indexes, and bibliographies discussed in Chapters 4 through 9.

Determining Where Copies Can Be Found

Nowadays the first sources for locating copies of books (and other sources) not held by your local library are the OCLC WorldCat and RLIN BIB databases (described in Chapter 11), each of which provides library locations. You have to be careful with the WorldCat file, as it appears within OCLC FirstSearch, however; as of this writing it is set up so it will usually show you only the holdings of other libraries in your own area, not the full list of all holdings in the international system. To get the latter, you have to search OCLC through a different software, known as PRISM; and this version, which is more expensive, usually will not be available on publicly accessible terminals. It may, however, be available to your library's catalogers and reference librarians; talk to them if you need a printout of all locations for an item in the entire system.

Other online sources, beyond OCLC and RLIN, for identifying library locations are the WLN (Western Library Network) and Utlas International databases. WLN includes about 10 million catalog records, with locations, from more than 600 libraries in the West and Northwest (including British Columbia). The Utlas database covers holdings from more than 2,000 libraries, mainly (but not exclusively) in Canada.

There are also a number of printed sources that identify library locations for books or journals; the most important point here is that these printed lists *are not superseded by the OCLC, RLIN, WLN, or Utlas* databases. They are called "union" lists or catalogs because they record the holdings of many libraries. They are often overlooked these days for much the same reason that published bibliographies (see Chapter 9) are neglected: researchers casually assume—mistakenly—that all the information in both printed bibliographies and union lists is now "included" in computers. While there is indeed some overlap, the printed lists continue to include a wealth of material that simply does not exist in digital formats and probably never will. While, in most cases, you will probably want to start with computer databases, remember that they do *not* have "every-thing" and that the print formats can identify sources—*and library loca-tions*—that cannot be found in any database. You have to be aware of both kinds of sources if you want to do efficient research in large libraries.

The most important printed union list is the *National Union Catalog: Pre-1956 Imprints*. It is a 754-volume set with more than 12 million entries (both catalog records and cross-references) reported to the project by about 1,100 research libraries throughout North America; and for each item it lists libraries that actually own a copy. (According to a 1994 brochure from OCLC, its WorldCat database contains just over 8.5 million records pub-lished between 1450 and 1959. Many of these are actually duplicates that are counted separately.) Since this set is so fundamental to scholarship, it is worth considering in some detail its capabilities, uses, and peccadilloes—espe-cially since these points are almost never taught in colleges and universities.

- The *National Union Catalog* (*NUC*) is basically arranged by author (not by subject), although anonymous works are included under titles. It is thus very useful for compiling a bibliography of an author's works and their various editions—which are displayed chronologically for each work. (Note, however, that this set does not list individual articles within journals.) Although there are supple-ments covering works published through 1993, the basic set includes only works published through the end of 1955. For this time period it includes many more works than can be found in any of the online union lists.

- It includes not only books but also pamphlets, maps, atlases, broad-sides, music (scores and print material rather than sound record-ings), government documents, microforms, and even some manuscripts. Audiovisual materials such as phonorecords, motion pictures, and filmstrips are excluded, as are Braille and Moon books for the blind. (These formats are not excluded in the various com-puter union catalogs.) Publications from all over the world are cov-ered, although the emphasis is on works in the Roman alphabet or Greek or Gaelic. But there are also many entries in Arabic, Cyrillic, Chinese, Japanese, Hebrew, Korean, the various Indic alphabets and other non-Latin characters. The works in the Near Eastern and Ori-

Wigram, *Sir* **James,** 1793–1866.

An examination of the rules of law, respecting the admission
- of extrinsic evidence in aid of the interpretation of wills. By
James Wigram ... 5th ed., by Charles Percy Sanger ... London, Sweet and Maxwell, limited; ¡etc., etc., 1914.

xlviii, 284 p.   front. (port.)   22½ᵐ.

"The text and author's notes are reprinted verbatim from the 3d ed.,
the paging of which is shown in the margin ... The 3d ed., being the last
rev. by the learned author himself, was pub. in 1840 ... The portrait of
Sir James Wigram is from a mezzotint by W. Walker, after John Watson
Gordon, A. R. A."—Pref. to 5th ed.

1. Wills—Gt. Brit. 2. Evidence (Law)—Gt. Brit.   i. Sanger,
Charles Percy, ed.

                                              15——4680

NW   0293187   DLC NcD-L PPB PU-L OU CtY CaBVaU IdU MH ◄━━━━━ **Library location symbols**

Fig. 11

ental alphabets are mainly those held in the vast collections of the
Library of Congress.

- While the basic print-format sources for determining library locations of journals and serials are the *Union List of Serials* and its supplement *New Serial Titles,* the *NUC* records many serials not listed
  in either of these; and it also covers conference proceedings and
  annual publications, which *ULS* and *NST* omit.
- The set provides very strong coverage of local, state, and federal
  government documents, and surprisingly good coverage of international and foreign government publications as well.
- Its overall coverage is so good that book dealers frequently raise the
  price of any item they come across that is not listed. "Not in *NUC*"
  is a strong selling point for a rare book.
- The library locations for each work are designated by symbols after
  the bibliographic description (see Figure 11). The most frequently
  used symbols are spelled out on the inside covers of each volume.
  Complete lists of all the symbols can be found in three volumes—
  200, 560, and 754—which are bound in brown cloth so they will
  stand out from the green of the others. (A common misconception
  regarding the *NUC* is that the Library of Congress owns every book
  listed in it. This is not true; LC owns only those items that have the
  symbol "DLC"—the "D" stands for District of Columbia.)

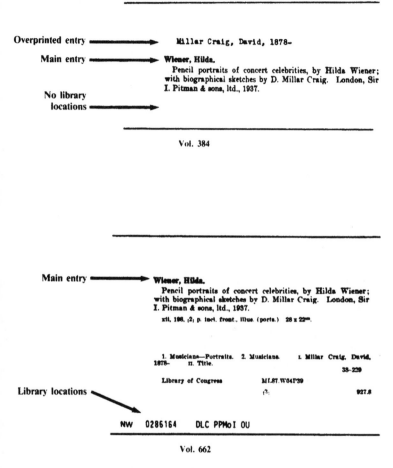

Overprinted entry ⟶ Millar Craig, David, 1878-

Main entry ⟶ **Wiener, Hilda.**
Pencil portraits of concert celebrities, by Hilda Wiener; with biographical sketches by D. Millar Craig. London, Sir I. Pitman & sons, ltd., 1937.

No library locations ⟶

Vol. 384

Main entry ⟶ **Wiener, Hilda.**
Pencil portraits of concert celebrities, by Hilda Wiener; with biographical sketches by D. Millar Craig. London, Sir I. Pitman & sons, ltd., 1937.

xii, 196, ₍2₎ p. incl. front., illus. (ports.) 28 x 22ᶜᵐ.

1. Musicians—Portraits. 2. Musicians. ɪ. Millar Craig, David, 1878- ɪɪ. Title.
38–229

Library of Congress   ML87.W64P39
₍3₎   927.8

Library locations ⟶ NW   0286164   DLC PPMoI OU

Vol. 662

Fig. 12

Some entries do not list locations; these are in the form of "overprinted" cards. In Figure 12, for example, a work providing David Millar Craig's biographical sketches of concert celebrities is listed under Millar Craig's name, but no library locations are listed. In this entry, however, "Millar Craig" is a typed-in (overprinted) line above the main entry, "Wiener, Hilda." When the main entry card is consulted directly, library locations are found. The overprinted entries thus serve as cross-references to main entries.

- If the book you want is not in the *NUC,* you should not assume that none of the participating libraries owns it. Most of the institutions did not report every item cataloged in their collections, but rather concentrated on those works they considered rare or unusual. Many participants, in fact, contributed very few reports. Several major libraries, however—the Library of Congress, Harvard, Yale, the University of Chicago, the John Crerar, and the New York Public—were extremely conscientious, reporting virtually every item cataloged in their collections. Indeed, the *NUC* lists *more* of LC's pre-1956 holdings than does LC's own computer or card catalogs. This is because the Library has many separate divisions that have their own catalogs, and these divisional files have large numbers of items that are not recorded in the main catalog. The *NUC* picks up some of these divisional items.

- The *Pre-'56 NUC* consists of *two separate* A–Z alphabets: volumes 1–685 (the main sequence) and volumes 686–754 (a supplement). The main sequence contains 11,637,350 entries and cross-references; the supplement, 949,385 (for a total of 12,586,735). The supplement was created because the publication of the main sequence, alone, took twenty years; and during this period reports kept coming in for additional items (and locations) falling into letters of the alphabet that had already been published. The supplement is thus especially valuable—i.e., it contains the most entries—for authors whose names fall in the earlier letters of the alphabet; coverage tapers off steeply as the supplement approaches the letter *Z*.

    It is important to note that the supplement includes many corrections and additional cross-references *to the main sequence*. My experience of years of helping people with the *NUC* is that most researchers—even those who have rather extensive prior familiarity with the set—*routinely overlook the second alphabet*. Be sure to check *both* sequences!

- Each of the supplementary volumes (686–754) has a separate numerically coded section that lists *additional library locations* for works already reported in the main sequence. But you should use

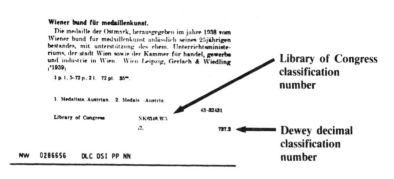

Fig. 13

both this numeric section *and* the alphabetical section of each supplement volume when looking for additional locations of items initially reported in volumes 1–685.

- Each entry is usually a reproduction of a full catalog card, including tracings (which are seldom found in other bibliographies). The subject headings in these can be useful in any library.
- The cards list not only Library of Congress call numbers but sometimes Dewey Decimal numbers as well (see Figure 13). These can help you locate browsing areas in the bookstacks of your own library. (Note, however, that call numbers given in the *NUC* may not work to retrieve the specific books you want. Even if your library used the LC classification scheme, the tail ends of its call numbers are likely to be different from LC's numbers for the same books. In fact, it is quite possible that your own library has assigned entirely different class numbers. LC class numbers, in other words, are not necessarily uniform from one library to the next. (This is true even today, but was especially the case in the pre-1956 period, when computer networks were not available to facilitate uniformity.)

When a call number is listed on an *NUC* card entry, it is usually the number assigned at the library whose location symbol appears first on the record.

- In addition to its use in locating actual copies of books, the *NUC* is especially helpful for verifying and filling out incomplete or questionable bibliographic citations. An important point to note: If you fail to find a book under an author's name as you have it in your original citation, *try slightly variant spellings*. It is the experience of librarians who must verify hundreds of interlibrary loan requests that frequently the initial citation that readers rely on—whether it comes from a footnote, bibliography, printout, or catalog—is itself inaccurate. In my own work, for example, I've found in the *NUC* works by "Lesse*m*" that were initially asked for under the name "Lesse*n*"; "B*u*lle*t*tino di Pisano" when "B*o*lle*t*ino" was cited; and "Abern*e*thy" when the original footnote read "Abern*a*thy." This approach works *with surprising frequency*.

- If an author has written a book under a pseudonym, you can often use the *NUC* to find his or her real name. If you look under the pen name you will find a cross-reference to the real name.
- Similarly, if an author signs initials rather than his full name, you can use the *NUC* to find the full form. "Eliot, T. S.," for example, refers you to "Eliot, Thomas Stearns, 1888– ." And various entries under the latter form fill in his death date at "–1965." Similarly, you can find that *G*ilbert *K*eith Chesterton lived from 1874 to 1936. Such entries and dates are useful in distinguishing among authors with similar names or initials. The first and last entry under an author's name will usually provide the fullest information.
- The *NUC* usually provides a quick way to find out if an old foreign-language book has been translated into English. If you look under the original author's name, you will find that entries include both original-language editions and translations. Similarly, you can often find out whether an English-language book has been translated into another language. (The same tack works in WorldCat or RLIN BIB, too—under any author's name both original works and translations will be listed together.)
- Although as a rule works are entered under authors' names or under titles for anonymous works, there are many cross-references in the set that often allow you to find them under other points of access (e.g., joint author, compiler, translator of poetry or drama, honoree of *Festschriften*, name of artist in cases of works with art reproduc-

tions). *Editors'* names, however, are usually *not* used as access points. The main entry point for most U.S. government documents (volumes 609–24) begins with the corporate designation "United States.," subdivided by department, bureau, or office—but since this makes items difficult to find, the editors also included rather liberal cross-references under titles or authors' personal names for these works. Similarly, the works in the "Bible" volumes (53–56) appear rather liberally under other entry points as well. (It is noteworthy that the U.S. document volumes and the Bible listings are such large catalogs in their own right that each has been republished as a separate set. The Bible reprint includes an index volume that cumulates the cross-references elsewhere in the *NUC*. There are also one-volume reprints of the extensive "Catholic Church" and "Freemasons" listings.) Cross-references are also provided in those cases in which there is confusion or disagreement regarding the spelling of an author's name. Again, researchers should remember always to check *both* alphabets, for the supplement may contain cross-references that did not make it into the main sequence. An example is provided by Ferdinand André's *Délibérations de l'administration* (Mende, 1882-84). In the main sequence this appears only under the main entry "Lozère, France (dept.)." However, if you look in the supplement under "André, Ferdinand" you will find a cross-reference that points you to the "Lozère" entry.

• The cross-reference structure of the *NUC*, all by itself, keeps the set valuable even in the age of computerized catalogs for older books. The online databases often do not include such linkages among alternative forms or entry; so if you do not guess precisely the right keywords for the item you are looking for, you can easily miss it. The *NUC*'s extensive cross-reference structure, however—which is not duplicated in any online catalog—can alert you to the existence of alternative keywords (variant spellings, or different names altogether) that you could never hit upon through online keyword guessing. (For instance, a cross-reference at "Geological Society of Denmark" refers you to "Dansk Geologisk Forening.") In other words, if you don't find what you are looking for in WorldCat or

RLIN BIB, you can often use the *NUC* cross-references to find unexpected forms of entry that you can then search for back in the online catalogs, to find additional locations not in the *NUC* itself.

- Researchers should be aware of five other national union catalogs in card-file format at the Library of Congress, which the regular *NUC* overlaps but does not supersede. These are for foreign-language materials in non-Roman scripts; they are:

  Chinese Union Catalog (ca. 160,000 cards representing pre-1958 imprints reported from ca. 10 major Chinese collections in American libraries)

  Hebraic/Yiddish Union Catalog (ca. 500,000 cards; stopped in the mid-1980s)

  Ladino Union Catalog (ca. 1,200 cards)

  Near East National Union List (Arabic, Persian, and Turkish; ca. 960,000 cards; pre-1979 imprints reported through the mid-1990s)

  Slavic/Cyrillic Union Catalog (more than 1 million cards; pre-1956 imprints reported up to 1980)

These files contain entries, with library locations, for materials in non-Roman scripts *originally cataloged by libraries other than LC*. They also contain items originally cataloged by LC and that therefore appear in the regular *NUC*; but the other non-LC entries—and there are literally millions of them—are not in the *NUC*. None of these card files is added to anymore, since all new cataloging is computerized. The *Near East National Union List* is also available in database form from the Library of Congress; and the *Slavic/Cyrillic Union Catalog* was also commercially published in two parts: the *Cyrillic Union Catalog* (Readex Microprint), reproducing more than 700,000 cards representing 178,226 pre-1956 monographic and serial titles reported by 185 North American libraries; and the *Slavic Cyrillic Union Catalog* on microfiche (Rowman and Littlefield) of 350,000 pre-1956 citations reported from 1956 to 1980 by 220 North American libraries. LC also maintains two other separate national union catalogs, one of talking books and books in Braille for blind and physically handicapped people; this exists in database form as the *NLS (National Library Services) Union Catalog*. The other, the *National Union Index to Architectural Records,* is a printout consisting of about 5,000 records reporting collections of architectural records, including drawings, renderings, blueprints, photographs, contracts, change orders, specifications, and so on, throughout the country; it is arranged by names of architects.[3]

- If you want to impress a librarian with a bit of trivia, mention that you've found a circular entry in the *Pre-'56*. When you look up Kaspar Hedio's *Chronica der Alten Christlichen Kirchen* (vol. 238, p. 43, col. 3) you'll find a note "See under Eusebius Pamphilii, bp. of Caesarea." But when you look this up (vol. 163, p. 442, col. 3) you'll find a "see" reference directing you right back to "Hedio, Kaspar." And then mention that your further research has discovered that the mistake is corrected in the supplement (vol. 773, p. 270, col. 2).

- If you want to be truly obnoxious in your expertise, mention that you strongly disagree with the scurrilous note written by a disgruntled *NUC* employee and inserted on the card for James Wolveridge's *Speculum Matricis* (vol. 671); and that you have grave doubts about the bibliographic veracity of entry NP0576549 (vol. 471), which you have determined is *not* owned by the University of Oregon.[4]

- The physical size of the *NUC* is amazing; it is one of the last of the great catalogs to be published in book format (CD-ROMs and licensed Web sites are now preferred by publishers). A complete set has 528,000 pages, taking up 125 linear feet of shelving. It has been estimated that, had the Wright Brothers' first airplane flight started at volume 1, it would have ended 5 feet short of the end of the set; and the world's record shot put would have landed about 49 feet short of it.

- The set is available on microfiche but has never been converted to machine-readable form. (The OCLC and RLIN databases overlap, but do not supersede, its coverage.)

- One of the interesting by-products of the compilation of the set was the discovery that some widely held assumptions about research libraries are false. Gordon R. Williams, chairman of the National

Union Catalog subcommittee within the American Library Association, has pointed out this surprising finding:

> In 1901 when Librarian of Congress Herbert Putnam started the union catalog, the implicit assumption was that—except where libraries had pursued special interests—the main differences between collections were determined by the age and size of the individual libraries in which they were housed. It was assumed that all comparable research libraries held in common virtually the same core collection and that it was essentially the older and larger libraries that were the repositories of books not generally to be found in the younger and smaller ones. This belief is implicit in Putnam's view, expressed in his annual report for 1900, that with the completion of the filing of cards from Harvard, the Boston Public Library, the New York Public Library, and a few others, the union catalog would "constitute the closest approximation now available to a complete record of books in American libraries."
>
> The following facts, which many librarians still find difficult to believe, did not become clear until much later. Research library collections, even those of about the same age, size, and purpose, hold many fewer titles in common than everyone thought. Far more titles and editions are held by only one or very few of them. And, anything even approaching a complete record of books in American Libraries requires a union catalog of hundreds of libraries.[5]

Scholars in America are therefore especially fortunate to have a resource such as the *NUC* at their disposal for tracking older books; no other nation has anything like it. (The largest printed catalogs of other countries—e.g., those for the British Library or the Bibliothèque Nationale—are not union lists; they are the catalogs of only the holdings of the one national library.)

There are various printed supplements of the *NUC* through 1982; afterward it exists on microform and in database format until 1993. With the printed supplements it is important to note that reports of locations of items (i.e., which libraries own a copy) are not always published on the bibliographic records themselves but appear instead in a supplemental list called the *Register of Additional Locations*. The *RAL* exists in two five-year bound sets, 1963–67 and 1968–72, with microfiche supplements thereafter until 1993. There is also an online version of the *NUC* from 1982 to 1993. These sometimes turn up locations not in OCLC or RLIN. On the whole, however, the *NUC* waned in importance as the commercial online union catalogs expanded in the 1970s and after. I never use it myself for anything beyond the 1968–72 set; the *NUC* ceased publication entirely in 1993.

The National Union Catalog of Manuscript Collections (NUCMC), in print format, is a listing of whose papers—both of individuals and corporate bodies and organizations—are held in which repositories. It has cumulative author, corporate body, and subject indexes covering all reports of collections through 1984; for subsequent years you must consult the individual annual volumes through 1993. The printed set ceased publication at that point; subsequent reports of manuscript holdings are now included in the AMC (Archives and manuscripts collections) file of the RLIN online catalog. The AMC file actually includes *NUCMC* records since 1987, so there is some overlap between print and online records. And a commercial database from Chadwyck-Healey, *ArchivesUSA,* now includes the entire *NUCMC* set from its beginning. (See Appendix.)

For locating copies of journals, especially older titles, two printed sources are often better than OCLC or RLIN; they are the *Union List of Serials (ULS)* and its supplements, called *New Serials Titles (NST)*. These are arranged by titles of journals, and for each they tell which libraries in North America own sets.

A number of specialized union lists cover journal holdings in particular regions (e.g., *California Union List of Periodicals, Journal Holdings of the Washington-Baltimore Area);* or on particular subjects (e.g., *Union List of Military Periodicals, Union List of Film Periodicals*). There are also union lists of serials for some other countries (e.g., *British Union-Catalogue of Periodicals, Catalog Collectif des Périodiques*). And then there are combinations of subject and area holdings (e.g., *Union List of Statistical Serials in British Libraries; Art Serials: Union List of Art Periodicals and Serials in Research Libraries in the Washington DC Metropolitan Area*). *Hundreds* of such specialized lists exist; they can be identified with the help of reference librarians. These specialized lists often provide library locations that do not show up in the large databases and catalogs.

Determining Which Libraries Have Special Collections on Your Subject

No matter how good the coverage of OCLC, RLIN, the *NUC*, and various other union catalogs and databases, libraries will always have many items that are recorded only on their own premises. If you cannot pinpoint the location of a desired item through a union list, the next best thing is to identify a collection that is *likely* to have it. There are several good sources for determing the existence and location of subject collections, both in the United States and internationally. The overall sources are:

1. *Subject Collections*, compiled by Lee Ash (New York: Bowker), revised irregularly. This is the basic guide to well over 65,000 special collections in university, college, public, and special libraries and museums in the United States and Canada. Entries are arranged alphabetically according to *Library of Congress Subject Headings* (with additional subject terms as needed); each provides the address of the library, an estimate of the number of items in the collections, and, frequently, descriptive notes.

2. *Directory of Special Libraries and Information Centers*, edited by Gwen E. Turecki (Detroit: Gale Research), revised irregularly. This describes more than 22,000 facilities in the United States and Canada; it lists them in alphabetical order and has a detailed subject index. A particularly useful feature is its geographic index, which will tell you quickly which libraries are in your area. A companion set, *Subject Directory of Special Libraries and Information Centers* (Gale), irregular, lists the same libraries in subject classified order (e.g., Business/Finance Libraries, Law Libraries, Health Sciences Libraries).

3. *World Guide to Special Libraries* (Munich: K. G. Saur), revised irregularly. This lists more than 32,000 libraries under about 1,000 subject terms; it also has an alphabetical index of library names.

4. *Directory of Special Collections in Western Europe*, edited by Alison Gallico (London and New York: Bowker-Saur, 1993). This is a listing of approximately 700 special collections in the arts, humanities, sciences, and social sciences. Details are given on time periods

covered, languages, formats, and accessibility (including loan policies); contact names and addresses, phone and fax numbers, hours, and availability of catalogs are also covered. Entries are arranged by country, then alphabetically by institution. Indexes are by subject and geographic location; the subject indexes are in English, French, German, and Spanish.

5. *The Aslib Directory of Information Sources in the United Kingdom* (London: Aslib, The Association for Information Management), revised irregularly, is an alphabetical listing of more than 6,800 libraries and organizations; it has a subject index.

As with union lists, there are also many specialized guides to libraries in particular regions within this country and to those of other countries (e.g., *Special Collections at Georgetown, Special Collections and Subject Area Strengths in Maine Libraries, Special Collections in German Libraries*). The librarians in your area can tell you which ones exist locally; the sources in Chapter 16 can be used to identify others. A good shortcut is to search for such publications under the LC subject heading forms "Library resources—[Place]" and "[Subject heading]—Library resources."

The United States, Canada, and Great Britain are particularly blessed with excellent interlibrary loan (ILL) networks. If you cannot find the book or article you want within your area, be sure to ask your librarians about the possibilities of borrowing the item from another facility, or of acquiring a photocopy. Some libraries nowadays also have access to document delivery services that provide copies of articles for a fee. It is best to first ask through a library; if this doesn't work, or if the item cannot be borrowed or photocopied through interlibrary loan, or isn't covered by a document delivery service, then contact the holding institution directly. Sometimes it will have photocopy or microfilming procedures outside the ILL network; or it can give you the names of local researchers for hire who can make photocopies for you.

The overall point to keep in mind is that if you have identified a good source that is not available in your local library, don't give up. The same local library is likely to have the means of identifying which other libraries either have the desired item or are likely to have it.

Notes

1. The Library of Congress did not save its old card catalog because the librarians were "sentimental" about the texture of cardboard or the smell of wood cabinets. They saved it because it is substantially different—and much more complete—*in content* than the PREMARC database that is available through the Internet. Unfortunately, many other libraries that have done retrospective conversions of their old catalogs to machine-readable form have chosen to proffer the myth that they have simply changed the format of the same file when in fact they have significantly diminished its contents (most notably in throwing away the entirety of the old network of elaborate cross-references). The consistency of subject heading terminology may also have suffered in such conversions.

2. Pre-1968 books that were received and cataloged after 1968 will show up in the LOCB database.

3. *The National Union Index to Architectural Records* once existed in database form, but the Library's Information Technology Services office lost the tape! It is being reconstructed as a project of the University of Maryland Library School. (There is a lesson here about the archival problems of electronic formats.)

4. Similar peculiarities appear in other reference sources. In the first (1980) printing of *The New Grove Dictionary of Music and Musicians*, a decidedly unconventional spelling of the word "Fugue" appears in vol. 7, p. 783, col. 1, l. 2; the obscenity is corrected in subsequent printings. Also in the 1980 *New Grove*, two hoax entries slipped past the editors, for the fictitious composers Guglielmo Baldini and Dag Henrik Esrum-Hellerup; in later printings these spaces are filled by illustrations. A hoax entry also appears in the 1971 edition of *Music Since 1900*, entered under 27 April 1905; subsequent printings reproduce the entry with an explanatory disclaimer note. In the *Congressional Record* of September 27, 1986, p. S14050, col. 1, a memorandum in support of a bill to outlaw indecent communications by means of telephone includes a full-paragraph transcription of a dial-a-porn message, thereby making the *Record* itself a printed means of indecent communication. Chapter 42 of Niels Horrebow's *Natural History of Iceland* (London: A. Linde, 1758), entitled "Concerning Owls," reads in toto: "There are no owls of any kind in the whole island." And all male readers will wince, and some feminists cheer, at the singular particulars of the death of Baron Delaval's son, as succinctly recorded in G. E. C. Cokayne's *Complete Peerage*, vol. 4, p. 139, note (b).

5. Gordon R. Williams, "*The National Union Catalog* and Research Libraries," in *In Celebration: The National Union Catalog, Pre-1956 Imprints*, ed. John Y. Cole (Washington, D.C.: Library of Congress, 1981), p. 14.

14

People Sources

So far we have examined seven major avenues of access to information: controlled-vocabulary searches, systematic browsing and scanning of subject-classified full texts, keyword searches, citation searches, related-record searches, searches through published bibliographies, and those done via computer databases. (Computer inquiries use elements of the other methods but add the possibility of postcoordinate Boolean combinations.) The eighth major avenue—that of talking to people—is the one most favored by journalists, but it is also valuable for anyone else.

It is particularly important for academic researchers not to overlook this method, as most academicians have an overly strong print bias—that is, they often unconsciously assume that if information cannot be found in print, then it cannot be found at all. In recent years this bias has expanded along parallel lines to include Internet sources, but the assumption is the same: "If it can't be found in print or on the Internet, then the information doesn't exist"—with the undesirable result that people change their questions to fit whatever information *is* found, and diminish the scope of their papers accordingly.

Such an assumption can be very detrimental to quality research, particularly if timeliness of information is important. Even the most recent journal articles may be several months old due to the time lag involved in submission, acceptance, and publication of manuscripts; and Internet sources may often be of questionable authority or provenance. Regardless of the time factor, however, talking to people will be valuable in any event because an expert can usually provide you with information that has never existed in print or electronic form.

It may seem obvious to state this; and, indeed, I have found few people who would say they disagree with these observations. Still—and this is the problem—many people who intellectually know that doing good research must take them outside the four walls of a library and beyond the reach of their computer workstation will not *act* as though they know it. When it finally comes to *doing* research, they are very shy about going beyond print and electronic sources to find what they want.

Part of the difficulty lies in the way "research methods" courses are taught in colleges. Very often they are confined to the discussion of a relatively few sources on a prescribed bibliography; and correlative assignments are frequently made with the stipulation that "you have to use the sources on this list" coupled with "don't bother the reference librarians—you should do your research on your own." Unfortunately, students tend unwittingly to learn more than they should from such experiences: They learn that "doing research" equals "playing library games"—or "using the Internet" *alone*—and that talking to people is "bothering" them and may even have a faint scent of "cheating" to it. Professors seem unaware of the long-term damage this does, not only to their students' subsequent academic careers but also to the future satisfaction of their curiosity about topics of personal interest. Reference librarians, on the other hand, notice the limiting effects of such "learning" all the time.

Genuine learning should obviously be a broadening rather than a limiting experience; and in doing research the most important lesson to learn is that *any* source is fair game. One should always go to wherever the information needed is most likely to be, and often this will be in someone's head rather than in a book or on a computer screen. (Remember, too, though, that you can travel full circle from talking to an expert to get back into the literature—for usually the expert will know the *best* written sources, and can offer shortcuts that will make library research more efficient.)

Talking to people can provide insights into one's own area of research, feedback on problem points, and a structure of perception that written sources often cannot match. Conversations can reveal quickly which areas of inquiry are valuable and worth pursuing, and which are likely to waste time. And people sources can often identify quickly what are the "crackpot" positions—something that's hard to grasp otherwise if the field you're entering is entirely new to you.

Experts, enthusiasts, and buffs are available without direct, one-to-one contact (at least initially) through the thousands of listservs and discussion groups available on the Internet; these services enable you to throw out a question to a wide variety of people interested in a particular subject area; usually you will receive direct e-mail responses from individuals who pick up on the question. As with other people sources, such contacts can provide you with either direct answers or possible additional contacts.

No matter what your means of contacting people, however, a common-sense word of caution is in order: A judicious mixture of personal and print sources is often the ideal in doing good research. Just as academics often overemphasize print, so journalists tend to overemphasize personal contacts to the outright neglect of print sources. Each can learn from the other.

Contrary to widespread assumption, it does not take special training or credentials to do research by telephone or interview. (Internet contacts will be discussed below.) Indeed, there is a notable research company in Washington, D.C., that has charged its clients more than $75 per hour to find information on anything from the market for golf carts in the United States, to eggplants, to abrasives, to the marketability of rubber-soled shoes in Eastern Europe—and without its researchers having any more background in these areas *than you do right now*. The president of the company has said:

> The information [that clients want] is usually somewhere in the federal government. The problem most people have is that they don't know how to find it. They make 10 calls, get transferred around and still don't get the right person. So they get frustrated and give up. . . .
>
> We have a former French pastry chef and an ex-seminarian. We look for people who make others want to talk to them and aren't intimidated by getting into a new topic every day.
>
> Sometimes you're better off if you're not a hotshot specialist. Then it's easy to know how hard it might be to find something. Ignorance is bliss in a lot of research projects.[1]

The fact that people without "credentials" can charge more than $75 per hour for making telephone calls points up two very important things: The technique of talking to people *does* produce good results, no matter what the subject; and *anyone can do it,* including *you*.

The key factors for success are not experience and credentials but rather your attitudes and assumptions. All you have to do is start somewhere, then follow through in asking questions. In other words, just jump in and do it. *It's okay.* The main stumbling block most researchers have is their own inhibiting belief that people will not respond. But most interviewees are flattered that you would consider them knowledgeable in some area, and they will usually respond helpfully. Experience will show you that the odds are in your favor—telephone or other contacts will usually be friendly, and people will sometimes volunteer much more information than you originally request.

If you start with *any* negative assumption, you will be defeating yourself before you begin. If the reasons for not making a phone call seem stronger than the reasons to go ahead and do it, then you're dooming yourself to failure. Most of these "reasons" will only be rationalizations to justify your own unwarranted shyness. Your attitude should be, simply, "What have I got to lose?" The answer is "Nothing"—or, at worst, a few dollars for a long-distance call; and frequently you'll spend much more than that on amusements that are much less important to your happiness than good information.

I've known researchers who use fictional heroes to good effect. When confronted with a puzzle, they would ask themselves, "What would [Sherlock Holmes, Perry Mason, Nancy Drew, V. I. Warshawsky, Miss Marple] do in this situation?" The detectives we admire so much in novels are not limited by print or Internet sources in solving their mysteries; neither should we be in solving ours!

The results are likely to repay you amply in time saved on complicated library searches. For example, one researcher who needed to find the address of a company in Japan couldn't find it in any of the library directories, so he just called the Japanese embassy and got the information from a staff member. Another student looking for information on the little-known winner of the Nobel Peace Prize, Adolfo Pérez Esquivel, could find nothing on him in library resources at the time he won the prize; but calls to Amnesty International and the Washington Office on Latin America turned up whole files of information.

Talking to people can provide you with a quick overview of a whole field; it can give you not only the answer to a question but also the larger context in which the question should be asked. For example, someone who was looking for information on the U.S. market for padlocks imported from India first did considerable library research; but only in talking to knowledgeable people in the field did he really get oriented. He was told that there are six different grades of padlocks, which have different markets; that it's best to concentrate on small areas, as data on large areas are unreliable; that there were forthcoming national standards for padlocks, which imported items might have to meet in another year or two; that he should first have the locks tested for quality (using current military specifications as interim standards, if applicable to the grade of item being imported) and to have a written contract that all other locks will be comparable, before paying for any; that he should incorporate to prevent personal bankruptcy in case a class action suit should result from the sale of a defective lock; that he must consider not only the price of the items but also the import duty and shipping charges; and that big chain stores will certainly be able to buy more cheaply than he, so his best bet is to market through independent "Mom and Pop"-type hardware stores.

The experts that this researcher talked to not only provided him with answers, they also alerted him to *whole new areas of questions* he had to consider, none of which he had thought of on his own. It's often impossible to get this kind of corrective feedback from printed sources, as they allow no interaction with the readers, nor can they be modified on the spot to accommodate slightly different inquiries. For this kind of thing you just have to talk to someone. (Note that even letter writing or e-mail is a poor substitute for a telephone call, although it's a good complement or means of follow-up.)

Some recalcitrant souls will undoubtedly still be intimidated by their lack of "credentials," even though lack of training is irrelevant to their success. For academics, it is hoped that the obvious will allay their fears: they already have research credentials precisely because of their university affiliation. The best way to start off a telephone conversation with a potential source is to mention this right up front: "I'm a student/grad student at _____ University, and I'm not sure whom I should talk to—maybe you could help, or direct me to the right person. I'm trying to find information on . . ."

Those who don't have any affiliation can do just as well.[2] In obtaining information from people, the "secret" that is so hard for so many people to believe is precisely this: *There is no secret. Just make the call anyway and be perfectly honest about your reasons. It's okay to ask for help. The odds are that you'll succeed if you are simply persistent in developing a chain of referrals.*

An easy way to circumvent the shyness factor in contacting other people is to use Internet listservs. A good way to identify which groups exist in which subject areas is to use the NetFirst database in the OCLC First-Search system. For example, I once needed to find out if the U.S. Army had ever used the phrase "Certified Disability Discharge" in reference to veterans' status. I could not find this exact phrase in printed sources, but upon discovering a veterans' information homepage through NetFirst, I sent the question to the group's e-mail address. The experts on the other end found some knowledgeable "old-timers" to talk to who clarified the use of the term.

As wonderful as Internet sites are, it is best not to be naive in using them. For example, one student sent a request to a Shakespeare discussion group, asking for the source of quotes such as "Alas, poor Yorick" and "Double, double toil and trouble"—and he even gave the list members a deadline! Needless to say, such an inquiry evoked several responses that can only be deemed less than charitable. Keep in mind that, while the enthusiasts who populate the various discussion groups are generally very helpful, they are often not kindly disposed toward questions creating an appearance that a student is simply trying to circumvent the work of real engagement with the subject of their list.

What is even more important to remember is that not every expert is available to begin with on the Internet—there are millions of knowledgeable people in different subject areas who simply do not participate in online listservs or discussion groups in their subject areas. (This may seem like common sense—but the view from a reference desk is that researchers often overlook it.) And even those who do participate will not choose to respond to every inquiry that gets tossed into their pool. (Most of these people have actual *lives*.) In other words, there is a vast ocean of experts who still can be reached only via telephone.

When using the phone, a few things must be kept in mind to make your calls more productive. First, if the nature of your inquiry is particularly complex, do a little homework first. At least talk to the reference librarians of your local library to see if they can suggest some background reading or orientation. An expert will be more helpful if you convey the impression that you've already done some work on your own and are willing to do more—and that you're not simply dumping the whole problem into his or her lap to solve for you. (This applies to Internet inquiries as well as to phone calls.)

Second, explain the purpose of your research—that is, what you're *ultimately* trying to do and what you will use the information for (e.g., personal curiosity, publication, broadcast, etc.). Be open and honest about it.

Third, try to be as specific as you can. If you ask specific questions, you're likely to get on-target answers; but if you ask only vague, general questions, you're likely to get only vague, general answers.

Fourth, respect the expert's intellectual property rights. Don't simply "milk" a person for information and then pass it off as your own—be careful not to infringe on your source's own potential use of the information. People who burn their sources in this way not only ruin their own chances for follow-up contacts, they also make the sources hesitant about helping other researchers. Anyone who uses "the network" has a responsibility to leave it in good or better shape for the next person.

Fifth, when you talk to people about a subject you're not familiar with, it is very important to ask for more contacts. Few researchers will rely exclusively on one printed source; it is similarly unwise to rely on only one spoken (or e-mailed) viewpoint. People's memories of events, and opinions, tend to be self-serving; it is therefore advisable to seek a balance of perspectives. (A related problem in some inquiries is that of "shrinkage of testimony." Private investigators and journalists frequently run into this. Sometimes a source will be very garrulous and free with statements when you first talk to him; but if he is later subject to cross-examination by an unsympathetic interrogator, or if he comes to realize that he will somehow be held accountable for his opinions, he may have much less to say. This points up one advantage of a printed source: It will be the same no matter how often you refer to it. There is also, of course, a corresponding disadvantage: The situation may have changed dramatically since the words were printed.)

And sixth, after you have talked to someone who has been helpful— especially if the person has gone out of his or her way for you—it is very important to write a thank-you note. There are several reasons for this:

- Above all, if a person has helped you it is simply appropriate to show your gratitude.
- A written record of your interest in a subject will enable your source to remember you, and to use *you* as a possible future source of information on your shared area of interest. This is how mutually beneficial contact networks are built up.
- You will frequently find that days later, when you are finally writing your report, new questions will occur to you that you did not think to ask the first time. When you call your source again for clarification, he will be more responsive if he's already received a good thank you in writing, for such notes are useful to him in very concrete ways. They provide proofs of good job performance he can readily refer to for justifying raises, program extensions, and so on.
- The *lack* of a thank-you note can positively hurt you when you want to use a source again. This writer is aware of more than one instance in which contacts who had no obligation to help researchers nevertheless went out of their way to provide information—sometimes a great deal of it—and never received any thanks for their efforts. The result was that, in each case, the contacts "dried up" when the same people sought them again for more information.

When you are paying someone to help you, you can call that person at any time. But when you are getting information for free, you must at all costs avoid the appearance of being thankless or pushy. It is therefore advisable to consider the sending of timely thank-you notes not simply as a nice thing to do, but rather as *an integral part of the research process*. If you haven't put a word of thanks *in writing,* you have not finished your contact with that source.

The problem remains, then, that even if you do want to talk to someone who knows about your subject, how do you find that person? Where do you start? If your own circle of acquaintances doesn't get you far enough, many sources will be useful, among them the following:

Encyclopedia of Associations   (Gale Research), annual. Associations, professional societies, and nonprofit organizations are excellent switchboards for connecting researchers with highly qualified sources. Indeed, the very purpose of most societies is to study and disseminate information or interpretations of particular subjects, so they will welcome inquiries that enable them to tell you more about themselves and their areas of interest. The annual *Encyclopedia*, from Gale Research, is the best list there is of such groups; it describes more than 23,000 nonprofit American membership organizations of national scope. Additional volumes cover international associations and those that are of local or regional interest. Each entry provides the address, telephone number, and name of the organization's chief official, plus a detailed description of the society's area of interest and purpose. There is also information on the society's publications, and dates and city locations of upcoming conventions. The volumes have comprehensive indexes by keywords and by geographic areas.

There is a society for everything under the sun. The following brief list gives only the slightest hint of the range and diversity of such groups:

American Accordionists' Association
American Society of Abdominal Surgeons
Baker Street Irregulars [Sherlock Holmes buffs]
Bald-Headed Men of America
Brotherhood of Knights of the Black Pudding Tasters
Carbonated Beverage Institute
International Chinese Snuff Bottle Society
Dance [more than 250 organizations]
Antique Doorknob Collectors of America
Estonian Educational Society
National Association of Franchise Companies
Frog Pond Frog Collectors Club
Gemological Institute of America
Association for Gravestone Studies
Great Books Foundation
Society for Austrian and Habsburg History
Society for Siberian Irises
Brewster Society [collectors of kaleidoscopes]
Milton Society of America
American Kitefliers Association
Federation of Historical Bottle Collectors

Life Insurances [more than two dozen groups]
Manuscript Society
American Medical Informatics Association
International Nanny Association
National Conference of Tuberculosis Secretaries
Institute of Outdoor Drama
American Frozen Food Institute
National Quartz Producers Council
National Ice Cream and Yogurt Retailers Association
National Schizophrenia Fellowship
Tapes for the Blind
American Institute of Ultrasound in Medicine
Veterinary Medicine [more than 150 societies]
Western Building Material Association
Stuntwomen's Association of Motion Pictures
Women Executives in Public Relations
American Registry of Radiologic Technologists
Young and the Restless Fan Club
American Association of Zoo Keepers

The *Encyclopedia of Associations* is a publication everyone should browse through; it's of interest not only for research but also for finding people who have the same hobby as you. (An additional useful volume that explains in detail how associations can help you is Charles S. Mack's *The Executive's Handbook of Trade and Business Associations: How They Work, and How to Make Them Work Effectively for You* [New York: Quorum Books, 1991].) There is also another annual set from Gale Research, the *Encyclopedia of Associations: International Organizations*. Two volumes from CBD Research Ltd. round out the list, the bienniel *Directory of British Associations* and the *Directory of European Professional and Learned Societies*.

Internet sources. These can be identified through the NetFirst database in the OCLC FirstSearch system, or through the various site directories and search engines on the Net itself. Good printed sources are the *Cyber-Hound's Guide to Internet Discussion Groups*, *CyberHound's Guide to*

Associations and Nonprofit Organizations on the Internet, and *Cyber-Hound's Guide to People on the Internet* (all from Gale Research). Print directories in this area tend to become dated rather quickly; nonetheless, their format allows a kind of "overview" scanning or browsing capability that is impossible to match on computer screen displays.

Yellow pages.   This incredible subject directory of the resources in your own area is one of the best starting points for handling many questions, yet it is often overlooked by those who think research can be done only in libraries or by computer. An added feature is a detailed subject index, which is the necessary key to the controlled-vocabulary subject headings used in the book. Remember, too, that your local library may have a set of yellow pages for other cities throughout the country—and may even have them in a computer database format. The OCLC FirstSearch System offers one database called Pro CD Biz that is, in effect, a national yellow pages listing of businesses, and another, Pro CD Home, that is a single white pages listing of all individual names from phone books across the country. There are also many free national phone directories of both residential and commerical listings on the World Wide Web; the various site directories and search engines usually offer you a "people finder" or "business" menu option that will lead to them. A good initial point of access to three major people-finder databases is *META-SITE* at <www.555-1212.com>. Gale Research also publishes two annual guides, *CyberHound's Guide to Companies on the Internet* and *CyberHound's Guide to People on the Internet*.

Directories in Print (Gale), annual.   This is a listing of more than 15,000 directories published in the United States, the United Kingdom, Canada, and Australia. It is arranged in 26 broad subject categories and has detailed subject and keyword indexes. Price and ordering information are included for each entry. Just as there is an organization for everything under the sun, so, too, there is a directory of contacts on any subject. The following is a sampling of the directories available:

Adventure Travel
National Directory of Adult Day Care Centers

Official ABMS Directory of Board Certified Medical Specialists
    (American Board of Medical Specialties)
Earthworm Buyer's Guide
Frog Collectors Club Members' Listing
Directory of Conventions
Minority Organizations: A National Directory
National Catalog of Occult Bookstores
Crematories Directory
Opportunities for Study in Hand Bookbinding and Calligraphy
International Directory of Published Market Research
British Performing Arts Yearbook
Meyer's Directory of Genealogical Societies in the U.S.A. and Canada
Directory of Historical Organizations in the United States and Canada
Mail Order Business Directory
Golf Course Guide to Britain and Ireland
Auto Museums Directory
Seasonal Employment (National Park Service)
Museums of Florence
Grants and Fellowships of Interest to Historians

Directories in Print also lists local directories for specific areas under
names of countries, regions, states, and cities in its subject index.

Current British Directories (CBD Research Ltd.), irregular.   This lists
4,000 publications, with indexes by publisher and subject.

Washington Information Directory (Congressional Quarterly), annual.
This is a subject guide to agencies in the executive branch, to Congress and
its committees and subcommittees, and to private and nongovernmental
organizations in the Washington, D.C., area. It describes each organization,
gives a summary of its area of interest, and provides specific phone numbers and addresses. Chapters include sources in eighteen broad categories:

    Communications and the Media
    Economics and Business
    Education and Culture
    Employment and Labor

Energy
Advocacy and Public Service
Government Personnel and Services
Health
Housing and Urban Affairs
Social Services and Veterans' Programs
International Affairs
Law and Justice
National Security
Agriculture
Environment and Natural Resources
Science and Space
Transportation
Congress and Politics

Each chapter has further subdivisions, and there is a detailed index to the whole volume.

The value of having this information network at your call (and it *is* available to anyone) is incalculable. The federal government is an especially good place to begin looking for subject experts, as it employs thousands in midlevel positions. These people spend their careers keeping abreast of information in limited areas, and all of these subject specialists can be reached by phone. (Note that you should first seek the specialists themselves in the department or agency—not the librarians in the agency's library.) They are quite helpful—and, in fact, *you* are helpful to *them,* since in answering inquiries from the public they justify their jobs, programs, and salaries. These are important considerations in an era of downsizing. They can also refer you to excellent private and nongovernmental contacts. The researcher mentioned above who was working on padlocks started out with the *Washington Information Directory* and then just followed a chain of referrals from the Commerce Department to various private sources.

Carroll Publishing Company directories.   There are a number of these: *Federal Executive Directory, Federal Regional Executive Directory, State Executive Directory, Municipal Executive Directory,* and *County Executive Directory.*

Monitor Publishing Company *Yellow Book* directories.   These include such titles as: *Federal Yellow Book, Federal Regional Yellow Book, Congressional Yellow Book, State Yellow Book, Municipal Yellow Book, News Media Yellow Book, Corporate Yellow Book, Associations Yellow Book.*

Authors of books or articles you've already read.   Writers who have published something on a particular subject usually keep up-to-date on new developments in the field. Such people can be located through various directories available in libraries and through publishers' offices. The various ISI indexes to scholarly journals discussed above (Chapters 5 through 7) are particularly useful in this regard; they will give you the institutional address of the authors of the journal articles they index.

Faculty of local universities.   The professors at institutions of higher learning are experts on an astonishing variety of topics, and most maintain regular office hours in which they are available for consultation or simply "chewing the fat." An advantage to researchers here is that there is no problem in getting past secretaries during these office hours—the scholars are there to be available to all comers.

These resources should be more than adequate for leading you to knowledgeable people in any field. Two additional sources with useful "how-to" tips are John Brady's *The Craft of Interviewing* (New York: Vintage Books, 1976) and Senator William S. Cohen and Kenneth Larson's *Getting the Most Out Of Washington* (New York: Facts On File, 1982). The latter describes, through many detailed case studies, what a member of Congress's office can do to pull strings for you.

A further word of advice has to do specifically with talking to reference librarians. Just as it is useful to match your book-retrieval techniques to the library's storage techniques, so it is often advisable to match the way you ask questions to the way librarians think (and any group that can hide books on "Moonshining" under "Distilling, Illicit" obviously doesn't think like most people).

Actually, it is the librarian's professional responsibility to find out what you're ultimately looking for—which may not be what you request initially—through a reference interview; so if you wind up being directed to an inappropriate source it may be more the librarian's fault than your own. Still, whatever the reason for any misdirection, you will nevertheless want to avoid it; and if you can make the librarian's job a little easier by knowing the sort of information he or she is listening for, then you will be the one to benefit. Going with the grain is more efficient than going against it.

Three examples of what to be aware of:

- A woman asked a librarian, "Where are your books on nineteenth-century English history?" The reference interview, however, elicited the fact that what she really wanted was, specifically, biographical information about her ancestor Samuel Earnshaw. Once this had been determined, the librarian could refer her directly to the multi-volume set *Modern English Biography,* which contained the necessary information. (*Biography and Genealogy Master Index* also provided other sources.) Had the librarian simply directed her to the library's bookstacks on nineteenth-century English history, the woman would have wasted much time.
- Another woman asked a graduate library assistant, "Where is *Chemical Abstracts*?" Further questioning could not elicit her ultimate aim, so she was indeed referred to *CA*. After about an hour, however, she came back and the assistant asked if she'd found what she needed. She had not. "What I'm really trying to find," she added, "is information on the side effects of Valium." Once the graduate student knew this, she could refer her directly to the *Physician's Desk Reference* manual, which the woman had never heard of.
- A student asked a reference librarian, "Where are your books on English literature?" After some discussion the librarian finally determined that he specifically wanted critical articles on Sir Walter Scott's *Heart of Midlothian*. The student could then be referred to *English Novel Explication: Criticism to 1972* (among other sources), which list such criticisms. Had the librarian simply referred him to the PR (English literature) section of the classified bookstacks, the student would have wasted a lot of time there and still would not have found what he needed. (Journal articles are difficult to find through browsing.)

In each of these cases—and librarians could cite thousands more—the inquirers asked *not for what they really wanted but for what they thought the library could provide*. The problem is that most people have grossly inadequate assumptions about what can or cannot be found in a library. Others tend to think that the few resources or databases they've heard about are the only or the best ones that exist. *They are usually wrong.*

Frequently, professors and graduate students are more inefficient than anyone else. This hearkens back to a point made earlier, that a large number of them have never critically challenged the dictum passed on to generation after generation of graduate students all over the country: "You shouldn't have to ask a librarian for help; if you can't find it on your own, you're no scholar." Researchers who have more common sense will not thus cut themselves off from a major source of help. The "find it on your own" imperative not only prevents scholars from asking for help, it also encourages them to settle for whatever they do find on their own, even when it's not exactly what they want. Even worse, when scholars can't think of a likely source offhand, this mentality encourages them to give up searching in the first place and to pretend that they don't really need what they think they can't get. Or just as bad—and this is a relatively new development—it encourages them to put inordinate trust in computer or Internet searches, which they wrongly assume will cover "everything."

That dictum is bad advice. Phrased positively, however—and understood positively—it is good advice: "The more you understand about library sources and systems, the better the scholar you will be." To the extent that you learn the range and depth of what you can expect from a library, you will allow yourself to ask more questions—and especially specific questions—you might otherwise think could not be answered efficiently. You will then find yourself asking, "Where can I find biographical information on my ancestor Samuel Earnshaw, who lived in nineteenth-century England?" rather than "Where are your books on nineteenth-century English history?" You will ask, "Where can I find information on the side effects of Valium?" rather than "Where is *Chemical Abstracts*?" You will inquire, "Where can I find criticisms of Scott's *Heart of Midlothian*?" rather than "Where are your books on English literature?"

What is most useful to a reference librarian is to know what you are *ultimately* trying to find. A good way to clarify your thoughts on this is to ask yourself, "If there were an absolutely perfect article on my subject, what would the title of that article be?"

In going *outside* the library to talk to people, however, you will need some good directories, and therefore your library should have an up-to-date shelf of them. (A good rule of thumb is that 30% of the entries in any directory of personal names changes from one year to the next, so a directory more than a few years old is not very trustworthy. A directory of institutions, however, may be good for much longer.)

The rule to remember in all of this is that somewhere along the line in your research you should ask yourself, "Who would be likely to know about this subject? Whose *business* is it to know? In whose *interest* would it be?" These questions, plus a browsing familiarity with the resources listed above, can get you started on some very valuable pathways, and lead you to important information that is not recorded in any print source.

Notes

1. Leila Kight, quoted in the *Washington Post* (Apr. 15, 1980), p. B5.
2. Unaffiliated scholars will find Ronald Gross's *The Independent Scholar's Handbook* (Berkeley, Calif.: Ten Speed Press, 1993) very useful.

15

Hidden Treasures

Four types of library holdings contain an incredible wealth of information in all subject areas, but are so neglected by most conventional indexes and databases that they are virtually unknown to most researchers. Discovering any one of them, however, can provide you with the reader's equivalent of tapping into Alaska's north shore oil reserves. The four are microform sets, CD-ROM collections, government documents, and special collections. These materials have several points in common:

- In addition to being neglected by most library catalogs, indexes, and databases, they are usually housed in quarters that are physically separate from a library's general collections.
- They are not shelved or "displayed" in a way that allows efficient subject access through browsing or scanning.
- They are each accessible only through a variety of special indexes, not through a single convenient source; and the identification of the best indexes may be a separate treasure hunt in itself.

It takes extra steps to get into these materials, in other words, and few people bother because to those lacking prior experience in these areas the paths are very obscure and the destination isn't foreseeable. Those who have enough faith to venture off the beaten track, however, are usually well rewarded. But you simply have to suspect in advance that microform sets, CD-ROM collections, government documents, and special collections will indeed yield remarkable results, and then actively look for them—for you cannot expect the normal channels of research to turn up adequate references to them. And in seeking these materials it is especially important to ask for help, for frequently the best initial access is through the experienced custodian's knowledge of what is likely to be found in the collections.

The ways to identify special collections have been discussed in Chapter 13 and so will not be repeated here.

Microform Sets

Many researchers are initially deterred from using microforms by the mistaken assumption that they cannot make quick photocopies on paper from such formats. But the truth is that such copies can be made very easily and that any library with microfilm or microfiche holdings will also have reader-printers immediately adjacent to them.

There are hundreds of large, prepackaged research collections in a bewildering variety of subject areas, and there is likely to be one or more of interest to any scholar. A good starting point for microforms is Suzanne Dodson's *Microform Research Collections: A Guide* (Meckler Publishing, 1984). It lists many of the major sets and describes them in detail; it also has a good subject index. Also useful is the annual *Subject Guide to Microforms in Print*, which lists collections, individual publications, and serials but does not describe or annotate them. You also want to simply ask the reference librarians if the library has a collection relevant to your topic. Another good source that lists and describes more than 800 microform sets is Patrick Frazier's *A Guide to the Microform Collections in the Humanities and Social Sciences Division of the Library of Congress* (Library of Congress, 1996), which is available on the Web at <gopher://marvel.loc.gov/11/research/collections.catalogs/collections/micro>. Most of these collections are commercially available sets that are duplicated in many other research libraries.

Once you've determined which collections exist, if your own library doesn't own them, then you have to find out which library does. The best way to check in your local area is through a few phone calls; or in some areas there may be a local union list of microform holdings. Nationally, the OCLC and RLIN networks may be of use; if you search under the title of a collection and find a record with the word "microform" added to the title, then that record will give you locations of the actual film or fiche sets, not just of the printed guide. (Libraries sometimes collect the guides without buying the microfilm.)

The range and variety of the sets that exist can be suggested by a brief listing of some of their titles.

African Library
American Architectural Books
American Natural History
American Fiction, 1774–1900; 1901–1910
American Periodical Literature, 1741–1900
American Poetry, 1609–1900
Archives of the Soviet Communist Party and Soviet State
Black Biographical Dictionaries, 1790–1950
Botany Library on Microfiche
British and Continental Rhetoric and Elocution
Civil War Unit Histories
City Directories of the United States [1786–1901]
Crime and Juvenile Delinquency
Early American Imprints, 1639–1800; 1801–1819
Early English Books, 1475–1640; 1641–1700
Eighteenth Century Collection
French Revolution: Critical Works and Historical Sources
Goldsmiths'-Kress Library of Economic Literature
Herstory
History of Medicine
History of Photography
History of Women
Human Relations Area Files
Human Rights Documents
Indians of North America
Kentucky Culture
Landmarks of Science
Labor Union Periodicals
Microbook *Library of American Civilization*
Musicache

The Negro: Emancipation to World War I
Records of Ante-Bellum Southern Plantations
Reports of Explorations in the Documents of the United States
     Government
Russian Revolutionary Literature
Slavery: Source Materials and Critical Literature
Sources Materials in the Field of Theatre
Southern Women and Their Families in the 19th Century: Papers and
     Diaries
Spanish Drama of the Golden Age
Travels in the Confederate States
Travels in the Old South I, II, III
Travels in the West and Southwest
Underground Press Collection
Western Americana
Witchcraft in Europe and America

Each of these sets may contain hundreds or thousands of publications. And there are many other collections; especially noteworthy are the complete sets of books published within various countries up to a certain date; the various exhaustive collections of literature, drama, or poetry for particular countries; and many collections of national and international government publications. A closer look at three of the above sets will give some indication of the riches that are covered.

Goldsmiths'-Kress Library of Economic Literature. This is a huge collection of 4,267 reels of microfilm containing 62,345 titles of monographs and serials: books published between 1460 and 1850 and serial literature (466 titles) whose publication began prior to 1850. (Entire runs of serials are included even when they extend well after 1850.) The material is in more than 10 European languages. The *Guide* to the set suggests its range:

> In addition to the standard, well-known works used in studying the history of economics and business, the microfilm library contains unusual and exceedingly rare items which offer unique possibilities for comparative and cross-cultural research in the history of economic thought. Moreover, the

collection is extremely rich in materials on political and social history in particular, and on history in general. Individual works are seldom confined to a single academic discipline, as the period antedates modern academic specialization. The micropublication thus constitutes a major research source for all social scientists and historians, as well as for economists.

Among the subjects covered are mercantilism, agriculture, emigration, European colonial expansion, slavery, demography in eighteenth-century England, the textile industry, socialism, trade unionism, piracy, dietary habits in various European countries, early business and technical education, commerce in Italy, penology, trade manuals, numismatics, the economy of eighteenth-century Scandinavia, Irish-English relations, social conditions, population, transport and transport technology, and even theology. The materials are in the range of European languages.

Human Relations Area Files.   This is a huge, ongoing collection of source materials (mainly published books and articles, although some unpublished manuscripts and reports of field research are included) for worldwide, comparative, cross-cultural study of human behavior and society as represented in more than 300 cultures. It is useful to students of anthropology, sociology, psychology, politics, literature, home economics, comparative religion, art, and agricultural development—and for anyone else who wishes to compare the perceptions, customs, social institutions, values, beliefs, and daily life of all peoples of the world, past and present. The microfiche source documents are arranged in more than 300 groups, each representing a different culture; and each culture is analyzed, insofar as the documentation permits, in more than 600 categories (e.g., mortality, recorded history, food production, architecture for various functions, humor, entertainment, trial procedures, recruitment of armed forces, old-age dependency, sexual practices and norms, views on abortion, drug use, division of labor by sex, sanitary facilities, power development, interpersonal relations, art, religion, political organization, etc.). Within each category is found, on microfiche, all relevant descriptive documentation drawn from more than 5,000 sources. (Foreign-language materials are translated into English.) The standardization of categories under each culture allows for ready comparisons of information, which in many cases can be statistically significant. The cultures are listed in the accompanying publication *Outline of World Cultures,* while the subdividing categories are listed in *Outline of Cultural Materials.* (A CD-ROM version of a portion of this set, covering 60 societies analyzed into about a dozen categories, is available under the title *Cross-Cultural CD.*)

Microbook *Library of American Civilization.* According to the guidebook that accompanies this set,

> it contains more than 6,500,000 pages of materials relating to all aspects of American life and literature, from the beginning to the outbreak of World War I. Included are pamphlets, periodicals, documents both public and private, biographies and autobiographies of persons both known and obscure, fiction and nonfiction, poetry, collected works and papers, material of foreign origin relating to America, and many rare books not generally available.

It is essentially a full historical library of approximately 10,000 books in a filing cabinet, covering early exploration, colonial history and records, politics and government, military history, foreign policy, constitutional history, law and law enforcement, the frontier, the South, local history, Indians and other minorities, agriculture, the city, business, labor, religion, education, reform, intellectual history, science and technology, literature, the various useful and performing arts, architecture, manners and customs, and so on. There are separate author, title, and subject index volumes.

Most of the other microform sets are equally amazing. Two important points to remember, however, are:

1. In most cases *none* of the individual items within a collection will be separately listed in your library's computer (or card) catalog. The only indication in the catalog will be a record of the printed *Guide* that accompanies the set and lists its contents; it will usually be found under the heading "[Subject]—Bibliography." If you miss this one entry, you will in effect miss all of the possibly thousands of relevant sources in the collection.
2. Some of the individual microform works within collections are recorded as such in the OCLC and RLIN systems; in other words, if

you find a record that says the work you want is available within a microform collection, check your local libraries to see if they own that collection.

One microform set that is not listed in Dodson's *Guide* but that should be of interest to any serious researcher is the aggregate of more than 1 million American doctoral dissertations available for purchase from University Microfilms International. The only library in the country that owns all of them is the Library of Congress; individual titles, however, can be ordered from UMI. A CD-ROM index, *Dissertation Abstracts,* provides keyword access to bibliographic citations and abstracts—but not to the full texts of the dissertations themselves. (Note that abstracts are searchable only from mid-1980 forward; prior to that date, the CD contains only citations without abstracts.) These studies provide a staggering array of knowledge in all areas of inquiry, and they also usually contain excellent bibliographies. (There is also a version of *Dissertation Abstracts* available online through OCLC FirstSearch.)

Another equally amazing set not in Dodson's *Guide* is the collection of National Technical Information Service (NTIS) reports. Again, the Library of Congress is the only facility that owns all of them; however, individual titles may be ordered directly from NTIS (see below, in the Government Documents section).

CD-ROM Collections

Many CD-ROMs are now available that contain entire research collections much like their microform counterparts; the advantage of the CD format is that it enables you to do keyword searching for virtually any significant word anywhere within any of the full-text documents on the disc. A good overview is Pat Ensor's *CD-ROM Research Collections: An Evaluative Guide to Bibliographic and Full-Text CD-ROM Databases* (Meckler, 1991). Also useful are Barbara Sorrow and Betty S. Lumpkin's *CD-ROM for Librarians and Educators: A Guide to Over 800 Instructional Resources,* 2d ed. (McFarland, 1996); Patrick R. Dewey's *303 CD-ROMs to Use in Your Library* (American Library Association, 1996); and *CD-ROMs in Print* (Meckler, annual).

Among the CD collections that are available are the following:

African-American Poetry, 1760–1900
American Poetry Full-Text Database [seventeenth century to ca. 1920]
Corpus des Oeuvres de Philosophie en Langue Française sur CD-ROM
Current Biography on CD-ROM
EIU Country Reports on Disc
English Poetry Full-Text Database
English Verse Drama [1,500 works by more than 450 authors]
Library of the Future, 3d ed.
Patrologia Latina Database
SEC Online on SilverPlatter [company filings with the Securities and
    Exchange Commission]

A closer look at two of these titles will suggest some of their search capabilities:

Library of the Future, 3d edition.   This is a kind of "great books" library on a single disc; it includes the full texts of more than 3,500 individual literary works by more than 200 authors, including poems, plays, novels, and epics as well as classic works of history, philosophy, science, biography, and religion. For example, it includes Jane Austen's *Pride and Prejudice* and *Sense and Sensibility;* Cervantes' *Don Quixote;* five full novels of Dickens; the *Complete Sherlock Holmes;* four novels of Melville; six of Mark Twain; four of Jules Verne; all of Shakespeare; nonfiction works by Aristotle, St. Augustine, Confucius, Emerson, Freud, Herodotus, Lincoln, Locke, Machiavelli, Marx, Montaigne, and Rousseau; philosophical works by Bacon, Marcus Aurelius, Descartes, Nietzsche, and Plato; scores of children's classics; scores of classic plays; major epics (including Homer, *Beowulf,* and the *Nibelungenlied*). The entire collection is keyword searchable. (Note, however, that the individual editions that were keyed in are seldom identified; almost all of them are old, copyright-free versions—rather than the best available editions and translations that have been assembled in, for example, the second edition [1990] of the printed set *Great Books of the Western World* published by Encyclopaedia Britannica, Inc.)

Patrologia Latina Database. The original printed version of the *Patrologia Latina* is a 221-volume set of the works of the Latin Fathers from A.D. 200 through 1216; it includes works by Tertullian, Hilary, Ambrose, Jerome, Boethius, Bede, Augustine, and hundreds of others. The database makes all of these texts, as well as the prefatory material critical apparatus, and indexes, keyword searchable. Boolean combinations, adjacency and proximity searching, and both right- and left-side truncation are possible. Scholars of patristics, Latin, medieval history, theology, philosophy, and linguistics have an enormous amount of material available for study in ways that could never be done before.

As wonderful as these collections are, researchers need to be aware of a major problem with them: the likelihood of technological obsolescence. These sets are very expensive, and libraries wishing to purchase them are confronted with the prospect that the machines needed to read today's CD-ROMs may not be functioning in another generation. Undoubtedly there will be future generations of CD machines that are even more sophisticated than those available now; and the discs that can be read on today's machines will not be readable on tomorrow's. With the inevitable changes in computer technology, libraries will be confronted by the very expensive prospect of having to convert existing CDs to new formats—or, more likely, of having to buy the same collections again in the new formats. Either way, they will in effect have to pay all over again for continued access to information they "already" own. Given that most libraries are chronically underfunded—a reality that is never likely to change substantially—CD-format collections are not as attractive in the long run as microfilm or microfiche sets. The latter involve a very simple magnification technology that is much less expensive to maintain and that will never become obsolete. And so libraries are justifiably reluctant to invest too much money on short-lived CD-ROM sets.

Government Documents

The term "document" is synonymous with "publication"; it can refer to just about any form, including monographs, magazines, reports, pamphlets, broadsides, maps, prints, photographs, posters, kits, CD-ROMs, and so on. Also included in government documents are many finding aids and reference sources such as catalogs, indexes, directories, dictionaries, and bibliographies.

The U.S. federal government—with whose publications this section is concerned—also produces films, sound recordings, audiovisuals, and microforms.

The range, variety, and depth of coverage of these materials are amazing. They are particularly thorough in scientific and technical areas, and in all the social sciences; but there are surprising contributions to the humanities as well (e.g., from the Smithsonian Institution, the Library of Congress, and the National Endowment for the Humanities). In using government documents, you can ask almost the same questions—and expect to find answers—as you can in using the more well-known research tools.

Since it is impossible to speak systematically of the range of these materials, let me offer a menu of titles, simply to suggest some of the possibilities available:

Camper's First Aid
Miro: Selected Paintings
Franchise Opportunities Handbook
Health Information for International Travel
Cruise Ships Health and Safety
Health and Safety of Professional Boxing
Poisonous Snakes of the World
Where to Write for Vital Records
The African American Mosaic: A Library of Congress Resource Guide for the Study of Black History and Culture
Library of Congress European Collections
Library of Congress Music, Theater, Dance: An Illustrated Guide
The Tradition of Science: Landmarks of Western Science in the Collections of the Library of Congress
The Tradition of Technology: Landmarks of Western Technology in the Collections of the Library of Congress
Cataloging and Classification Quality at the Library of Congress
Doing Research at the Library of Congress: A Guide to Subject Searching in a Closed Stacks Library

Environmental Planning for Small Communities: A Guide for Local Decision-Makers

Polish Genealogy and Heraldry

Preparing Your Child for College: A Resource Book for Parents

Guide to Federal Government Sales

Falconry

How to Buy Surplus Property from the Department of Defense

How to Sell to Government Agencies

Selling to the Military

Backyard Bird Problems

Basic Electricity

Family Therapy: A Summary of Selected Literature

The Education System of Switzerland

Midlife Women: Policy Proposals for Their Problems

Occupational Outlook Handbook

How Basic Research Reaps Unexpected Rewards

Marijuana: A Study of State Policies and Penalties

Handbook of North American Indians

Beekeeping in the United States

Growing Vegetables in the Home Garden

Sex and the Spinal Cord Injured

Annotated Bibliography and Subject Index on the Shortnose Sturgeon, Acipenser Brevirestrum

Solar Hot Water Handbook

Delightful Places: A Book Tour of English Country Houses and Gardens

Great Houses and Their Treasures: A Bibliographic Guide

Guide to High Speed Patrol Car Tires

The Murals of Harold Weston

The Effects of Nuclear War

Photographer's Mate [training manual]

Journalist [training manual]

Low-Cost Wood Homes for Rural America: Construction Manual

Building the Solar Home

A Descriptive List of Treasure Maps and Charts in the Library of Congress

Nutritive Value of Foods

The Calibration of a Burn Room for Fire Tests on Furnishings

Cantonese: Basic Course [also similar books for French, German, Spanish, Swahili, Hebrew, Greek, Sinhala, etc.]

Diplomatic Hebrew

What You Should Know About Smoke Detectors

Survival, Evasion, and Escape

Drug Paraphernalia

Project MKUltra: the CIA's Program of Research in Behavior Modification

Economic Problems of Rural America

Radiologic Technology

A Barefoot Doctor's Manual

Fundamentals of COBOL: Programmer's Reference

A Study of Lumber Used for Bracing Trenches in the United States

Harpsichords and Clavichords

Wildlife Portrait Series

The Ship's Medicine Chest and Medical Aid at Sea

The Star of Bethlehem [LC bibliography]

A Reader's Guide for Parents of Children with Mental, Physical, or Emotional Disabilities

Children's Literature: A Guide to Reference Sources

Occupational Diseases: A Guide to Their Recognition

The Back-Yard Mechanic

The Translation of Poetry

The Social and Economic Status of the Black Population in the U.S.: An Historical View, 1790–1978

Family Folklore: Interviewing Guide and Questionnaire

Homebuyer's Information Package: A Guidebook for Buying and Owning a Home

Angler's Guide to the United States Atlantic Coast [also *Pacific Coast* volume]

Marine Life Posters

Fifty Birds of Town and City

Ducks at a Distance: Waterfowl Identification Guide

Research on Sleep and Dreams

The Martian Landscape [with 3-D stereo viewer]
A Guide to the Study and Use of Military History
Literary Recordings: A Checklist of the Archives of Recorded Poetry
     and Literature in the Library of Congress
Catalog of Federal Domestic Assistance
Standard Industrial Classification Manual
A Study of Global Sand Seas
NOAA Diving Manual
Farm Structure: A Historical Perspective on Changes in the Number
     and Sizes of Farms
Small Business Location and Layout
Drug Themes in Science Fiction
Career Opportunities in Art Museums, Zoos, and Other Interesting
     Places
Crime Scene Search and Physical Evidence Handbook
Raising a Small Flock of Sheep
Defining Death: A Report on the Medical, Legal, and Ethical Issues in
     the Determination of Death
For Women: Managing Your Own Business
Fermentation Guide to Potatoes
The Bark Canoes and Skin Boats of North America
Books That Help Children Deal with a Hospital Experience
How to Buy a Christmas Tree
How Trees Help Clean the Air
Report of the Commission on Obscenity and Pornography
Chinese Herbal Medicine
The Hammered Dulcimer in America

Many of these publications are themselves but the tip of an iceberg—
whenever you find one document on a subject that interests you, you can
usually figure that there are many others waiting to be discovered (see
especially the *Subject Bibiographies* series, described below). The Government Printing Office has published more than 40,000 titles per year in
recent years.

   If you have not tried documents before, you almost have to make a leap
of faith to start looking for them; but it is probable that you will be pleas-

antly surprised. (And students who use documents will almost invariably find that none of their classmates has found the same sources.)

A number of reasons account for the general neglect of government publications by academic and other researchers; let me extend a few points made at the beginning of this chapter.

- Although the government spends millions of dollars a year to publish these materials, it spends very little to advertise or market them. Some enterprising private companies republish documents for a wider audience—which is perfectly allowable, since virtually nothing printed by the Government Printing Office is copyrighted—but such efforts pick up only a fraction of what is available.
- Libraries that own collections of government documents often shelve them separately rather than integrate them into the general collections. This is done because the best access to documents is provided by their own special indexes, which are keyed to Superintendent of Documents (SuDocs) call numbers rather than Library of Congress or Dewey Decimal numbers; and SuDocs numbers cannot be interfiled with such traditional shelf-arrangement schemes. The result is that you will not find documents through the two major avenues of subject access to the library's books—the computer (or card) catalog and shelf browsing. (And even in its own section a documents collection cannot be browsed very efficiently because the SuDocs scheme arranges items according to the agencies that produced them and *not* according to the *subjects* of the documents. This is the difference between an archival scheme of arrangement and a subject classification scheme.)
- Documents are not covered by the most commonly used databases, indexes, and catalogs.
- Documents are not sold in most bookstores, so even avid readers have little opportunity to become aware of their existence.
- Courses in government publications are not required in library schools. One result is that not all librarians are themselves aware of their potential. This is unfortunate for researchers, because you probably won't be referred to documents in the first place unless you chance upon someone with experience in using them.

There are two types of government documents collections: regional depositories and selective depositories. The regionals are required by law to receive and permanently retain copies of *all* federal documents available through the depository program. Selective depositories are just that—they can choose which categories of publications they wish to receive and can weed their collections. A directory of which depositories are in which cities—including where the regionals are—is available in any public library; the same information is available on the Web at <www.gpo.gov/su_docs/dpos/adpos002.html>.

Law school libraries are usually selective depositories, but they generally confine their selections to series of law-related materials and administrative decisions.

It is noteworthy for researchers that all depositories (including those at law schools) must admit the general public to their documents collections. The law that allows them to receive free federal publications carries the condition that access must be open to all; schools that permit only their own students to have access to the documents can lose their depository status. In other words, you can use the demand "I want to use your documents collection" to get in the door of law or medical libraries that are otherwise closed to you.

For those who wish to undertake systematic research in U.S. government documents there are a variety of indexes that have different strengths and weaknesses and must therefore be used in combination.

Monthly Catalog of U.S. Government Publications.   The *MoCat* is the basic "umbrella" index to government documents, excluding NTIS reports (for which, see below). It is intended to be a complete list, with cumulated annual indexes, to all federal publications. Currently, the paper-copy version allows access through LC subject headings, titles, title keywords, authors, and report/series numbers. Most people nowadays use a CD-ROM version called *GPO CAT* or the online version called *GPO* within the OCLC FirstSearch system. Both of these computer versions cover only from 1976 to date. For retrospective searches of earlier years you have to use printed formats. The best resource for this is a separate publication called *Cumulative Subject Index to the Monthly Catalog of United States*

Government Publications 1900–1971 (Carrollton Press, 1973–1975). There is also a *Cumulative Title Index to United States Public Documents 1789–1976* (U.S. Historical Documents Institute, 1971–79) and a *United States Government Publications Monthly Catalog: Cumulative Personal Author Index, 1941–1975* (Pierian Press, 1971–79). A cumulative approach through corporate author or agency name is provided by volumes 606–24 of the *National Union Catalog: Pre-1956 Imprints,* which has also been republished as a separate set. The OCLC and RLIN databases can also be useful, but they do not supersede these printed sources. Several other indexes and catalogs for historical approaches are ably discussed in Joe Morehead's *Introduction to United States Government Information Sources* (Libraries Unlimited), revised irregularly, which is the bible for documents researchers.

Publications Reference File (PRF). This is a Web database that is, in effect, the "Books in Print" list for Government Printing Office publications. It allows access to documents through titles, keywords, key phrases, series, personal authors, SuDocs numbers, and GPO stock numbers. Although not as extensive in its coverage as the *Monthly Catalog,* its listings are more current. The *PRF* is available on the Internet—searches are free—at <www.access.gpo.gov/su_docs/sale/prf/prf.html>.

CIS/Index (Washington, D.C.: Congressional Information Service, Inc., 1970–), monthly with annual and five-year cumulations. Also CD-ROM version, (*CIS 2,* 1970–). This is the most thorough index to all Congressional publications since 1970, including hearings, committee prints, and House and Senate reports and documents. It is especially useful because Congress has so many oversight interests and responsibilites that generate detailed studies; these investigations monitor all areas of U.S. society and world relations. Most people are aware, simply from newspaper coverage, of Congress's investigations of regulatory reform, military spending, Social Security problems, nuclear energy, and foreign policy, but the many hearings it conducts on smaller issues are underpublicized and underutilized. The value of hearings is that they usually assemble top experts and interested parties on all sides of an issue to testify on the current state of a problem and recommend specific courses of action. Often there is extensive documentary material appended. This kind of overview is not often available elsewhere. Some examples of hearings include:

Acid Rain
Assessing the Effects of Nasal Radium Treatments
*The Impact of HIV/AIDS on the Social and Economic Development in
     Africa*
Youth Violence and Gangs
Violence in Video Games
Rating Video Games: A Parent's Guide to Games
Exploitation of Young Adults in Door-to-Door Sales
Scientific Fraud
*Review of Production and Marketing Challenges Facing U.S. Fruit and
     Vegetable Industries*
Computer Viruses
Status of the African Elephant
Elephant, Rhino, and Tiger Conservation
Cranial Deformities: Giving Our Kids a Fighting Chance
The Role of Basic Research in Economic Competitiveness
Airworthiness of the DC-10
Life on Mars?
Preservation of Petroglyphs in Albuquerque, New Mexico
Competitiveness in the Glassware Industry
Telemarketing Practices
*Shaping Our Responses to Violent and Demeaning Imagery in Popular
     Music*
Innovation in Telemarketing Frauds and Scams
Medical and Psychological Impact of Abortion
*Hearing on the Rights of Artists and Scholars to Freedom of Expression
     and the Rights of Taxpayers to Determine the Use of Public Fund[s]*
Superconductivity
Asian Organized Crime
Samoan White-Collar Crime
Atlantic Swordfish Oversight
Mailing of Dangerous Martial Arts Weapons

Recent Trends in Dubious and Quack Medical Devices

Mass Mortality of Bottle-Nose Dolphins in 1987–88

Degradable Six-Pack Rings

Persecution of Albanian Minority in Yugoslavia

Cartoon All-Stars to the Rescue

The Beretta Pistol: Should it Be the Defense Department's Standard Handgun?

Public Safety Issues Surrounding Marijuana Production in National Forests

Organ Transplants, Choices and Criteria, Who Lives, Who Dies, Who Pays?

Global Change Research: The Role of Clouds in Climate Change

Babies and Briefcases: Creating a Family-Friendly Workplace for Fathers

Turn it Down: Effects of Noise on Hearing Loss in Children and Youth

New Research on the Potential Health Risks of Carpets

Racial Discrimination in Awarding Toyota Dealerships

Breastfeeding in the U.S.

Sleep Disorders

The Effects of Traffic Radar Guns on Law Enforcement Officers

Insurance Redlining Practices

Auto Repair Fraud

Parental Kidnapping

Sex and Violence on TV

Street People

Severe Storms Research

Effect of Pornography on Women and Children

As should be obvious, Congressional hearings provide rich materials for student term papers, and researchers who simply browse through the *CIS/Index* have an advantage in selecting topics that their classmates usually will overlook. Thousands of topics have been covered; a 1994 article notes that "over the past 16 years the House committees alone held a total of 54,034 hearings—about 20 each day the chamber was in session."[1]

Retrospective coverage of hearings from 1833 to 1969 is provided by the *CIS U.S. Congressional Committee Hearings Index;* of prints from

1830 to 1969, by the *CIS U.S. Congressional Committee Prints Index;* and of miscellaneous congressional reports and documents from 1789 to 1969, by the *CIS U.S. Serial Set Index.* (Coverage of all three from 1970 onward is provided by the basic *CIS/Index* or *CIS 2* CD-ROM.) All three of these pre-1970 paper copy indexes—along with additional coverage of older Congressional hearings and Executive branch documents and reports— have also been combined in a CD-ROM called *CIS 1.* Additional related print-format sets (each linked to a microfiche collection of documents) from the same publisher are the *CIS Unpublished U.S. Senate Hearings: Early 1800s through 1964*; the *CIS Index to U.S. Executive Branch Documents, 1789–1909; Reports Required by Congress; Congressional Member Organizations and Caucuses;* and *American Foreign Policy.*

Note that the various indexes to hearings provide not just subject access but also access by names of witnesses.

All of these various indexes are keyed to microfiche sets of the corresponding documents; when you use any of them, be sure to ask your librarian if the fiche is also available.

Committee prints are particularly noteworthy, as they are often in-depth studies commissioned by Congress to provide an overview and detailed analysis of particular subjects, many being written by the Congressional Research Service of the Library of Congress.

Most of the investigative and background reports written by the Congressional Research Service, however, are theoretically available only to members of Congress—or are available to the public only through requests directly to Congressional offices. Those picked up by the CIS indexes are only a minority of the ones actually written. But another publisher—University Publications of America—is acquiring and publishing on microfilm the majority of these CRS studies (see Chapter 8).

American Statistics Index, or ***ASI*** (Congressional Information Service, 1974–),   monthly with annual and five-year cumulations; also entirely on CD-ROM as part of *Statistical Masterfile.* Although it only began publication in 1974, the first volume of this index picks up statistics back to the early 1960s. Statistics are the backbone of documents research, and the federal government either counts everything imaginable itself or assembles figures from others who do. *ASI* provides detailed subject access to *every* statistical table, list, or publication produced by the government. Especially useful are its many category indexes (e.g., "By State," "By Industry," "By Occupation," "By Sex," etc.), which greatly facilitate finding comparative figures. Through the *ASI* you can find answers to such questions as "How much advertising do Chicago TV stations sell?"; "How much of the coal used in U.S. coke plants comes from Fayette County, Pa.?"; "How many children of unemployed parents are on welfare in California?"; "How much did the chemicals industry invest in pollution control equipment in New Jersey?"; and "How many people are killed each year in bombing incidents and what are the motives of such incidents?"[2] Almost any question that involves counting, pricing, or categorizing can be approached through this index.

CIS also produces two similar indexes: *Statistical Reference Index* (1980–) and *Index to International Statistics* (1983–). The first is a wide-ranging index to statistics produced by nonfederal U.S. agencies such as state and municipal governments, universities, trade and industry groups, think tanks, private pollster companies, and so on; the latter covers the statistical publications of approximately 100 international agencies, such as the United Nations system, the European Union, the Organization for Economic Cooperation and Development, the Organization of American States, and so on.

As with the *CIS/Index,* any library that owns the *ASI, SRI,* or *IIS* may also own a corresponding microfiche set that provides the full text of the documents indexed; but remember that none of the fiche will be recorded in the library's computer or card catalog. (*SRI* is especially useful to business researchers, as it often provides rankings of companies by name; and its fiche will also include full texts of various market studies.)

The complete runs of the *ASI, SRI*, and *IIS* printed indexes have been combined into a single CD-ROM called *Statistical Masterfile*. While there are obvious advantages to computer access, there are also drawbacks in this case. The *Masterfile* does not have a very friendly software, and users of it are often inundated with too much retrieval. Many researchers actually prefer the paper copy versions, which allow much easier scanning of index columns and (lengthy) abstracts.

Statistical Abstract of the United States. This annual volume from the Government Printing Office is a smorgasbord of statistical information on thousands of subjects. Usually you will want to look here first, before getting into any of the *ASI*, *SRI*, or *IIS* indexes. *Statistical Abstract* all by itself will answer many questions, without reference to complicated indexes or microfiche sets. (See also the section on "Statistics" in the Appendix.)

U.S. Government Periodicals Index (Congressional Information Service, 1992–).   An index to more than 180 periodicals published by the federal government, this service is available in paper format (quarterly with annual cumulations) or on CD-ROM. Most of the titles it covers are not indexed elsewhere, and subject coverage spans everything from abortion to zoology. Anyone who uses *Readers' Guide to Periodical Literature* or *P.A.I.S.* would find this source useful in the same ways. It is a gold mine for student researchers in particular, as they can safely assume that no one else in their class will use it. The years 1970 to 1987 are covered by the old *Index to U.S. Government Periodicals* (Chicago: Infordata).

Subject Bibliographies, SB-series (GPO).   This series provides an excellent shortcut in documents research. There are more than 150 such bibliographies, each revised irregularly, each listing in one place a whole range of in-print government publications on a particular subject. (See Chapter 9.)

Government Reports Announcements & Index (GRA&I) (Department of Commerce, National Technical Information Service, 1946–), semi-monthly with annual cumulations. Every year the federal government spends millions of dollars on grants and contracts for research; and each recipient of such funding is required to submit a report on the result of his or her work. The *GRA&I* is the overall index to these reports; it provides access by keyword, personal author, corporate author, report number, and contract number. Each citation includes a full abstract of the work. (There is a database version available through commercial systems covering 1964 to date, and a CD-ROM version covering 1983 to date [see below].)

   NTIS studies cover virtually all subject areas in science, technology, and social sciences; there is even some surprising coverage in humanities, too. Since more than 60,000 titles are added annually, you can expect to find a government-funded research report on just about anything. There are studies of air pollution, anchor chains, drug abuse, educational philosophy, food contamination, foreign military forces, Greenland's ice cap, junction transistors, leadership, personnel management, quark models, seafloor spreading, sex behavior, and the sociology of Peruvian squatter settlements. There is even a study of one of Lord Byron's poems—it was done as a master's thesis at the Air Force Institute of Technology; and since government money paid for it, it got picked up by NTIS.

The vast majority of NTIS reports are not depository items in documents collections, although the *GRA&I* itself is, if the depository library chooses to receive it. If you need a copy of a particular report, you can either buy it from the National Technical Information Service or read it for free at the Library of Congress, which is the only library that owns a full set. The address of the NTIS is:

U.S. Department of Commerce
Technology Administration
National Technical Information Service
Springfield, VA 22161
Tel.: 703-487-4780

Although there is an NTIS Web site (<www.ntis.gov/>), it does not provide free access to the *GRA&I*.

NTIS Title Index on Microfiche. This is no longer published, but it is still useful for its cumulative indexing of earlier years of NTIS reports. It is a cumulated keyword-from-titles index to reports from 1964 to 1978, with annual supplements through 1992. While the first cumulation makes it easier to use than *GRA&I* for retrospective searches, it does not include the abstracts you will find there.

NTIS CD-ROM. Silver Platter Information Service offers the NTIS index in CD-ROM format from 1983 to date. Additional computer access to the NTIS database is available, for a fee, through Dialog and other online services; this remotely accessible version of the file extends back to 1964.

National Security Archive. The National Security Archive is an independent nongovernmental organization founded by investigative reporters;

its purpose is to make available copies of any previously secret or classified documents released by the federal government through Freedom of Information Act requests. About 35,000 of these documents, in 12 separate collections, have now been published on microfilm from Chadwyck-Healey in a series called *The Making of U.S. Policy*. A cumulative index to all 12 collections, the *National Security Archive Index on CD-ROM*, also has been published. The Archive's work is ongoing, so additional documents are available through its office in Washington, D.C., at (202) 994-7000.

The indexes listed above are the major avenues of access to government documents; several other sources, however, deserve particular mention.

- A number of indexes published through government funding are some of the best in their fields:

  STAR (Scientific and Technical Aerospace Reports), 1962–
  A.I.D. Research and Development Abstracts, 1976– (Agency for International Development)
  Energy Research Abstracts (ERA), 1975–
  INIS Atomindex, 1969–
  EPA Publications Bibliography Quarterly Abstract Bulletin, 1977–

  (It is perhaps worth noting, however, that the current climate of downsizing in federal agencies may affect the continued availability of such sources.)
- There are federally produced maps, charts, and aerial photographs of every section of the United States and many regions of the rest of the world. For information on these sources, see the "Maps" section of the Appendix.
- The federal government also produces English-language translations of many foreign newspapers, journal articles, and radio broadcasts. See the "Translations" section of the Appendix.
- There are many researchers who, understandably, throw up their hands at the prospect of doing documents research in a library. Often it is the case, however, that those who balk at library research are whizzes at using the telephone to find out what they need. A

very useful but obscure guide to phone numbers and addresses of contacts for seekers of federal publications is the Defense Technical Center's *How to Get It: A Guide to Defense-Related Information Resources* (Alexandria, Va.: The Center), revised irregularly. This 500-page directory lists contacts for all sorts of information in federal (and other) sources for reports, maps, pamphlets, documents, translations, and databases; it also tells you which forms are necessary for placing orders and gives information on costs, restrictions on access, and where particular types of reports or publications are indexed. It is especially good at explaining report numbers—if all you have is such a number, this guide will explain what it means and tell you whom to contact for a copy of the report. A free electronic version of the whole book is available on the Internet at <www. dtic.mil/gils-input/htgi/>.

- If you need to locate regional or other depositories for federal documents, or those for state, local, U.N., or other international and foreign documents, there is a very good directory that will identify almost all such collections in the United States. This is the *Directory of Government Documents Collections and Librarians* (CIS), revised irregularly. Its arrangement is by state, then by city; and it has a particularly good index to special subject collections.

- Government documents produced by cities and counties are often extremely useful for local information. An excellent index, by subject or by locale, to such documents is the *Index to Current Urban Documents* (Greenwood, 1972–) and its corresponding *Urban Documents Microfiche Collections* of the actual reports themselves. These local documents include planning studies for stadiums, environmental studies, plans for redeveloping downtown areas, statistical reports on crime, and so on. Nearly 300 U.S. and Canadian city and county jurisdictions are covered.

- One of the persistent problems that documents researchers have is that of trying to cite federal publications in a formal manner; many style sheets don't adequately deal with documents. The problem is solved by Diane Garner and Diane Smith's *The Complete Guide to Citing Government Information Resources: A Manual for Writers & Librarians,* rev. ed. (Congressional Information Service, 1993).

It should be obvious at this point that few researchers would get very far into microforms, CD-ROM collections, or government documents (and the same could be said of special collections) if left to only the most widely known library indexes. What is required is that you actively seek out these collections. This will often mean making a leap of faith that the effort will be worthwhile; but you should give it a try anyway—the results may be spectacular.

Notes

1. "Legislative Oversights," *Wilson Quarterly* 18, no. 3 (Summer 1994): 128.
2. These examples come from some of the publisher's own promotional literature.

16

Reference Sources: Searching by Types of Literature

So far we have been concerned mainly to delineate the options for pursuing *research* questions rather than *reference* questions. The former are more open-ended, in the sense of not having definite "right" or "wrong" answers. For example, "What information exists on land reform in seventeenth-century China?" or "What is available on U.S.-Israeli relations after the Six-Day War?" are research questions, in the sense that I'm using the term here. Reference questions, in contrast, are those looking for a specific bit of information—for example, "What is the height of the Washington Monument?" "Who won the Oscar for Best Actor in 1932?"—and that have a more ascertainable "right" answer.

In dealing with research questions, the overall point of the discussion so far is that there are eight different methods of subject searching:

- Controlled-vocabulary subject-heading searches
- Systematic browsing or scanning of classified full texts
- Keyword searches
- Citation searches
- Related-record searches
- Boolean combination searches (especially, but not exclusively, via computers)
- Searches through published bibliographies
- Using people sources[1]

Browsing or scanning classified full texts, and using published bibiographies, are techniques that cannot be done via computers—the texts and bibliographies I'm referring to here are precisely the bulk of library records that are not *on* computers (and never will be) to begin with. Most of the other kinds of searches can be done using either computer or print sources, although with different results, since the electronic sources only partially overlap the contents of the printed sources. "People" sources can be identified by either computer or print means, too—or, obviously, by questioning other people themselves.

Each method of searching is potentially applicable in any subject area; each has distinct advantages and disadvantages (both strengths *and* weaknesses); and each is capable of turning up information that cannot be reached by the other seven. Information that lies in a blind spot to any one method of searching, however, usually lies within an area of light to one or more of the others.

It is especially advisable to remember that all computer searches have noteworthy limitations; that Boolean combinations of subjects can be accomplished by both computers and printed sources; that published bibliographies are not superseded by computer printouts; and that particular treasures lie in special collections, microform sets, CD-ROM collections, and government documents—which must be sought out more actively than other sources.

A knowledge of these few distinct search techniques—and of the advantages and limitations of each—will enable most researchers to increase substantially the range and efficiency of their investigations in any subject area. Most scholars, unfortunately, do most of their research within much more limited frameworks of perception—they too often act as though their research options consist only of (1) looking at footnotes in sources they already have, (2) general browsing in bookstacks, and (3) using *any* electronic (computer or Internet) sources that are conveniently available. Those in the sciences tend to minimize even these pursuits, relying instead on talking to acquaintances. Very few researchers use databases, catalogs, or indexes efficiently because they so frequently search under the wrong terms to begin with (confusing keywords with category terms, or searching under general rather than specific headings); because they are familiar with only a small fraction of the range of sources that exist; and because they are entirely unaware of methods (citation and related-record searches) that don't rely on direct verbal attempts to specify subjects in the first place. Familiarity with the outline of procedures sketched above, however, will enable most researchers to gain a simple overview of the *full range of options* available in any research inquiry, and (I hope) also assist them to achieve a sense of "closure" in making estimates of what options remain to be pursued.

The framework of options available for research questions, however, is not fully adequate for dealing with reference questions. A ninth method of searching is usually preferable here:

- Type of literature searches

This kind of searching is based on the fact that within any subject or disciplinary field, certain distinct types of reference sources can, predictably, be expected to exist. By "reference sources" I mean those that either point the way into the core literature contained in books, journals, reports, dissertations, etc., or those that summarize, abstract, digest, or review it. Reference sources tend to be those forms of publication that are simply consulted rather than read from beginning to end. These various types of sources form a kind of structure within the literature of any subject area; and a foreknowledge of the existence of this predictable structure can alert you to distribute your efforts among a variety of paths of inquiry, each tailored to answering certain kinds of questions.

It must be emphasized that the line between open-ended and specific-fact questions is not always sharp. In general, however, there is a useful distinction here, and as a reference librarian I find that in pursuing research questions it is best to think in terms of a framework of the eight "methods of searching," while in pursuing the fact questions it is usually better to think in terms of "types of literature." In other words, you can think of two different conceptual structures here; or you can simply regard the "types" framework as an add-on, ninth method of searching, still within a single "methods" model. (This is a distinction that may be more of a concern to instructors who are trying to structure a class on "library use" than to anyone else.)

The structure of reference sources defined by types of literature[2] has several "bones" within it. You can reasonably expect to find any of these types of literature within a wide range of very different subject areas:

- *Almanacs*. These are general fact books and compendiums of miscellaneous information. They are particularly good for answering questions having to do with statistics, awards, brief news or historical data, dates and anniversaries, geography, city or country data, sports, and so on.
- *Atlases*. These are compendiums of maps or tables that graphically display information not just on geopolitical matters but also on subjects such as crop production, spread of diseases, military power balances, climate variation, ecological conditions, status of women, literacy levels, technological levels, population trends, soil conditions, occupational distributions, area histories, trade patterns, and the like.
- *Bibliographies*. These are compendiums of citations (sometimes with annotations) to books, journal articles, conference papers, dissertations, reports, and so on, on particular subjects. They are especially important in historical or literary research, as they frequently include references to works that are overlooked by computer databases. Their arrangement, too, often provides an overview of the structure of a topic—which cannot be duplicated by computer printouts.
- *Catalogs*. Catalogs provide listings of merchandise, art objects, publications, equipment, and so forth that are located at particular places or that are available in a particular market; they often provide descriptive details, specifications, and prices.
- *Chronologies*. These present facts arranged by the time sequence of their occurrence. Often chronologies present parallel listings that display temporal contexts of different areas of study (e.g., politics, arts, technology, religion) simultaneously, so that a reader may correlate the events of one area with contemporaneous, earlier, or later developments in the other subject areas.
- *Computer databases* and *Web sites*. See Chapter 11 for an overview of these.
- *Concordances*. These are word lists associated with particular texts (usually literary or philosophical classics) that enable researchers to determine exactly where any particular word or words appear within the text.

- *Dictionaries.* These reference sources provide an alphabetically arranged list of words with their definitions, pronunciations, etymology, scope of usage, and so on. Often they contain biographical and geographical information. The term "dictionary" is often synonymous with "encyclopedia," referring simply to an alphabetical (rather than a systematic) arrangement of entries, regardless of their length.
- *Directories.* Directories provide information for identifying or locating knowledgeable people, organizations, or institutions in various subject areas. They list names, addresses, and telephone or fax numbers; many now list electronic addresses on the Internet.
- *Encyclopedias.* The purpose of an encyclopedia is to summarize established knowledge in a given subject area and to provide a starting point for more extensive research; it seeks to present an overview of a subject written for nonspecialists (unlike a review article). (Note that encyclopedias specialized in a particular *subject area* still tend to be written with a nonspecialist *audience* in mind.) An encyclopedia may be contrasted to a *treatise,* which attempts to provide all knowledge on a subject in a systematic (rather than an alphabetical) arrangement, and which may be written for specialists rather than laypeople. Encyclopedias usually can be counted on to have detailed keyword indexes that will reveal more of their contents than can be found through the simple alphabetical arrangement of their articles. (See Chapter 1.)
- *Gazetteers.* These are alphabetical dictionaries of geographic placenames; entries often include descriptions of the history, population, economic characteristics, and natural resources of the places listed. They are also useful for identifying which larger geopolitical units a smaller locale is part of (e.g., they will tell you which county a town is in—often of interest to genealogists).
- *Guides to the literature.* The literature of any subject area may be thought of in terms of different levels. *Primary literature* deals directly with a particular problem or concern, presenting original testimony or insights about it or creative expression of it. *Secondary literature* generally comprises both scholarly analyses and popularizations of the primary literature. *Tertiary literature* consists of reference

works (the various types of literature: dictionaries, encyclopedias, handbooks, etc.) that identify, point out, summarize, abstract, or repackage the information provided by the other two levels. Guides to the literature ideally seek to provide an intellectual structure that orients a researcher to the most important sources at all three levels of literature for a given subject. In practice, however, many such "guides" fall short of this mark, and present instead an overview of only the tertiary reference literature for their field. (See Chapter 9.)

- *Handbooks and manuals*. These are a type of reference source intended to be easily transportable for actual use "in the field" rather than just in libraries. They are related to encyclopedias and treatises in that they try to provide the principles and important facts of a subject area, and in that they can be arranged alphabetically or systematically. Their major distinction from these other forms is their emphasis on practice, procedures, and other "how to" directions for producing actual results rather than just intellectual understanding. Also, they tend to be much more concisely written, again, so as to be more easily carried about in field situations.

- *Newsletters*. These are current sources, providing up-to-date information in fields that tend to develop or change with some rapidity. They appear daily, weekly, or monthly.

- *Review articles*. These should not be confused with book reviews. They are articles that appear in journals, annuals, or essay anthologies that seek to provide a "state of the art" or "state of the situation" overview or assessment of a particular subject. Unlike encyclopedia articles, they are usually written for specialists, and so may assume familiarity with technical or occupational jargon. They also include a bibliography that seeks to be comprehensive rather than merely selective. Review articles, too, tend to place a greater emphasis on the current state of a subject, whereas encyclopedia articles tend to emphasize its historical aspects. (See Chapter 8.)

- *Treatises*. Like encyclopedias, these try to present a comprehensive summation of the established knowledge of a particular subject; unlike encyclopedias, however, they tend to be arranged systematically rather than alphabetically, and they tend to be written for specialists rather than laypeople.

- *Union lists*. These are location devices; they enable researchers who have already identified specific sources to identify which libraries actually own a copy of the desired works. (See Chapter 13.)
- *Yearbooks*. This type of literature seeks to provide a historical record of, and usually an evaluative commentary on, the year's developments in a particular field. Such annuals often provide a more permanent and better-indexed cumulation of the updating information contained in newsletters.

A foreknowledge of the existence of this structure of reference-source options can greatly increase the efficiency of your searches by enabling you to focus your inquiries, to begin with, in the types of literature most likely to answer them.

There are other types—indexes and abstracts, for example—that are geared much more toward research rather than reference questions; so, again, the line between questions that can be handled by "methods of searching" and "types of literature" is not hard and fast; both models of options can sometimes be used for either research or reference inquiries. The "indexes and abstracts" type, however, whether referring to print or electronic formats, does not adequately distinguish among those geared toward controlled-vocabulary, keyword, citation, or related-record searching; so it isn't *enough* to simply think of type-category "indexes" as a research option; further distinctions must be made at a concrete level, and the "methods" framework of options is preferable in such situations.

The overall point here is that if you understand the trade-offs and the strengths and weaknesses of all the different methods of searching and types of literature, then just from this knowledge of the *formal properties* of the retrieval systems—even without knowing any specific sources, titles, or databases in advance—you can ask much better questions to start with, and also have much better expectations of answering those questions, than if you start out with merely a knowledge of a few particular "subject" sources. You can map out a likely strategy on a formal level before looking at any particular source by making distinctions such as these:

- This question requires a published bibliography that will enable me to recognize a whole group of citations whose keywords I cannot specify in advance in a computer search.

- This question requires an arrangement of full-text sources in a classified order, rather than just a catalog of superficial surrogate records arranged alphabetically by subject headings.
- This question demands an index or database that allows keyword access rather than just subject-heading approaches.
- This question requires some kind of categorization of related sources—whether by subject headings or by compilation within a bibliography produced by an expert—rather than keyword or citation searching.
- This question requires citation searches to find subsequent sources in addition to previous sources listed in footnotes.
- This question requires a database that allows citation searching coupled with postcoordinate limitations by keywords.
- This source requires related-record searching because there isn't any good subject heading, and keyword searching is not adequate to round up variant phrasings of the same subject.
- This question requires talking with someone who can get me oriented in the field.
- This question requires use of printed bibliographies, catalogs, and indexes that can reach into the earlier literature not covered by computer databases.
- This question sounds like it could be answered more efficiently by an encyclopedia article than by browsing the bookstacks.
- This question sounds like the kind of thing some experts will know about; therefore it requires a directory that will enable me to find such people.
- This question requires a union list (or database) that will tell me who owns a copy of a particular source that my local library does not have.

It is possible to frame scores of observations like this that entail a combined knowledge of both methods of searching and types of literature—even without knowing in advance the titles or names of particular indexes, databases, encyclopedias, people sources, and so on, that will meet the desired criteria. Simply knowing the *kinds* of sources that exist within *any* subject area will make you more proficient in finding specific instantiations of them geared toward whatever particular inquiry you may be pursuing.

Such knowledge also will enable you to *eliminate* whole areas of options with which you might otherwise waste time (e.g., in trying to use controlled-vocabulary sources for a topic that does not have an established subject heading; in trying to use printed or electronic sources when the information you need exists only in some person's head; in trying to use computer databases rather than classified bookstacks when the needed information exists only at the page or paragraph level within printed, copyrighted books).

It is this kind of foreknowledge of the formal properties of the several retrieval options that usually makes reference librarians much more efficient in finding information on a subject than even full professors within the discipline.

Students within a particular subject area usually learn its information resources from a particular list they are given to study. The result is that they often learn the individual trees very well without perceiving the arrangement of the forest or the variety of methods available for getting through it, whether by walking, riding, flying over, swinging from branch to branch, or burrowing underneath. The training of reference librarians, on the other hand, is more from the top down than from the bottom up. They learn first the overall arrangement that can be expected in *any* forest—here the analogy is not perfect—and the various methods of moving around in it. They learn overall *methods of searching* and *types of literature*; and they thereby usually understand the *full range of options* for finding information even—or rather, especially—in unfamiliar subject areas. The librarians may not understand the content of the discipline in which they are searching as well as professors within it; but the librarians probably will have a better grasp of the range of options for *finding* the content, which is a distinct and different skill.

The study of the categorization, arrangement, storage, and retrieval of information is a discipline unto itself; it is called library and information science. Those who have not studied it formally should be wary of assuming that they are doing fully efficient research "on their own," for there will always be more options in searching than they realize. The moral of the story is brief: The more you know of what your options are, the better the searcher you will be; but remember to ask for help, since the probability is that you will miss something important if you work entirely on your own.

Librarians have four major aids that help them to exploit the internal type-of-literature structure of the information sources within any given field. The first two can be considered the basic sources; the others, updates. They are:

1. *Guide to Reference Books*, currently edited by Robert Balay (American Library Association, revised irregularly). This volume is often considered the reference librarian's bible. It enables a searcher to look up any subject field and find within it a listing of virtually all its important reference sources arranged according to types of literature. The citations provide full bibliographic descriptions of each source—both current and time-tested older works—with descriptive annotations. The overall arrangement of the volume is by broad subject groups, with an index by authors, titles, and subjects.

2. *Walford's Guide to Reference Material* (London: Library Association Publishing, revised irregularly). This is a multivolume set comparable to the American Library Association *Guide* but with more of an emphasis on British sources.

3. *ARBA: American Reference Books Annual* (Libraries Unlimited, 1970–). Each annual volume in this series presents a listing of all reference books published in the United States within the preceding year. The distinctive feature of the series is that it provides a detailed review of each work listed. Indexes are by author, title, and subject. *ARBA* thus serves as an excellent update of the ALA *Guide* volume. Various five-year cumulative indexes have appeared since the beginning of the series, and these cumulations are themselves major guides to reference books. Some libraries keep them next to their *Guide* volume.

4. The library's own card catalog or computer catalog. Subject headings within the catalog are subdivided by form subdivisions that correspond to the various types of literature; for example:

          [LC Subject Heading]—Atlases
                              —Bibliography

—Case studies
—Catalogs
—Charts, diagrams, etc.
—Chronology
—Concordances
—Dictionaries
—Directories
—Discography
—Encyclopedias
—Film catalogs
—Guidebooks
—Handbooks, manuals, etc.
—Illustrations
—Indexes
—Manuscripts—Catalogs
—Periodicals—Bibliography
—Periodicals—Bibliography—
    Union lists
—Periodicals—Indexes
—Photograph collections
—Pictorial works
—Posters
—Quotations
—Statistics
—Tables
—Textbooks
—Union lists
—Yearbooks

The predictability of this kind of "form" cataloging enables librarians to identify quickly new instances of familiar types of literature within any subject area, because the catalog is updated daily.[3]

The above four sources enable researchers to find types of literature in monographic or printed-book formats. There are other types of literature, however, that exist "within" journals and report literature; these include such things as book reviews, database reviews, software reviews, hardware reviews, film reviews, editorials, letters to the editor, curriculum guides, bilingual materials, and state-of-the art reviews. Many online or CD-ROM databases enable you to specify these kinds of formats within the literature they cover; but there is no convenient overall listing of which types are searchable within which databases. Usually, however, there will be "Help" or "Limit" menu options within the individual databases themselves that will bring to your attention the "document type" search options for whatever file you're in.

Researchers who have never seen a copy of the *Guide to Reference Books* or Walford are well advised to spend some time browsing through them. Either is likely to alert you to the existence of so many good sources that, right there, you may start allowing yourself to ask questions you never thought could be answered. And it is the hallmark of a good researcher to start out by assuming that every question has its answer somewhere.

Perhaps the most important point overall, however, is the observation with which this book began: If you want to do serious research, you cannot confine yourself to "virtual libraries" alone. The information universe of the future, no matter how its contents may change and grow, is best understood in terms of unavoidable trade-offs among *what, who,* and *where* restrictions. The Internet will never include everything in real libraries until such time as human nature itself changes, in the direction of selfless benevolence, and all writers, artists, and creators forgo the advantages of intellectual property to voluntarily contribute their work products to the good of the socialist whole. History has not been kind to systems based on the assumption that most human beings will act in this manner. Within the world of learning, however, history has also witnessed the creation of a marvelous mechanism for protecting the rights of the authors while also making the universe of knowledge freely available to anyone who will travel to certain locations. I hope this book will lead to a more efficient use, and greater appreciation, of that mechanism: real libraries.

Notes

1. Other techniques, such as original observation and analysis, controlled experimentation, and statistical surveying or sampling, are beyond the scope of this book. Research in archives and manuscripts is discussed in the Appendix.

2. The descriptions given here are derived largely from another book of mine, *Library Research Models* (Oxford University Press, 1993).

3. A fuller listing of hundreds of form subdivisions used in library catalogs may be found in my *Library Research Models*, Appendix 2.

Appendix: Special Cases

The sources discussed in this section have proven themselves useful in providing answers to many specialized questions. They are by no means the only materials available; others can be found by using the approaches discussed elsewhere in this book.

The special cases covered are:

Archives, manuscripts, and public records
Biography
Book reviews
Business and economics
Conference proceedings
Consumer product evaluations
Current awareness sources
Films and audiovisual material
Genealogy and local history
Illustrations, pictures, and photographs
Literary criticism
Maps
Newspapers and newspaper indexes
Out-of-print and secondhand books
Primary sources
Psychological and educational tests
Reports
Standards and specifications

Statistics
Tabular data
Translations

Archives, Manuscripts, and Public Records

It is useful to consider unpublished primary sources as falling into two classes: archives or manuscript collections that have been assembled in special historical repositories, and current sources that are still with the people or agencies that originally created or received the records. Both offer gold mines of historical and biographical information.

Research in archives or historical manuscript collections is unlike research in books or journal articles in libraries. The latter sources are comparatively well cataloged and indexed, and there is subject access to individual items. Not so with unpublished sources—there may be broad subject access to large groups of items but not to individual papers or documents within the groups. A major reason for this is that most individual unpublished sources are simply not worth the time and expense it would take to catalog or index them fully, for most of them make sense only within the larger context of the other items they are stored with. The strategy for working with such materials involves four levels of searching:

1. Identifying which repositories have collections or archival manuscript materials that are relevant to your subject
2. Determining if there is a separate repository guide that will give you an overview of the holdings of a particular repository you're interested in
3. Finding out if that repository has an archival inventory or manuscript register for a particular series of documents you wish to examine
4. Browsing through the documents themselves, which will be grouped according to who wrote or received them, or which agency produced them—often regardless of what their subject may be

At the first level, several good sources will help you identify which collections exist. Philip M. Hamer's *A Guide to Archives and Manuscripts in the*

United States (Yale University Press, 1961) is a standard source, listing about 1,300 repositories and describing their holdings. It has an index of names and subjects. The National Historical Publications and Research Commission's *Directory of Archives and Manuscripts Repositories in the United States*, 2d ed. (National Archives, 1988), supplements but does not supersede Hamer. The *Directory* describes 4,225 repositories and reports minimally on another 335, for a total of 4,560. It covers not just papers and documents but also architectural drawings, photographs, oral history collections, sound recordings and motion pictures, microforms, and machine-readable collections. It has an index providing name and subject access.

Also on the first level is the *National Union Catalog of Manuscript Collections*, or *NUCMC* (Library of Congress, 1959–), which exists in printed volumes from 1959 to 1993; thereafter it is updated only in computer form. It is the largest national listing of whose papers are where, including the records of both individuals and corporate bodies. The electronic version covers from 1986 forward; it is accessible as part of OCLC and within the AMC (Archives and Manuscript Collections) file within RLIN. There is also a free Web site for the electronic *NUCMC* at <lcweb.loc.gov/coll/nucmc/> or <lcweb.loc.gov/z3950/rlinamc.html>. These addresses actually grant free access to the entire AMC file within the RLIN system, not just to the *NUCMC* portion of it. The printed *NUCMC* has two cumulative indexes, both published by Chadwyck-Healey: *Index to Personal Names in the National Union Catalog of Manuscript Collections 1959–1984*, listing more than 200,000 personal and family names; and *Index to Subjects and Corporate Names in the National Union Catalog of Manuscript Collections 1959–1984*, with almost 300,000 entries. Note that the "1959" date is simply the year in which the *NUCMC* began publication; it does not mean that only sources written since 1959 are included. The *NUCMC* lists records from all places and all time periods insofar as they are collected in publicly accessible repositories in the United States.

An online database from Chadwyck-Healey called *ArchivesUSA* provides cumulative access to many of the above printed sources. This file includes an updated version of the *Directory of Archives and Manuscript Repositories in the United States* and the entire *NUCMC* from 1959 to 1995 (i.e., not just the 1986 and later part in the RLIN AMC file; the current 1995 cutoff may change in the future). It also includes full descriptions and subject indexing of more than 42,000 collections contained in the 300 repositories whose finding aids have been published in microfiche format in the *National Inventory of Documentary Sources in the United States* (see below). Note that while the finding guides are indexed here, their full texts are available only through the microfiche set.

Lee Ash's *Subject Collections* (Bowker, revised irregularly) is a subject guide to more than 65,000 special library collections in the United States and Canada, and many of these include unpublished or manuscript materials. The Modern Language Association also publishes two relevant sources, John A. Robbins's *American Literary Manuscripts,* 2d ed. (1977), a directory of 2,800 authors' papers in 600 repositories, and James Thorpe's *The Use of Manuscripts in Literary Research,* 2d ed. (1979), a handbook explaining problems of access and literary property rights. Philip C. Brooks's *Research in Archives: The Use of Unpublished Primary Sources* (University of Chicago Press, 1969) is also good for an overview.

The first of two British sources at this level is the *Index of English Literary Manuscripts* (a multisection set still in process, being published in London by Mansell and in New York by Bowker); Volume 1 covers 1450 to 1625; Volume 2, 1625 to 1700; Volume 3, 1700 to 1800; Volume 4, 1800 to 1900. The second is the *Location Register of Twentieth-Century English Literary Manuscripts and Letters: A Union List of Papers of Modern English, Irish, Scottish, and Welsh Authors in the British Isles,* 2 vols. (G. K. Hall, 1988). There is also the *International Directory of Archives* (K. G. Saur, 1992; also published as Volume 38 of the journal *Archivum*).

At the second level, the *Guide to Federal Records in the National Archives of the United States,* 3 vols. (National Archives and Records Administration, 1995) may serve as an example of a particular repository guide. This book describes the various Record Groups held by the National Archives; these groups of government records are arranged not by subject but rather by agency or bureau. If you wish to find out which agencies' records have material on your subject, you must use some imagination in thinking how the federal government would have become involved with your area of interest—for, with very rare exceptions, there are no subject or name indexes to the records. For this reason alone you must work closely with the archivists, who have a good sense of what types of things can be found in the various agencies' documents. The same rule applies at other repositories: Use the expertise of the staff as much as you can, and be sure that they understand *clearly*—not just in vague, general terms—what you are *ultimately* trying to research. Note especially that many repositories—including the National Archives itself—are now publishing guides at this second level of depth directly on the World Wide Web. (The National Archives' site is at <www.nara.gov>.)

The third level of guide is that of the archival inventory or manuscript register; usually it is a typed finding aid that describes one particular collection with an introductory note followed by a listing of the parts of the collection down to the box or folder level (but rarely to the level of individual items within boxes or folders). Most of these inventories and registers are themselves unpublished and are available only at the repository; as with guides at the second level, however, these third-level resources are now starting to show up irregularly on the Web sites of the various repositories. The best printed listing of which ones exist is Donald L. DeWitt's *Guides to Archives and Manuscript Collections in the United States: An Annotated Bibliography* (Greenwood Press, 1994). It lists more than 2,000 inventories, checklists, and registers (at this third level), as well as repository guides at the second level. Dewitt has also compiled *Articles Describing Archives and Manuscript Collections in the United States: An Annotated Bibliography* (Greenwood Press, 1997). Both the OCLC and RLIN systems include records for manuscript collections, too; and these online records often include information about finding aids and registers for the collections.

A good Web site for information on British finding aids is the National Register of Archives at <www.hmc.gov.uk>.

The Chadwyck-Healey company is printing several microfiche collections of the actual guides themselves, filmed at large repositories in the United States and the United Kingdom. Part 1 of their *National Inventory of Documentary Sources in the United States: Federal Records* reproduces finding aids for collections in the National Archives, the Presidential Libraries, and the Smithsonian Institution. Part 2, the *National Inventory of Documentary Collections in the United States: Manuscript Division, Library of Congress*, reproduces hundreds of finding aids for many (not all) collections in LC. Part 3 is *State Archives, State Libraries, State His-*

torical Societies, Academic Libraries and Other Repositories. All three parts are ongoing projects, with both new finding aids and new institutions being added. The publisher is also producing Name and Subject indexes for each part; these indexes reach the level of "main entry" for each collection but do not include every name and subject referred to *within* each finding aid. The indexes, in other words, must be used in conjunction with the microfiche sets of the actual finding aids, to get down to a level beyond that of the collection as a whole. The indexes themselves are published in both microfiche and CD-ROM formats, and they are included within Chadwyck-Healey's online *ArchivesUSA* database.

The same company is also publishing a comparable microfiche set for British manuscript collections, the *National Inventory of Documentary Resources in the United Kingdom and Ireland.* This set covers the contents of more than 14,000 archives and manuscript collections in more than 80 repositories, with a single master index of names and subjects. (Chadwyck-Healey's CD-ROM format index covers all of the U.S. and U.K. *Inventory* sets together.)

Keep in mind, again, that many repositories are now creating homepages on the World Wide Web; and eventually these sites will include copies of many of their local manuscript registers. Examples may be found at the Library of Congress's Manuscript Division site at <lcweb.loc.gov>; and at the National Archives' NARA Archival Information Locator (NAIL) at <www.nara.gov/nara/nail.html>. Remember, however, that these Internet sources are not even nearly complete rosters of either institution's holdings. Be aware, too, that the National Security Archive (see Chapter 15) can be a shortcut for obtaining documents secured from the U.S. federal government via Freedom of Information Act requests.

As helpful as the archival inventories and manuscript registers may be, only at the fourth level of research—reading through the documents themselves—can you really know what is in a collection. You cannot do archival or manuscript research quickly; you must be prepared for much browsing and many dead ends before you come to any nuggets. Plan your time accordingly.

If you plan to visit an archival or manuscript repository, it is especially important to read as many secondary or published sources as you can on your subject *before* you inquire into the unpublished sources. Since these are not cataloged or arranged by subject, you will have to have in advance a rather clear idea of what you're looking for in order to recognize it when you're browsing. (It is especially useful to know in advance the names of any people connected with your area of interest; names are easy to look for in the records.) If you are planning a research trip, it is a good idea to write to the archives in advance, stating what you are interested in and asking for suggestions on what to read before you come in personally.

And once you are at the repository and are looking through the boxes of manuscripts or documents it has, *it is essential that you replace in the correct box any material you photocopy.* The individual papers are *not cataloged,* so if you misplace an item it is *permanently lost for other researchers.*

As with the other three levels, some of this fourth-level material—actual records, not just finding aids—is now starting to appear on the World Wide Web. An example is the California Heritage Digital Image Access Project at <http://sunsite.Berkeley.edu/Calheritage>; it includes digital images of primary sources themselves embedded within the searchable finding aids.

Research in public records—those that are still with the agency that produced or collected them and not yet sent to an archival repository—is another very valuable avenue of inquiry for studying individuals, businesses, or government itself. A good guide to finding such records is *The Reporter's Handbook: An Investigator's Guide to Documents and Techniques,* 3d ed., by Steve Weinberg (St. Martin's Press, 1996).

The above sources are helpful in finding unpublished primary sources. Remember, however, that many have been published in book form and are available in regular libraries. For shortcuts in finding them—especially if you are a student given an assignment to use primary sources in a term paper—see the "Primary Sources" section below.

Other useful resources for locating manuscripts or archival records are discussed below in the "Biography," "Business and Economics," and "Genealogy and Local History" sections. A good introduction to research in archives is a class that is usually offered every year in Washington, D.C., by the National Archives and Records Administration, called "Going to the Source." For information on when it will be offered, called the Education Branch of the National Archives at (202) 501-6172.

Biography

Two excellent starting points for biographical information are the *Biography & Genealogy Master Index* (Gale Research, 1980), with ongoing supplement sets, and *Biography Index* (H. W. Wilson Company, 1946–). The former is a cumulative index to more than 9 million biographical sketches in more than 1,030 current and retrospective biographical dictionaries, including scores of *Who's Who* publications. (The CD-ROM version does not index all of the older sources covered by the print version of *B&GMI*.) *Biography Index* is the largest ongoing index to biographical books, pamphlets, and journal articles (covering more than 1,000 periodicals).

K. G. Saur, Inc., has published a number of *Biographical Archive* printed index sets for various countries. Each of these is an index to a few hundred old biographical encyclopedias or works of collective biography; and each index is also keyed to a microfiche set of the actual articles from all of the various sources. The indexes, in other words, can refer you either to paper copy sets (if your library owns them) or to cumulative microfiche collections. The *American Biographical Index* (first series), for example, is a "single-alphabet cumulation of 367 original biographical reference works cover[ing] 360,000 individuals from the earliest period of North American history through the early 20th century." The other sets in the *Biographical Archive* series are the following:

Australasian Biographical Index
   (microfiche: *Australasian Biographical Archive*)
British Biographical Index
   (microfiche: *British Biographical Archive*, Series I and II)
Deutscher Biographischer Index and supplement *Neue Folge* (microfiche: *Deutsches Biographisches Archiv*, and supplement *Neue Folge*)
Indice Biografico de Espana, Portugal e Iberoamerica
   (microfiche: *Archivo Biografico de Espana, Portugal e Iberoamerica,* Series I and II)
Indice Biografico Italiano
   (microfiche: *Archivio Biografico Italiano,* and supplement *Nuevo Serie*)

> *Index Biographique Français*
> > (microfiche: *Archives Biographiques Français,* Series I and II)
> *Scandinavian Biographical Index*
> > (microfiche: *Scandinavian Biographical Archive*)

Saur has several other microfiche *Archive* sets in preparation, with a separate *Index* for each; these include *African, Arab-Islamic, American* (Series II), *Baltic, Benelux, Chinese, Classical World, Czech/Slovak, Hungarian, Jewish,* and *Polish* compilations. The indexes to all of these *Biographical Archive* sets have been cumulated in one CD-ROM, the *Internationaler Biographischer Index/World Biographical Database,* revised irregularly. (The actual articles, however, are not available electronically.)

Current Biography, an ongoing hard-copy series, is the best place to look for articles on people currently in the news; each article is accompanied by a photograph. The *New York Times Biographical Service*, which reproduces biographical articles from that paper, is somewhat comparable.

The two largest quick-reference sources on American biography for historical coverage are the multivolume sets *Dictionary of American Biography* and *National Cyclopedia of American Biography*. The former is the standard in the field; the second is especially good for picking up noteworthy people (e.g., business executives, military officers, clergy) who are otherwise neglected by the history books. The *Cyclopedia* articles tend to be authorized or approved by the biographees themselves.

If these sources don't cover the individual you want, often the various national or specialized subject encyclopedias pick up obscure people, as does the *Personal Name Index to the New York Times Index 1851–1974* and *1975–1984* supplement. Robert B. Slocum's two-volume *Biographical Dictionaries and Related Works,* 2d ed. (Gale Research, 1986), is a bibliography of more than 16,000 biographical sources categorized by country and by occupation; it can alert you to many sources not covered by the *Biography and Genealogy Master Index*. The *ARBA Guide to Biographical Dictionaries* (Libraries Unlimited, 1986) is a comparable but smaller annotated listing of 718 biographical sources.

Directories are also frequently useful for information on people. American academics will certainly want to be aware of the *National Faculty Directory* (Gale Research, annual), which locates colleagues, although it does not provide sketches of them. City directories, such as those published by the R. L. Polk Company, can be used to find a surprising amount of information about a person. Among the questions they can often answer are: Is the individual married? If so, what is the spouse's name? If a widow, what was the husband's name? Who else lives at the same address? Who are the neighbors? What is the individual's occupation, and where is he or she employed? Is the individual a "head of house" or a resident? Retrospective searching of old volumes can also indicate how long an individual has been employed at a job, what previous jobs or business associations were, how long a person lived at an address, who were previous neighbors, and so on. (Researchers who want to learn to milk old directories to the last drop should study pages 158–60 of Harry J. Murphy's *Where's What: Sources of Information for Federal Investigators* [Quadrangle/New York Times Book Company, 1976]; Murphy quotes a previous publication listing about 50 questions city directories can answer.) The one drawback: Polk directories are no longer published for very large cities; they are mainly good for small towns and suburbs. The various city directories now published for large cities are strictly "crisscross": You have to start out with either a phone number or an address, and the directory will give you the name connected with either (without any occupational information).

The LEXIS system contains various databases with information on individuals (as well as corporations). Its ALLOWN file, for example, combines real-estate tax assessment records from more than 350 counties or townships in more than 30 states; you can use it to see who owns what property, and how much it's worth.

Most of the site directories and search engines for the World Wide Web now include "People Finder," "WhoWhere," or "People Search" options; these usually allow you to search any name from any telephone book in the United States to find a current listing. (They also enable you to find e-mail addresses.) One of the services, the Database America *PeopleFinder* engine, enables you to do crisscross searches starting from phone numbers, to identify who has the number you key in. It is available at <www.databaseamerica.com/>. Another site is <www.555-1212.com>.

Book Reviews

Each of the Wilson indexes (see Chapter 4) has a separate "Book Reviews" section, but there are also several other indexes specifically for such articles. Among them are *Book Review Digest* (1905–), *Book Review Index* (1965–), *Index to Book Reviews in the Humanities* (1960–), *Combined Retrospective Index to Book Reviews in Scholarly Journals 1886–1974*, and *Combined Retrospective Index to Book Reviews in Humanities Journals 1802–1974*. The ISI citation indexes (see Chapters 5 and 6) also pick up book reviews, as well as footnote citations to books and articles. *Book Review Digest* picks up reviews from only about 80 periodicals (published in the United States, Canada, and Great Britain); but, unlike the others, it provides abstracts from the texts of the reviews and not just bibliographic citations. The *Digest* is also especially useful in that it provides a subject index (using *LC Subject Headings*) to the books being reviewed.

Note that these sources are generally not the best ones for students who want scholarly criticisms of individual books, stories, plays, or poems (see the "Literary Criticism" section below).

Business and Economics

Two books that everyone in this field should be familiar with are the *Encyclopedia of Business Information Sources* (Gale Research, revised irregularly), and Lorna Daniells's *Business Information Sources,* 3d ed., rev. (University of California Press, 1993) The *Encyclopedia* is arranged by very specific subjects (e.g., Boat Industry, Computers in Accounting, Condominiums, Dental Supply Industry, Economic Entomology, Financial Ratios, General Agreement on Tariffs and Trade [GATT], House Organs, Inheritance Tax, Location of Industry, Molasses Industry, Retirement, Solar Energy, Sweet Potato Industry, etc.), and under each provides a good list of both print and electronic sources and—especially useful—names of associations and industry groups, with addresses and phone numbers. The Daniells book, in contrast, is arranged by broad topic (e.g., Chapter 6:

Industry Statistics; 7: Locating Information on Companies, Organizations, and Individuals; 8: Investment Sources; 10: Management; 18: Marketing). Each chapter then provides a good overview of the specific research resources in its area, with evaluative annotations. (The entries in the Gale *Encyclopedia* are not annotated.) Both books arrange their sources, within their topic categories, by types of literature (e.g., books, encyclopedias, bibliographies, handbooks, periodicals, directories, online databases, etc.).

In locating information on an individual company it is very important to first put the firm into one of three categories: those that sell stock and are *publicly owned,* those that are *privately owned* and don't sell stock to the public, and those that are *nonprofit* organizations. A fourth category is that of *foreign* companies. Another distinction to keep in mind is that information can be of two types: what the company says about itself, and what others say about it. For the former you will use such things as annual reports and filings with government regulatory agencies. For the second you will use articles in business (or other) magazines and newspapers, or commercially prepared research reports. Business reference books tend to be excerpts or compilations of the self-reported data, or indexes to the articles and reports generated by others, or some form of combination.

Business databases are extremely varied. Some are indexes that point out articles in printed sources. Some are full-text directories. Some provide keyword-searchable full texts of government filings (such as SEC reports) or texts of business-related sources produced by the U.S. federal government; others provide the full texts of selected business journals and newsletters. (Note, though, that the databases providing bibliographic citations to printed articles are much more extensive in scope—while shallower in depth—than those that provide the actual articles themselves; the former may cover thousands of journals, the latter only scores or hundreds.)

Several very useful "general" CD-ROM databases are available as components of the *InfoTrac* system; these include the following:

- *Business Index* covers 850 business periodicals, including the *Wall Street Journal* and the financial section of the *New York Times*. Most references contain abstracts.
- *Company ProFile* provides directory information for more than 50,000 public and 100,000 private companies.

- *Business & Company ProFile—Academic Edition* is a CD-ROM that combines the coverage of both *Business Index* and *Company ProFile*.
- *Investext Academic Library Version* provides the full texts of company and industry research reports from scores of Wall Street firms and regional and international brokerage and financial analysis companies.
- *General Business File—Academic Edition* is another monthly-updated CD-ROM. This database includes everything in the *Business & Company Profile* and *Investext Academic Library Version*. It covers the current year plus three previous years. (This is the most comprehensive single business database.)
- *Business ASAP* is a companion CD-ROM that provides the full texts of more than 350 of the journals indexed in the above files; coverage is for the current year plus two previous years.
- *Business Collection* is a set of microfilm cartridges that provide the full texts of more than 350 journals indexed in the above files—but not the same 350 as in *Business ASAP* (although there is some overlap).

A categorization of business databases prepared by the Library of Congress's Business Reference section is useful as a road map to other CD-ROMs.

For directory and financial information on companies or products, search the following:

- *Compact Disclosure/SEC*. This CD provides the full texts of the filings of 12,500 U.S. public companies with the Securities and Exchange Commission.
- *InfoTrac* business databases (see above).
- *Dun's Million Dollar Disc*. Updated quarterly, this file contains information on more than 230,000 U.S. public and private companies that report $25 million or more in sales, or have 250 or more individuals at the company's headquarters, or have a net worth of more than $500,000. Also included is biographical information on 450,000 executives. (This database includes all of the information in the paper-copy *Million Dollar Directory* series and the *Reference Book of Corporate Managements*.)

- *National Trade Data Bank.* This is sometimes thought of as a "government documents depository collection on a disc" because it puts trade promotion and international economics data from 15 U.S. federal agencies—more than 100,000 documents, full text—on one disc, updated monthly. It is divided into two separate files, *NTDB (Reports)* and *NTDB (Foreign Traders)*. The former provides full texts of documents and data from government publications pertaining to international trade; these are searchable by topic or by source agency. These include *Country Commercial Guides* from the Department of Commerce, State Department *Background Notes,* and *Market Research Reports* from the International Trade Administration.

  The *NTDB (Foreign Traders)* segment contains an *Export Yellow Pages* section with directory and product/service information on more than 12,000 U.S. companies interested in exporting; and a *Foreign Trader's* section with similar information on foreign importers, agents, and distributors of interest to U.S. companies that want to do export business. Both the *Export Yellow Pages* and the *Foreign Traders* parts can be searched by geographic region, company, product, or keywords. (There is also an Internet version of the *NTDB* at <www.stat-usa.gov/BEN/databases.html>, but it is not as complete as the CD-ROM version. There is talk about making the Internet version a subscription rather than a free service.)

- *Worldscope* is a CD that provides descriptive information on more than 12,000 major corporations in 25 countries.

- *Gale Business Resources*, updated quarterly, cumulates the information in several printed sources: *Ward's Business Directory, Encyclopedia of Associations (U.S.), Business Rankings Annual, Companies and Their Brands, Market Share Reporter, International Directory of Company Histories*, and others. It provides detailed information on more than 200,000 U.S. businesses and gives industry overviews and analyses, financial ratios, market share reports, and company rankings.

- *Companies International,* also from Gale, is a combination of the printed *Ward's Business Directory* and the *World Trade Centers Association World Business Directory;* it provides basic information on 280,000 businesses from more than 180 countries. With this source you can answer questions such as "How many companies manufacture paper in Argentina?"; "Where can I find international rankings by sales of companies outside the United States in SIC 5044?"; or "How many Dallas companies compete with Mind Path Technologies?"[1]

- *Hoover's Company and Industry Database on CD-ROM* is also an electronic compilation of several printed sources: *Hoover's Handbook of American Business, Hoover's Handbook of Emerging Companies, Hoover's Handbook of World Business, Hoover's Guide to Computer Companies,* Hoover's regional guides (e.g., Northeast, Mid-Atlantic, West), and *Hoover's Guide to Private Companies,* with hundreds of additional company profiles not available in printed form. The database provides in-depth profiles of 2,500 companies and 200 detailed industry profiles.

For magazine or newspaper articles about companies, products, or business topics, search the following:

- *InfoTrac* databases (above)
- *ABI/INFORM* provides subject indexing, with abstracts, of articles from 800 business and management journals for the past five years
- *Wilson Business Abstracts,* a CD comparable to Wilson's printed *Business Periodicals Index,* but with abstracts
- *Business Dateline* provides full texts (not just citations or abstracts) of about 350 U.S. regional business journals, newspapers, and wire services, updated monthly with backfile discs from 1985 forward. Fully keyword searchable, it is an extremely powerful tool for finding information on very obscure private companies
- *EconLit* provides subject indexing of about 300 scholarly economics journals, with abstracts of articles from 1968 to the present. It corresponds to both the printed sources *Index of Economic Articles in Journals and Collective Volumes* and the *Journal of Economic Literature* index.
- *National Trade Data Bank* (above)
- *Worldscope* (above); this contains citations to some newspaper articles about companies, to be found at the end of the "Complete Company Records" display format for most of the company entries.

For investment reports and market research on companies or industries, search the following:

- *InfoTrac General Business File* or *Investext Academic Library Version* (above)
- *National Trade Data Bank* (above); select "Market Research Reports" in Program search

For U.S. statistical information, search the following:

- *Census Summary* contains summary data from the most recent decennial Census of Population and Housing. It can be searched for data at many different levels, from the country as a whole, to states, counties, or places with 10,000 or more people, as well as Metropolitan Statistical Areas and Indian reservations.
- *County Business Patterns* provides data on agriculture, construction, mining, manufacturing, public utitilities, wholesale and retail trade, insurance, real estate, and finance. Summary data (i.e., not naming individual companies) are provided on number of establishments and of employees. The CD can be searched at different geographic levels from the whole country, to states (including the District of Columbia), to counties.
- *Sourcebook of Census Demographics*, from Gale Research, is another index to U.S. federal census data. It is searchable by zip codes or counties and can provide breakdowns of information by age, housing, employment, income, education, and poverty status.

There are dozens of databases relating to business within the Dialog system (see Chapter 11); these, however, unlike the above CD-ROMs, require direct payment at the point of use.

The OCLC FirstSearch system (see Chapter 11) contains several databases of interest to business researchers, including ABI/INFORM (with the advantage that the FirstSearch version extends coverage back to 1971), *DataTimes* (which abstracts recent articles from more than 90 regional U.S. newspapers, updated daily), *NewsAbs* (an index to more than two dozen major U.S. newspapers from 1989 to date), *Pro CD Biz* (a kind of national yellow pages listing of products and services), and *WilBusAbs* (the Wilson index, with abstracts, to more than 300 business journals since 1982).

The Internet's resources for business research are growing exponentially; a good guide from Gale Research is the *CyberHound's Guide to Companies on the Internet*. Keep in mind the obvious, however: Homepages mounted by the companies themselves will naturally be very positive in their presentations.

Not every business or company question requires a computer search; there are many printed indexes and directories that are widely available in libraries and that may be just as useful.

For information on public companies, some libraries will have microfiche sets of 10-K reports (filed with the Securities & Exchange Commission) rather than CD-ROM versions. A private company called Disclosure, Inc., provides free copies of some very useful booklets such as *A Guide to SEC Corporate Filings: What They Are, What They Tell You* and *List of SEC Filing Companies*. Their toll-free number is 1-800-777-3272; their Marketing Department is at 301-718-2393. You can also order copies of any SEC documents from them.

Other good sources of information about publicly owned companies are the annual reports they issue to stockholders. These can be obtained directly from companies; they are also available in a microfiche set that may be owned by local libraries. Many companies also have their own Web sites that provide current information—but you'll still need real libraries if you want their histories.

Paper-copy resources in libraries can supply quite a bit of information on public companies. Factual, objective information on companies that sell stock is available from two loose-leaf services, *Standard & Poor's Corporation Records* and Moody's Investors Service's *Moody's Manuals*. The former exists only in loose-leaf binders and does not cumulate (i.e., outdated pages are discarded as new ones come in). Moody's loose-leaf service is similar; however, Moody's is backed by permanent, bound annual volumes of reports on companies, and these are useful for researching the history of a company. A third loose-leaf service, *Value Line Investment Service*, provides analytical and evaluative ratings of companies and advice on investment, which *S&P* and *Moody's* do not.

Private securities and investment firms also prepare reports on individual public companies. Many of these are available, in full text, in the *InfoTrac* databases discussed above; but libraries without these CD-ROMs may still subscribe to the weekly *Wall Street Transcript,* which provides excerpts of many of these studies. The *Transcript* is indexed in *Predicasts* (see below). An annual directory called *Findex* (London: Euromonitor) is the largest international listing of commercially prepared studies of particular companies, industries, or markets; it will give you price and ordering information. (Note, however, that most of these reports are very expensive.) The annual *Nelson's Directory of Investment Research* (Nelson Publications) is somewhat comparable.

Four basic printed sources for directory information (company name, address, phone number, names of top executives, SIC codes, sales and employment figures, etc.) are *Standard & Poor's Register of Corporations, Directors, and Executives*, Dun & Bradstreet's *Million Dollar Directory*, *Ward's Business Directory of U.S. Private and Public Companies,* and *Hoover's Billion Dollar Directory.* The names of other such print-format directories, specialized in certain industries or regions, are listed above, their electronic versions being included within the coverage of different CD-ROMs. These sources cover both public and private companies.

Private companies are not required to file information with the Securities and Exchange Commission; however, in many states they are required to file annual reports with the Secretary of State's office of the state in which they are incorporated. Usually these are not findable within public libraries; many of them, however, are available online—at rather stiff fees—in the COMPNY file in LEXIS/NEXIS. The ALLOWN file within LEXIS is another useful (albeit expensive) source; it enables you to search real property tax assessment and deed records in more than 30 states.

A good overall source listing public agencies that may have information on private (and other) companies is Washington Researcher's *How to Find Information About Companies* (revised irregularly). Two volumes from Oryx Press also provide good overviews: *Business Information: How to Find It, How to Use It* and *International Business Information: How to Find It, How to Use It. Analyzing Your Competition*, from Find/SVP, is also a good guide, not just for sources but also for spelling out which questions you should ask of them. The volume mentioned above in the Archives section, *Reporter's Handbook*, is also a good guide to the range of public records available on any company. Directory-type information can be found in *Hoover's Guide to Private Companies,* the *Directory of Leading Private Companies,* and *Owners and Officers of Private Companies.*

The R. L. Polk company's annual city directories for many U.S. cities are often good for providing the names and officers of small private companies.

Country Reports from the Economist Intelligence Unit provide business information for any of 180 countries worldwide.

For nonprofit organizations, a good overview source is Gale Research's annual *Encyclopedia of Associations*, which lists and describes more than 23,000 of them. Additional information on nonprofits can be obtained from the Internal Revenue Service, for the information returns of nonprofit organizations—unlike those of public or private companies—are considered public records. The IRS publishes a list of these nonprofits called *Cumulative List of Organizations Described in Section 170(c) of the Internal Revenue Code of 1954*; it is annual with quarterly supplements, and it may be found in many local libraries. It is no more than a list of corporate names with the city and state of each, however, and offers no further information. To actually see the IRS filings of a listed company, you must send a request *in writing* to:

Internal Revenue Service
Freedom of Information Reading Room
CP:EX:GLD:D:T:RR, Room 1619
P.O. Box 795, Benjamin Franklin Station
Washington, DC 20024
Tel.: 202-622-5164; Fax: 202-622-9069

When making your request, it is best to include two separate letters in the same envelope; in the first, request a copy of the "annual return" of the organization in which you are interested; in the second, request a copy of its "application for recognition of exemption."

Several paper-copy indexes to business journals are very useful, and may be more readily findable in libraries than their more expensive CD-ROM counterparts. These include the Wilson Company's *Business Period-*

icals Index, the *Wall Street Journal Index*, and *Predicasts F&S Index: United States, Predicasts F&S Index: Europe,* and *Predicasts F&S Index: International*. For information on local companies it is advisable to check your local newspaper, many of which have published indexes (see the "Newspaper Indexes" section below); and a telephone call to the editor of the business section of the newspaper may turn up leads that have not been published. Your local public library may also have clipping files on local businesses. The full-text *Business Dateline* CD-ROM (described above) is also unusually good for locating information on local companies. And the *DataTimes* file within the OCLC FirstSearch system, being an index to more than 90 local newspapers, is also an excellent source.

If you are interested in a larger perspective on whole industries rather than just individual companies, the same indexes are useful. A better starting point, however, is *Standard & Poor's Industry Surveys* (semiannual, with monthly supplements). Gale Research's *Manufacturing USA* (biennial) and *Service Industries USA* (biennial) are somewhat comparable. The *Encyclopedia of Business Information Sources* is also good for listing specific sources of information on whole industries.

The *Thomas Register* is an annual directory of 150,000 U.S. and Canadian industrial companies categorized under 52,000 alphabetical subject headings; it also has a detailed cross-reference index at the end, in case you can't find the subject you're looking for in the regular A–Z sequence. It's sort of like a huge yellow pages for manufacturers and manufacturing-related services. If you want to know who makes what, and where they are, this will tell you.

Specialized directories often appear as annual issues within various business journals. The two best indexes to these are the *Guide to Special Issues and Indexes of Periodicals* (Special Libraries Association, revised irregularly), and the *Directory of Business Periodical Special Issues: The Definitive Guide to Indexed Business, Science, and Technology Periodicals* (Reference Press, 1st ed., 1995; will probably be revised in subsequent years). The overall *Directories in Print* (Gale, annual) is also a standard source.

The multivolume *International Directory of Company Histories* (Gale) is an ongoing set that brings together histories of more than 2,000 firms. Another good source is Francis Goodall's 668-page *International Bibliogra-*

phy of Business History (Routledge, 1997). A good researcher's trick in doing company histories is first to find the founding date of the company (often provided in the various directories listed above) and then check indexes to business journals and newspapers at important "anniversary" years for the company (especially their twenty-fifth and fortieth years); often there will be write-ups on the company's history at those points. For very old firms, founded in the United States between 1687 and 1915, Etna M. Kelley's *The Business Founding Date Directory* (Morgan & Morgan, 1954) will be helpful; its *Supplement* (1956) covers foundings up to 1933.

Two good sources for commodities information are the *Commodity Price Locator* (Oryx Press, 1989) and *Commodity Prices: A Source Book and Index Providing References to Wholesale, Retail, and Other Quotations for More Than 1,000 Agricultural, Commercial, Industrial, and Consumer Products* (Gale, revised irregularly).

A good source of information on how to find financial ratios and ratings is *R3 = Ratios, Ratings and Reference* (American Library Association, 1997). A very good guidebook through the difficulties of successful exporting is Julie Ann Clowes and Sarah McCue's *Trade Secrets: The Export Answer Book* (Michigan Small Business Development Center, 1995).

The best guide for job hunters is the annual *What Color Is Your Parachute?* by Richard Nelson Bolles (Ten Speed Press). Its basic advice is first to decide where you want to be, then get to know the person or persons who can hire you. (This really does work much better than sending out dozens of résumés or relying on want ads and posted job vacancies. I've gotten three jobs myself—including my present one—by following what this book says to do.)

Business researchers need to be aware of a change in indexing that will affect many business sources: Standard Industrial Classification (SIC) codes for designating products and services are now gradually being replaced by the North American Industry Classification System (NAICS). European sources will likely continue with the International Standard Industrial Classification ("ISIC revised 3").

Needless to say at this point, the field of business reference sources is very large and very changeable. Although the above listings should give you a good overview of the more important sources, no such roster can ever be either complete or current. When you are doing business research, then, don't just go to the sources you know about from this or any other list; be sure to talk to the business reference librarians at your library, too, and ask them for other suggestions.

Conference Proceedings

The best printed indexes to these elusive sources are produced by the same company that offers the citation indexes; they are: *Index to Scientific and Technical Proceedings (ISTP)*, 1978 to date; and *Index to Social Sciences and Humanities Proceedings (ISSHP)*, 1979 to date. Each has several sections: Category Index (general subjects), Sponsor Index (agencies or societies that sponsor meetings), Corporate Index (organizational affiliations of individual authors), Permuterm Subject Index (keywords from book titles and subtitles, conference titles, and titles of individual papers), Author and Editor Index, and Meeting Locator Index (by country and city). They are published quarterly, with annual cumulations.

Another good printed source is the annual *Bibliographic Guide to Conference Publications* (1974–) from G. K. Hall.

For earlier years, use *Directory of Published Proceedings* (1965–) and *Proceedings in Print* (1964–). Also useful is *International Congresses and Conferences 1840–1937: A Union List of Their Publications Available in Libraries of the United States and Canada,* ed. Winifred Gregory (H. W. Wilson Company, 1938). The *National Union Catalog of Pre-1956 Imprints* also covers proceedings.

A number of computer databases also enable you to search for conference papers. In the OCLC FirstSearch system the *Papers First* file indexes more than 500,000 scholarly papers received by the British Library since 1993; and the *Proceedings* file covers thousands of listings of scholarly meetings, also since 1993. The basic *WorldCat* database in FirstSearch is also useful. In the RLG Eureka system, the *Scientific Conference Papers* file indexes more than 70,000 papers annually since 1988; and the general RLIN BIB file is also worth checking.

If none of these identifies the paper you want, the best thing to do is to consult the *National Faculty Directory, American Men and Women of Science,* the *Directory of American Scholars*, or various *Who's Who*-type publications. These will usually enable you to locate the current address of the author of the paper in which you are interested, and you can then contact the person directly for a copy or a reprint. (Authors usually provide these routinely.)

Consumer Product Evaluations

A good source to start with is the annual *Consumer Reports Buying Guide Issue,* which provides rankings of specific products and comparison information in all areas from autofocus cameras and cars (including used cars) to stereo equipment and videocassette recorders. Food items are included, too, and brand names are rated. (Copies are available in public libraries and local bookstores.) Sometimes whole books are published that compare and rate particular types of products, and these can be found through *Subject Guide to Books in Print, Paperbound Books in Print*, and *Subject Guide to Forthcoming Books*. The ever-changing World Wide Web also offers a variety of consumer information sources; consult the annual *Cyberhound's Guide to Internet Databases* (Gale) for a listing by subject.

Current Awareness Sources

Libraries—particularly specialized corporate or legal libraries—are capable of offering "Selective Dissemination of Information," or SDI, services. (Special libraries may offer these to company employees as part of their regular service; nonaffiliated persons would have to pay fees.) An SDI service enables you to have a particular search strategy stored in a computer system and automatically run against new update files as they come into the databases you've selected. The result will be a bibliography, tailored to your specified interests, usually every month, alerting you to new publications. If you want to set up an SDI account, talk to your librarian.

Another source researchers should be aware of is the *Current Contents* series from the Institute for Scientific Information. There are several different *Current Contents* journals, each with a subtitle denoting its subject area:

Agriculture, Biology & Environmental Sciences
Arts & Humanities
Clinical Medicine
Engineering, Computing & Technology
Life Sciences
Physical, Chemical & Earth Sciences
Social & Behavioral Sciences

Each of these is a weekly publication that reproduces the table of contents from each of hundreds of journals within its subject area; and each issue has a keyword index at the back. They're great for browsing if you want to find the *most* recent articles in your field (and don't want to pay the costs of an SDI service); these weeklies will alert you to the articles that have not yet been covered by the conventional indexes.

There are also a number of yearbooks in various subjects that are useful in updating one's knowledge; see Chapters 8 and 16 for information on identifying which ones exist.

Films and Audiovisual Material

Teachers seeking educational A/V material should consult a group of sources known collectively as the NICEM indexes. The National Information Center for Educational Media publishes separate indexes to the following:

Film & Video Finder (more than 115,000 entries)
Audiocassette & Compact Disc Finder (ca. 40,000 entries)
Filmstrip & Slide Set Finder (more than 80,000 entries)

These provide subject and title access to the materials, plus addresses of producers and distributors. NICEM also publishes a separate *Index to AV Producers and Distributors*. A CD-ROM cumulation of all of the NICEM indexes, called *A-V Online,* is available from SilverPlatter; the database is also available as File 46 in the Dialog system.

The largest roster of theatrical films available on videocassette is the *Movies Unlimited Video Catalog* (annual), which lists and annotates tens of thousands of titles that can be ordered in VHS format. It is updated during the year by various supplements. Copies can be ordered from 1-800-4-MOVIES; as of this writing, the cost is $7.95 plus $3.00 shipping.

Genealogy and Local History

The best two books for genealogists to start with are Val D. Greenwood's *Researcher's Guide to American Genealogy,* 2d ed. (Genealogical Publishing Company, Inc., 1990), which you should read completely before you do anything else; and *The Source: A Guidebook of American Genealogy*, rev. ed., ed. Loretto Dennis Szucs and Sandra Hargreaves Luebking (Ancestry Publishing Company, 1997), which provides the most extensive overview of what sorts of historical records exist on people and where they are. And there are several other books that you should at least browse through:

- *American & British Genealogy and Heraldry,* 3d ed., comp. P. William Filby (New England Historic Genealogical Society, 1983) and *1982–1985 Supplement* (1987).
- *The Genealogist's Address Book,* 3d ed., by Elizabeth Petty Bentley (Genealogical Publishing Company, 1995).
- *Ancestry's Red Book: American State, County, & Town Sources*, ed. Alice Eichholz (Ancestry, 1992).
- *The Genealogist's Handbook: Modern Methods for Researching Family History,* by Raymond S. Wright (American Library Association, 1995).
- *The Handy Book for Genealogists,* ed. George B. Everton (Everton Publishers, revised irregularly).
- *Genealogical and Local History Books in Print: Family History Volume,* 5th ed., ed. Marian Hoffman (Genealogical Publishing Company, 1997).
- *Genealogical and Local History Books in Print: General Reference and World Resources,* ed. Marian Hoffman (Genealogical Publishing Company, 1997).
- *Genealogical and Local History Books in Print: U.S. Sources and Resources, A Through N,* ed. Marian Hoffman (Genealogical Publishing Company, 1997).

- *Genealogical and Local History Books in Print: U.S. Sources and Resources, N through W,* ed. by Marian Hoffman (Genealogical Publishing Company, 1997).
- *The [Year] Genealogy Annual,* 1st ed. 1995, by Thomas Kemp (Scholarly Resources, annual).

Oftentimes material on particular families or individuals can be found in local or county histories; two good sources for these are P. William Filby's *A Bibliography of American County Histories* (Genealogical Publishing Company, 1985) and Arthur P. Young's *Cities and Towns in American History: A Bibliography of Doctoral Dissertations* (Greenwood, 1989).

Two books with a focus on the Washington, D.C., area are also noteworthy: *The Center: A Guide to Genealogical Research in the National Capital Area* by Christina K. Schaefer (Genealogical Publishing Company, 1996) and *American Genealogical Research at the DAR* by Eric G. Grundset and Steven B. Rhodes (National Society Daughters of the American Revolution, 1997).

There are two week-long classes on how to do genealogical research that are offered regularly at the National Archives in Washington, D.C. One is called "Introduction to Genealogy"; to learn when it is scheduled, call the Education Branch of the National Archives at (202) 501-6694. The second is sponsored by the National Institute on Genealogical Research, a private organization, but the program is offered at the National Archives building. For information on the NIGR program write to the National Institute at P.O. Box 14274, Washington, DC 20044-4274.

Many genealogical resources are now appearing on the World Wide Web. The following sites are taken from a longer list prepared by Judith P. Reid of the Library of Congress (the term "GenWeb" refers to a project to provide linkages to the various genealogical URLs on the Web):

General Sources

Afrigeneas
  <www.msstate.edu/Archives/History/afrigen/>
Cemetery Listing Association (U.S. records)
  <http://mininet.systems.smu.edu/cla/>

GENDEX - WWW Genealogical Index
  <www.gendex.com/gendex/>
Genealogy Home Page
  <www.genhomepage.com>
Index of Genealogy Resources on the Internet
  <www.family-tree.com/www.index.htm>
Online Genealogical Database Index
ROOTS-L Home Page
  <www.rootsweb.com/roots-l/>
Rootsweb Genealogical Data Cooperative
Searchable Genealogy Links
  <http://www.bc1.com/users/sgl/>
Social Security Death Index (records from U.S. Social
  Security system)
  <www.ancestry.com/ssdi/advanced.htm>
U.S. GenWeb Project
  <www.usgenweb.com>
Vital Records State Index
  <www.inlink.com/~nomi/vitalrec/vitalrec.html>

By Country

Australia
  Australian Family History Compendium
    <www.cohsoft.com.au/afhc>
  Genealogy in Australia
    <www.pcug.org.au/~mpahlow/welcome.html>
Canada
  Canadian Genealogy Resources
    <www.iosphere.net/~jholwell/cangene/gene.html>
  National Archives of Canada
  National Library of Canada

France
  Genealogy of French-Speaking People
    <http://www.cam.org/~beaur/gen/welcome.html>
Germany
  German Genealogy Home Page
    <www.genealogy.com/gene/>
  Internet Sources of German Genealogy
    <www.bawue.de/~hanacek/info/edatbase.htm>
Ireland
  IRLGEN
    <www.bess.tcd.ie/roots_ie.htm>
  National Archives of Ireland
    <www.kst.dit.ie/nat-arch//>
Italy
  Italian Genealogy
    <www.italgen.com>
  Resources & References (Italian Genealogy)
    <http://homepage.interaccess.com/~arduinif/tools01.htm>
Latin America/Hispanic
  Puerto Rican/Hispanic Genealogical Society
    <www.linkdirect.com/hispsoc/>
United Kingdom
  UK+Ireland Genealogy
    <http://midas.ac.uk/genuki>
United States
  Library of Congress Local History & Genealogy Room
    <lcweb.loc.gov/rr/genealogy
  New York Public Library
    <www.nypl.org/research/chss/lhg/genea.html>
  National Archives
    <www.nara.gov>
  National Genealogical Society Home Page
    <www.genealogy.org/~ngs/>
  New England Historic Genealogical Society
    <www.nehgs.org>

An interesting sideline by which genealogists can enrich their understanding of the past is through the study of the history of neighborhoods and of individual buildings or sites. One especially noteworthy source is the huge collection of fire insurance maps housed at the Library of Congress. At LC itself, the maps are accessible through the book *Fire Insurance Maps in the Library of Congress: Plans of North American Cities and Towns Produced by the Sanborn Map Company* (Library of Congress, 1981). This entire map collection is now also available in a microfilm set, from Chadwyck-Healey, covering the period 1867 to 1970. There is also another microfilm set, called *Fire Insurance Maps from the Sanborn Map Company Archives, 1900s–1990,* from University Publications of America; it contains, from the Sanborn Company's own archives, maps that were never deposited in the Library of Congress.

The LC collection—623,000 maps covering 10,000 American cities and towns—are of interest because they can tell you who previously owned the land on which you live, where your ancestors lived in the given city at the time of the map (some cities had as many as seven maps published at different times), how many rooms each building had, the number of windows, the kind of roof, and the materials the walls were made of. You can use them to identify which businesses were located in a community (when and exactly where), the location and denomination of churches, and where the groceries, banks, hotels, and saloons were. In short, these maps can show you the neighborhoods your ancestors lived in, and how those neighborhoods changed over the years.

Illustrations, Pictures, and Photographs

The *Library of Congress Subject Headings* system currently has four standard subdivisions that are useful for finding pictures in books:

[Subject heading]—Illustrations
    —Pictorial works
    —Portraits
    —Caricatures and cartoons

In searching for older books, also try two additional forms that used to be used under names of places:

[Name of place]—Description—Views
        —Description and travel—Views

The Wilson indexes also note whether or not a journal article is accompanied by illustrations. And there are several one-volume indexes specifically for illustrations or reproductions of paintings, among them *Illustration Index* (Scarecrow, 1973) and irregularly issued supplements (e.g., *Illustration Index VII, 1987–1991*), *Index to Illustrations* (Faxon, 1966), *Index to Illustrations of the Natural World* (Gaylord, 1977), *Index to Illustrations of Animals & Plants* (Neal-Schuman, 1991), and *Index to Illustrations of Living Things Outside North America* (Shoe String, 1981).

Facts On File publishes a wide variety of three-ring loose-leaf binders with copyright-free illustrations, pictures, diagrams, charts, and maps, all intended for easy photocopying. There are several such series:

African History On File
American Historical Images On File
   The Black Experience
   Colonial and Revolutionary America
   The Civil War
   The Faces of America (I and II)
   Key Issues in Constitutional History
   The Native American Experience
Animal Anatomy On File
Charts On File
CIS and Eastern Europe On File
Design On File
Earth Sciences On File
Environment On File
Forms On File
   Business Forms On File
   Personal Forms On File
Geography On File

Hazardous Chemicals On File
Historical Inventions On File
Historical Maps On File
Historical Science Experiments On File
Human Body On File
Junior Science Experiments On File
Junior Science On File
Life Sciences On File
Maps On File
More Science Experiments On File
Nature Projects On File
Physical Sciences On File
Religions On File
Science Experiments On File
State Maps On File
Surgery On File
Time Lines On File

The various specialized encyclopedias are also frequently useful for pictures, as is the technique of scanning subject-grouped books on classified bookshelves (see Chapter 3). Paula Berinstein's *Finding Images Online: Online User's Guide to Image Searching in Cyberspace* (Pemberton Press, 1996) will help with Internet sources.

Literary Criticism

The *best* way to locate criticisms of a particular literary work is not through the computerized *MLA International Bibliography* (even though many professors will uncritically refer you to it); better results usually can be obtained by finding a published bibliography of works about the particular author, then checking its index for the particular story, play, or poem title you have in mind. Published bibliographies compiled by literary scholars will usually give you a much better overview than the *MLA* of the range of criticism that exists. For example, a student who wants to find a close reading of John Donne's *Holy Sonnet #10* ("Death Be Not Proud") will find three critical articles on it listed in the *MLA;* however, if he checks his library catalog under "Donne, John, 1572–1631—Bibliography" he is likely to find two compilations by John R. Roberts, *John Donne: An Annotated Bibliography of Modern Criticism, 1912–1967* and *John Donne . . . 1968–1978* (University of Missouri Press, 1973 and 1982). The first lists five close readings of this one sonnet; the second, sixteen.

Similarly, a student interested in Edgar Allan Poe and cryptography would find citations to four articles (and a reprint of one of them) by crossing "Poe" and "cryptography" in the *MLA* database. In consulting J. Lasley Dameron and Irby B. Cauthen's *Edgar Allan Poe: A Bibliography of Criticism 1827–1967* (University Press of Virginia, 1974), however, she would find thirteen.

The *MLA International Bibliography* database, which is available on CD-ROM or through the OCLC FirstSearch system, indexes literary criticism journals from 1963 to date; the paper copy of the same index goes back to 1921. Students who confine their searching to the computer version should be aware that the more recent years of literary studies journals may have a bias toward "politically correct" readings.

Although somewhat dated, F. W. Bateson and Harrison T. Meserole's *A Guide to English and American Literature,* 3d ed. (Longman, 1976) has a peculiar strength in its survey of older critical sources: It will tell you quickly what is the *best* scholarly edition of an author's works, the best biography, and the best overall criticism. This is very helpful for graduate students, but less so for undergraduates who want detailed criticisms of individual works.

For the latter purpose (assuming that individual author bibliographies have already been checked), there are dozens of published bibliographies of criticisms that are not confined to a single author; among these are such titles as the following:

- *Poetry Explication: A Checklist of Interpretation Since 1925 of British and American Poems Past and Present* (G. K. Hall, 1980).
- *English Novel Explication* (Shoe String Press, 1973) and *Supplement* volumes.
- *The American Novel: A Checklist of Twentieth Century Criticisms on Novels Written Since 1789,* 2 vols. (Swallow Press, 1961–70).

- *Twentieth Century Short Story Explication,* 3d ed. (Shoe String Press, 1977), with five supplements. (This set has a cumulative index: *Twentieth-Century Short Story Explication: An Index to the Third Edition and Its Five Supplements, 1961–1991* [Shoe String Press, 1992].)
- *Magill's Bibliography of Literary Criticism,* 4 vols. (Salem Press, 1979). (This covers world literature.)
- *Black American Writers Past and Present: A Biographical and Bibliographical Dictionary,* 2 vols. (Scarecrow Press, 1975).

Each of these is arranged by author and then subdivided by individual work, listing particular criticisms of each work.

The best overall index to such compilations of citations to critical articles on individual stories, plays, or poems is Alan R. Weiner and Spencer Means's *Literary Criticism Index,* 2d ed. (Scarecrow Press, 1994); this is a cumulative index to 146 volumes such as the six listed above. *Literary Criticism Index,* be it noted, is another source that often produces better results than a simple computer search of the *MLA* database.

One of the very best shortcuts to critical articles on major literary works is through the Prentice-Hall *Twentieth Century Interpretations* series. Look in your library's catalog under the title *Twentieth Century Interpretations of [Title of work].* (Within the brackets you can enter such titles as *A Farewell to Arms, The Crucible, Doctor Faustus, Gray's Elegy, Julius Caesar, Moby Dick, Oedipus Rex, Pride and Prejudice,* etc.) There are about 90 volumes like this, each about 120 pages long, and each presenting an excellent collection of scholarly analyses.

Another comparable series is Prentice-Hall's *Twentieth Century Views.* These tend to have titles of the format *[name of author]: A Collection of Critical Essays.* The best entry into the content of this series is an obscure but remarkably useful volume entitled *Reader's Index to the Twentieth Century Views Literary Criticism Series, Volumes 1–100* (Prentice-Hall, 1973). This book reproduces the index pages from the end of each volume in the series. It thus offers an excellent way to find articles on *particular topics* connected with authors (as opposed to particular works), such as "Negative capability in Keats," "Inscape and instress in Hopkins," "Irony in Mann," and "Puritan influences on Hawthorne." In a sense you can use this compilation of indexes to do Boolean combinations of "specific topic and specific author" to find sources that lie beyond any computer database.

Assuming your library has a computer catalog that can do Boolean combinations of keywords, you can easily find either of the Prentice-Hall series by telling the machine to find "Twentieth Century" combined with either the name of a literary work or the name of the literary author.

Three new, comparable series published by Chelsea House are *Modern Critical Views* (each volume of which is entitled with the name of a literary author, e.g., *John Le Carré* or *Homer*); *Major Literary Characters* (each with a title, such as *Hester Prynne* or *Huck Finn*); and *Modern Critical Interpretations* (each with the title of a particular work, such as *Jane Eyre* or *The Scarlet Letter*). These volumes are compilations of critical articles, often more recent than those in the Prentice-Hall series. All three of the Chelsea House series have Harold Bloom as their general editor. This makes computer searching relatively easy: Just combine "Bloom" and ([author] or [title] or [character]) to find if there is a volume relevant to your interest.

G. K. Hall publishes several comparable "Critical Essays" series; these can be found by searching for titles of the form *Critical Essays on [name of author; e.g., Christopher Marlowe, Albert Camus, Virginia Woolf]*.

Two ongoing series of critical overviews of authors and their works are the *Dictionary of Literary Biography* and *Contemporary Authors,* both from Gale Research. The former set has a cumulative index to the whole series at the back of whatever is the most recent volume. An excellent cumulative index to both of these sets (and to several other related series of reference sources) is the *Contemporary Authors Cumulative Index;* it is issued irregularly to subscribers of the set.

A number of "serial bibliographies" are published annually, covering the year's work in various fields, and literature is well represented among them. The best guides to these ongoing serial bibliographies are William A. Wortman's *A Guide to Serial Bibliographies for Modern Literatures,* 2d ed. (Modern Language Association, 1995), Richard Gray's *Serial Bibliographies in the Humanities and Social Sciences* (Pierian Press, 1969), and the annual *Bibliographic Index.*

Perhaps the most important thing for an undergraduate to keep in mind when doing an analysis of a literary work, however, is that quite possibly no research at all is required, or even desired, by the professor. Often the purpose of such assignments is to stretch your analytical powers rather than your research abilities. Another problem with critical articles is that—as most graduate students in English will tell you—much of what you find simply won't be worth reading. (The Prentice-Hall and Chelsea House series, above, are certainly exceptions.) Few things are more frustrating to a student than expending a lot of time and energy on research and getting only mediocre or off-target articles as a result. The time involved would often be more profitably and efficiently spent devising your own analysis—for by going in that direction you can often have your paper completely written while your colleagues are still compiling notes in the library.

Maps

Good starting points for determining what kinds of maps are currently available for any part of the world are two publications from Map Link in Santa Barbara, California: *Map Link Catalog* (1995) and *Map Link Academic Section* (1995). The *Catalog* covers more than 5,000 U.S. and international maps, from both governmental and commercial sources, with complete ordering information; the *Academic* publication covers the more obscure maps "for explorers, libraries, and engineers."

The three-volume *Inventory of World Topographic Mapping* (Elsevier, 1989) gives an overview of the history of mapping in each country and a list of the current map scales and map series in each. *World Mapping Today* (Butterworth, 1987) is another overview of sources worldwide for topographic and thematic maps that were in print as of the mid-1980s. For the United States, the loose-leaf *Manual of Federal Geographic Data Products* (Federal Geographic Data Committee and ViGYAN, Inc., 1992; updates planned) describes current "maps, digital data, aerial photographs and multispectral imagery, earth sciences, and other geographically-referenced data sets"; it illustrates many of them and gives you addresses and phone numbers to contact. The U.S. Geological Survey's Earth Science Information Center maintains a toll-free telephone number (1-800-USA-MAPS) from which you can obtain information about, and order copies of, maps, digital data, and aerial photographs.

Useful sources more readily findable in public libraries are *Maps for America: Cartographic Products of the U.S. Geological Survey and Others,* 3d ed. (U.S. Government Printing Office, 1988) and Joel Makower's *Map Catalog: Every Kind of Map and Chart on Earth and Even Some Above It,* 3d ed. (Random House, 1993). Makower provides addresses and phone numbers of suppliers, both governmental and commercial.

Kister's Atlas Buying Guide (Oryx Press, 1984) compares and evaluates more than 100 general and world atlases currently available in the United States and Canada. A larger, international listing—but without comparative evaluations—is Gerard L. Alexander's *Guide to Atlases: World, Regional, National, Thematic—An International Listing of Atlases Published Since 1950* (Scarecrow Press, 1971), and, by the same author, *Guide to Atlases Supplement* (Scarecrow Press, 1977) covering those published from 1971 through 1975.

The *Maps on File, Historical Maps On File,* and *Charts On File* compilations of copyright-free, photocopyable illustrations from Facts On File are also useful (see the above section on illustrations), and probably can be found in a local library.

A good Web site for road map displays is <www.mapquest.com>; if you plug in a departure address and a destination, it will show you a route between the two.

Newspapers and Newspaper Indexes

There are both printed and electronic indexes to newspapers, as well as many full-text databases of the actual papers. As is usually the case, the electronic sources are good mainly for recent years, while the printed may cover many earlier decades.

Three indexes (with corresponding microfilm of the newspapers) are likely to be found in many libraries—the *New York Times* is indexed back to 1851; the *Times* of London from 1790 to date; and the *Wall Street Journal* from 1959 forward.

You can often use the *New York Times Index* to gain some access to other papers that do not have their own indexes. Through it you can often determine the dates of relevant events, and use that time frame to narrow your search to particular issues of other papers. An especially useful additional avenue of approach in this regard is the *Personal Name Index to the New York Times Index 1851–1974,* with a *1975–1979* supplement, which lists all names in the *Index* for the designated years.

There are now printed indexes to dozens of American newspapers, among them the *Washington Post, USA Today,* the *Chicago Tribune,* the *Chicago Sun-Times,* the *Christian Science Monitor,* the *Los Angeles Times,* the *Atlanta Constitution,* the *New Orleans Times-Picayune,* the *Detroit News,* the *Boston Globe,* the *Houston Post,* and the *San Francisco Chronicle.* None of these, however, covers years earlier than 1972; many don't go back even that far.

The *National Newspaper Index,* a CD-ROM that is part of the InfoTrac system, covers the *New York Times,* the *Wall Street Journal,* the *Christian Science Monitor,* the *Washington Post,* and the *Los Angeles Times;* it covers the current year plus three earlier years and is updated monthly. A Web version is also available for a subscription fee.

Newspaper Abstracts is a database covering more than two dozen major U.S. papers, with abstracts of their articles, from 1989 to date; it is available in both the FirstSearch and the Eureka systems. *DataTimes* is a First-Search index to more than 90 regional U.S. newspapers and over 30 regional papers from outside the United States; it covers from 1996 to date and is available in FirstSearch. *Business Dateline* is a CD-ROM that provides the full texts of more than 350 regional business magazines and newspapers; the current disc always covers the most recent year's articles and is updated monthly.

The NewsBank/Readex company of New Canaan, Connecticut, produces dozens of CD-ROM editions of the full texts of newspapers throughout the United States (coverage usually does not extend earlier than the 1990s or mid-1980s). Your library may subscribe to the title or titles relevant to your local area.

If you want to locate a library that owns a particular backfile of a U.S. newspaper, the best source is OCLC's *United States Newspaper Program National Union List* (revised irregularly), on microfiche. It's a national listing of who owns more than 100,000 titles, and it includes specific holdings information. It also has four indexes: Beginning Date–Ending Date; Place of Publication/Printing; Subject Topical; and Subject Geographic.

The Subject Topical index includes headings such as "Trade-Union—Newspapers—Ohio—Dayton," "Afro-Americans," and "Episcopal Church." The Subject Geographic index provides access by the name of the community served, or the area of news covered, such as "Chicago (Ill.)—Newspapers" or "Hawaii—Newspapers."[2]

Many newspaper indexes exist in unpublished form throughout the country in libraries, newspaper offices, and historical and genealogical societies. The best guide to these is Anita Cheek Milner's *Newspaper Indexes: A Location and Subject Guide for Researchers,* 3 vols. (Scarecrow Press, 1977–82); Grace D. Parch's *Directory of Newspaper Libraries in the U.S. and Canada* (Special Libraries Association, 1976); and the *Lathrop Report on Newspaper Indexes* (Norman Lathrop Enterprises, 1979–80).

If your local library does not have a CD-ROM newspaper index, or access to FirstSearch or Eureka, there is another printed source that may still be of use. This is *Facts On File*, a weekly news digest series that cumulates in permanent annual volumes. It is usually up to date to within about ten days, and you can use it to find the exact dates of very recent events, which will cut down the number of newspaper issues you have to scan for the article you want.

Remember that newspapers are valuable research tools not only for their "news" items but also for their features, reviews, product evaluations, general essays on art and culture, and editorials. Regarding the latter, some libraries subscribe to a service called *Editorials On File* (Facts On File, 1970–) which reprints full editorials, and some editorial cartoons, from more than 125 U.S. and Canadian newspapers. The issues appear twice a month and are very valuable for providing "pro and con" arguments about current issues.

An excellent guide to the literature on American newspapers in general is Richard A. Schwarzlose's 417-page *Newspapers: A Reference Guide* (Greenwood Press, 1987).

Out-of-Print and Secondhand Books

While the emphasis of this book has been on sources that are available for free within libraries, those who haunt such places will sometimes have an unavoidable urge to own personal copies of some of the books they find. Five excellent Web sites let you search the holdings of thousands of book-stores specializing in rare, out-of-print, and secondhand books:

<www.mxbf.com>
<www.interloc.com>
<www.abebooks.com>
<www.bibliocity.com>
<www.bibliofind.com>

These sites are international in coverage, and each allows you to search by author, title, or keywords. Prices and ordering information are given for any works you find.

Primary Sources

Sometimes students are given assignments to use "primary sources" in their papers. A good shortcut for finding such sources published in book formats is through a simple computer Boolean combination of several *Library of Congress Subject Headings* elements. First find the right *LCSH* heading for your subject, such as "World War, 1939–1945" or "Civil War, 1861–1865." (The "Civil War" element is actually a subdivision of the full heading "United States—History—Civil War, 1861–1865," but most softwares can pick out the subdivision directly.) Then combine that element with three others that are standard subdivisions within the *LCSH* system: "Diaries" or "Personal narratives" or "Sources." The final statement, then, should look like "[LC Subject Heading] AND (Diaries OR Personal narratives OR Sources)." It's a lot easier to find primary sources this way than to have to search through archives and manuscript collections.

There is a qualification regarding "Personal narratives"; this subdivision is usually further specified, in the printed *LCSH* list, by a national designation, as in the following:

Personal narratives, American
Personal narratives, Armenian

Personal narratives, Australian
Personal narratives, Confederate
Personal narratives, Danish
Personal narratives, East Indian

There are scores of such national qualifiers. In selecting "Personal narratives" as an element for combination, then, you will want to use the computer catalog's keyword search capability to retrieve all of these terms together; in the Library of Congress's LOCIS system (available through <http://lcweb.loc.gov>), the command would be *Find s "personal narratives"* to create one set containing all of them; the "s" indicates that you want the words found together in any of the subject fields, and the quotation marks around "personal narratives" are necessary both to mask the word "personal," which, otherwise, is a "stop" word, and to get "personal" and "narratives" adjacent to each other.

Another good shortcut to primary sources lies in consulting bibliographies of published diaries. These are especially useful:

- *American Diaries: An Annotated Bibliography of Published Diaries and Journals,* 2 vols., by Laura Arksey, Nancy Pries, and Marcia Reed (Gale Research, 1983–87).
- *British Diaries: An Annotated Bibliography of British Diaries Written Between 1442 and 1942,* by William Matthews (P. Smith, 1967).
- *And So to Bed: A Bibliography of Diaries Published in English,* by Patricia Pate Havlice (Scarecrow Press, 1987).

These have useful subject indexes that connect the diaries to various historical events or periods.

Psychological and Educational Tests

A good place to start your search for these is *Tests: A Comprehensive Reference for Assessments in Psychology, Education, and Business,* 3d ed. (Pro-Ed, 1991); it describes, but does not evaluate, more than 3,000 English-language tests and provides information on costs and availability. (For reviews of these tests, see the ongoing *Test Critiques* series below.) Subject access is possible through browsing the 87 categories into which the citations are arranged; there are also multiple indexes (by title, hearing-impaired, computer-scored, etc.).

Another avenue of approach is through two series from Oscar Buros and his successors, *Tests in Print* (three editions so far, which do not supersede each other) and *Mental Measurements Yearbook* (eleven so far); the title indexes from *Tests in Print II* and *III* are, in effect, a master index to all of the test titles in the first eight *Mental Measurements Yearbooks*. These will give you more detailed information about tests published throughout the English-speaking world and will present critical reviews and extensive bibliographies on their use and validity. These volumes, like *Tests* above, do not reproduce copies of the tests, however; for those you must write to the publisher of the test (the Buros sources include a directory of addresses), or try one of the other sources listed below. Buros's subject indexes leave something to be desired; for older instruments, two volumes that are easier to approach by subject are William A. Mehrens and Irving J. Lehmann's *Using Standardized Tests in Education,* 4th ed. (Longman, 1987); Ki-Taek Chun et al., *Measures for Psychological Assessment* (Survey Research Center for the Institute for Social Research, University of Michigan, 1975); and A. L. Comrey et al., *Sourcebook for Mental Health Measures* (Human Interaction Institute, 1973). These can bring to your attention tests for which you will then turn to the Buros sources for further information.

Test Critiques is an ongoing series currently published in Austin, Texas, (Pro-Ed, 1984–), with irregular new volumes, that presents detailed criticisms and reviews—not just citations, but the actual reviews—of hundreds of tests.

A good overall index to all kinds of tests is available for free at the Web site of the Educational Testing Service (<http://www.ets.org>, then click on "Other Tests and Services"; under "Special Services" click on "Test Collection"). ETS also publishes an ongoing set of *Tests in Microfiche;* each of these includes 25 to 100 measures, spanning a wide range of topics. Note, however, that these microfiche tests are generally unpublished instruments, not the commercially available tests listed in *Tests* or Buros; and unpublished instruments usually have not been subjected to the intensive scutiny of published tests. A cumulative index to the first thirteen microfiche sets (sets A through M) is John C. Hepner's *ETS Test Collection Cumulative Index to Tests in Microfiche, 1975–1987* (ETS, 1988). (Set T was published in 1994.) Note, too, that the Educational Testing Service, in Princeton, New Jersey, maintains a library of *20,000* tests and other measurement devices and that not all of these are reproduced in the *Tests in Microfiche* set; nor are they all recorded in the various printed catalogs and indexes; nor are they all indexed in the "Test Collection" Web site, which now lists more than 10,000 test descriptions. Oryx Press publishes an ongoing *ETS Test Collection Catalog* in hardcopy format; it includes tests not recorded in the Web site.

Psychological Abstracts (or its various online and CD-ROM versions) can be used for updating information on tests; and for earlier years, the set has a cumulative *Author Index* for the years 1927 to 1983 that can be very useful if you already know the name of the author of the instrument you want. The subject heading "Tests and scales" is also valuable in both *Education Index* and *Social Sciences Index*.

Three works by John P. Robinson et al. reproduce the full text of tests: *Measures of Political Attitudes* (Survey Research Center, 1968), *Measures of Occupational Attitudes and Occupational Characteristics* (Survey Research Center, 1969) and *Measures of Personality and Social Psychological Attitudes* (Academic Press, 1991). Three others that reproduce the actual tests are Marvin E. Shaw's *Scales for the Measurement of Attitudes* (McGraw-Hill, 1967); Anita Simon and Gil Boyer's *Mirrors for Behavior III: An Anthology of Observation Instruments* (Philadelphia: Communication Materials Center, 1974); and Gil Boyer et al., *Measures of Maturation: An Anthology of Early Childhood Instruments* (Philadelphia: Research for Better Schools, 1973). William Goodwin and Laura A. Driscoll's *Handbook for Measurement and Evaluation in Early Childhood Education* (Jossey-Bass, 1980) presents a good explanation and overview of relevant tests.

Other sources that sometimes are useful for researchers are doctoral dissertations—those in education and psychology sometimes reproduce in appendices the texts of the instruments they've used. Emily Fabiano's *Index to Tests Used in Educational Dissertations* (Oryx Press, 1989) should be consulted to identify relevant tests used in dissertations from 1938 to 1980; it is derived from a study of the paper copy abstracts of dissertations for those years that are not searchable in the online *Dissertation Abstracts*. The latter database includes abstracts from 1980 forward and can thus be used to search tests referred to in later years. Note, however, that instruments published within dissertations are usually "unpublished" tests created for the study. Standardized tests are usually not reproduced because of copyright restrictions.

The *ERIC* database in education is also worth searching for tests; sometimes the various microfiche reports include texts of instruments.

Reports

Reports are records of research findings much like journal articles, except that they have not been published in a journal and are usually available only in microfiche or photocopied formats. Copies usually can be obtained from a central clearinghouse such as the National Technical Information Service (NTIS) in Springfield, Virginia, or directly from their authors (whose addresses can be obtained through various directories). Those that are done with federal grant or contract money are usually in the public domain. The largest overall index to reports is the NTIS's *Government Reports Announcements & Index* (1946–); this is an ongoing index, with abstracts, of almost all nonclassified research reports generated by U.S. government funding in all subject areas (see Chapter 15). There is also a cumulated version, *NTIS Title Index on Microfiche,* covering the years 1964 through 1978 in one sequence, with annual supplements until 1992. A CD-ROM version of the index is *NTIS on SilverPlatter,* covering from 1983 to date; the online Dialog and DataStar versions of the file cover from 1964 to date. Although the NTIS has its own home page (<www.ntis.gov/>), there is, as of this writing, no free index to its material on the Internet; you have to use a commercially available CD or online file.

Many other indexes to reports, however, are more comprehensive in specialized fields such as aeronautics and astronautics, agriculture, education, energy, environment, and transportation; these can be identified through the reference sources discussed in Chapter 16. Another excellent finding aid for material in report format is a publication called *How to Get*

It: A Guide to Defense-Related Information Sources (see Chapter 15). A free Internet version can be searched at <www.dtic.mil/gils-input/htgi/>.

Standards and Specifications

A source that is readily available in public libraries is *Architectural Graphic Standards* (revised irregularly). It provides diagrams and standard measurements of such things as tennis courts, horseshoe pits, swimming pools, door frames, fireplaces, etc.; it even diagrams the profiles of major trees, listing their average heights and spreads.

If you need to obtain a technical, engineering, industrial, military, or governmental standard, you first want to see if you can get it from a library; document delivery companies can supply copies, but they may be very expensive. The largest library collection is that of the Library of Congress, which comprehensively collects standards issued or endorsed by the American National Standards Institute (ANSI), the Institute of Electrical and Electronic Engineers (IEEE), the Society of Automotive Engineers (SAE), Underwriters Laboratory (UL), and others; LC also systematically collects documents issued by the major international standards-producing organizations, such as International Standards Organization (ISO), the International Electrochemical Commission (IEC), the International Telecommunications Union (ITU), and the European Community, as well as the national standards of the major industrialized countries, such as Great Britain, Germany, France, Japan, the People's Republic of China, and South Africa. Although the Library, because of copyright restrictions, does not itself make copies of standards, the fair-use provision of the copyright law does permit on-site visitors to make a reproduction of relevant portions of any standard they need. The specialists at LC also can help you to identify standards appropriate to your needs and suggest libraries or other sources where they may be obtained. The LC experts can be reached at 202-707-5655, by fax at 202-707-0253, or in writing at:

Technical Reports & Standards Section
Science & Technology Division
The Library of Congress
Washington, DC 20540-4750

The National Institute of Standards and Technology (formerly the National Bureau of Standards) maintains the National Center for Standards and Certification Information; according to its Web page (<http://ts.nist.gov>), it "provides information on U.S., foreign and international voluntary standards; government regulations; and rules of conformity assessment for nonagricultural products. The Center serves as a referral service and focal point in the United States for information about standards and standards-related information." They can also be reached at:

National Center for Standards and Certification Information
National Institute of Standards and Technology
Building 820, Room 164
Gaithersburg, MD 20899
Tel.: 301-975-4040, -4038, -4036, or -5155

Two sister companies that provide standards for a fee are Global Engineering Services (800-854-7179; <http://global.ihs.com>) and Information Handling Service (800-525-7052; <www.ihs.com>). Global is preferable for ordering a copy of an individual standard; IHS for ordering a large set or an ongoing subcription. IHS also publishes CD-ROM indexes to standards worldwide.

Statistics

The most useful compendium of statistics on all sorts of things is the federal government's annual *Statistical Abstract of the United States*. There is also a large collection of searchable federal statistics mounted on the Fed-Stats Web site at <www.fedstats.gov>.

Several compendiums are good for historical statistics:

- *Historical Statistics of the United States, Colonial Times to 1970* (U.S. Government Printing Office, 1975).
- *International Historical Statistics: The Americas and Australia*, by B. R. Mitchell (Gale, 1983).
- *International Historical Statistics: Europe 1750–1988*, by B. R. Mitchell (Stockton Press, 1992).

- *International Historical Statistics: Africa and Asia*, by B. R. Mitchell (New York University Press, 1982).
- *British Historical Statistics*, by B. R. Mitchell (Cambridge University Press, 1988).
- *Historical Statistics of Canada,* ed. M. C. Urquhart (Macmillan, 1965).
- *Australians Historical Statistics,* ed. Wray Vamplew (Fairfax, Syme & Weldon Associates, 1987).
- *The Arab World, Turkey, and the Balkans (1878–1914): A Handbook of Historical Statistics*, by Justin McCarthy (G. K. Hall, 1982).
- *Value of a Dollar 1860–1989,* ed. Scott Derks (Gale, 1994).

The best ongoing indexes to statistical publications are from the Congressional Information Service. One is *American Statistics Index* (or *ASI,* 1974–); the second is *Statistical Reference Index* (*SRI*, 1980–); and the third is *Index to International Statistics* (*IIS,* 1983–). All three exist in paper copy, and also in a cumulated CD-ROM version called *Statistical Masterfile.* The first is an index with abstracts of *all* statistics produced by the U.S. federal government; the second covers thousands of statistical sources from nonfederal sources (state and local governments, business, trade associations, institutes, university research centers, private polling organizations, etc.); the third indexes publications of international governmental organizations, including 59 U.N. organs, the European Community, the Organization of Petroleum Exporting Countries, and the Organization of American States.

Each of these three is an index by subject or title; and each has an extremely useful Index by Categories that lists sources giving comparative data according to any of a score of geographic, economic, or demographic breakdowns (e.g., by city, state, industry, individual company, occupation, age, race, sex, etc.—the *SRI* is especially useful in providing *rankings* of companies). Each is updated monthly, with annual cumulations. And for each index there is a corresponding microfiche set of the actual documents that are indexed. The CD-ROM version is a single cumulation of all of the years of all three indexes together. (Unfortunately it has a rather unfriendly software, so many researchers still justifiably find the printed indexes easier to use.)

Rankings of various sorts can be found in sources such as these:

- *Places Rated Almanac* (Macmillan, revised irregularly), which ranks the "most livable" cities and towns in North America
- *Retirement Places Rated* (Macmillan, irregular)
- *Gale Country & World Rankings Reporter* (Gale, 1995).
- *Gale State Rankings Reporter* (Gale, irregular)
- *Gale City & Metro Rankings Reporter* (Gale, irregular).
- *Educational Rankings Annual* (Gale, annual)

Other good compendiums include the United Nations' *Statistical Yearbook* and its *Demographic Yearbook* and the *UNESCO Statistical Yearbook*. *Statistics Sources: A Subject Guide to Data on Industrial, Business, Social, Educational, Financial and Other Topics for the United States and Internationally* (Gale, revised irregularly) is an excellent guide to sources of statistics on more than 20,000 subjects.

The Inter-University Consortium for Political and Social Research in Ann Arbor, Michigan, is a nonprofit organization that maintains the world's largest archive of machine-readable data files in the social sciences; both current and historical statistics are available (for a price) in manipulable formats. Their homepage is at <www.icpsr.umich.edu/>.

Tabular Data

The Chemical Rubber Company of Cleveland, Ohio, publishes more than 50 handbooks that present tabular data in such fields as chemistry and physics, mathematics, optics, probability and statistics, microbiology, nutrition and food, and so on. The best avenue of access into this bewildering maze of data is the *Composite Index for CRC Handbooks* (CRC Press, revised irregularly), which covers all the volumes. *Handbooks and Tables in Science and Technology* (Oryx Press, revised irregularly) also is useful.

Translations

The easiest way to find out if a foreign-language book has been translated into English is to look under the original author's name in one of the big printed or online union catalogs of books; these include the WorldCat database in the FirstSearch system, the RLIN BIB file, and the printed *National Union Catalog: Pre-1956 Imprints.*

There are also various specific indexes listing translations of books or journal articles. For works of a technical nature, the *Consolidated Index of Translations into English* (National Translations Center, 1969) is supplemented by the *Translations Register-Index* (1967–86) and the *World Translations Index* (1987–). The *World Index of Scientific Translations* (1972–), the National Institute of Health's *N.I.H. Library Translations Index, 1954–1963* and its ongoing supplements, the annual *Index Translationum* (1932–40; new series 1948–), also should be kept in mind. There is a cumulative index to *Index Translationum* for 1948 to 1968.

In the humanities, *The Literatures of the World in English Translation: A Bibliography,* 3 vols. (Frederick Ungar, 1967–70) should be consulted. Another good way to find translations of major foreign authors' works— especially if you want to find what is considered the best English collected set—is to consult the *Reader's Advisor*, a multivolume set, revised irregularly, from R. R. Bowker. A new series from Boulevard Books in London also is useful; it includes *The Babel Guide to Italian Fiction in English Translation* (1994), *The Babel Guide to the Fiction of Portugal, Brazil & Africa in English Translation* (1995), and *The Babel Guide to French Fiction in English Translation* (1996). For older sources, consult *Bibliography of English Translations from Medieval Sources* (Columbia University Press, 1946) and *Bibliography of English Translations from Medieval Sources, 1943-1967* (Columbia University Press, 1974).

Good subject headings to look for in library catalogs are of this form:

> [Name or subject]—Translations into English [or French, German, etc.]

Two U.S. federal government sources offer ongoing translation series. The Joint Publications Research Service (JPRS) translates foreign newspapers, journal articles, and some speeches. Three indexes exist:

- *Bibliography-Index to Current U.S. JPRS Translations,* vols. 1–8, (1962–70)

- *Transdex: Bibliography and Index to United States Joint Publications Research Service (JPRS) Translations,* vols. 9–12 (1970–74)
- *Transdex Index* (Bell & Howell, 1975–); monthly paper indexes with annual cumulations on microfiche

As of this writing there are no computer indexes to JPRS translations. The actual texts indexed by the above sources are available in a microfiche set.

The Foreign Broadcast Information Service (FBIS) has translated foreign radio broadcasts from around the world since 1941. The best index to the more recent years is the *FBIS Index on CD-ROM* (NewsBank/Readex, 1975–96), which contains 2.4 million citations. Texts are available on microfiche up to 1996; thereafter, access to FBIS material (indexing and texts) is available only through the World News Connection (WNC), an online news service accessible on the World Wide Web only to subscribers (which may, of course, include libraries). The WNC service includes only a rolling two-year back file, however. Plans for access to material older than two years remain to be worked out.

A good list of which journals internationally are regularly translated into English is *Journals in Translation* (British Library Document Supply Centre, revised irregularly).

Notes

1. These examples, as well as many of the descriptions in this section, are derived from the company's own promotional literature.

2. These examples come from a promotional booklet for the project, *United States Newspaper Program National Union List,* 4th ed. (OCLC, 1993), p. 4.

Index

*Where multiple page references are listed,
page numbers of the major discussion are in italics.*